TAKE A HIKE
MINNEAPOLIS
& ST. PAUL

JAKE KULJU

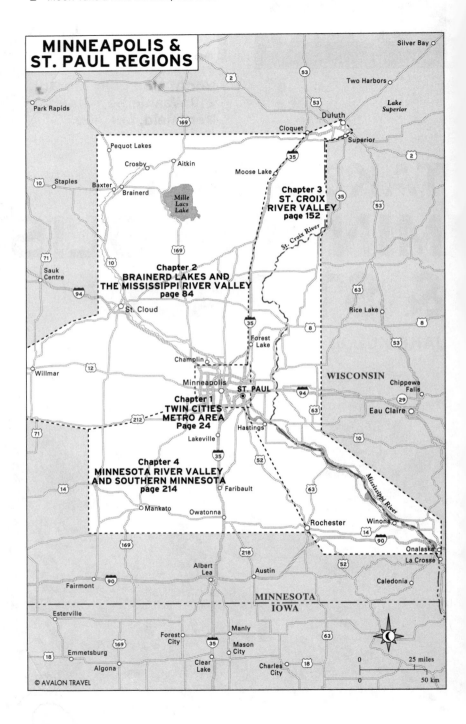

MINNEAPOLIS & ST. PAUL REGIONS

Silver Bay

Park Rapids

Two Harbors

Lake Superior

Duluth

Cloquet

Superior

Pequot Lakes

Crosby

Aitkin

Moose Lake

Staples

Baxter

Brainerd

Mille Lacs Lake

**Chapter 3
ST. CROIX
RIVER VALLEY
page 152**

St. Croix River

Rice Lake

Sauk Centre

**Chapter 2
BRAINERD LAKES AND
THE MISSISSIPPI RIVER VALLEY
page 84**

St. Cloud

Forest Lake

Willmar

Champlin

WISCONSIN

Chippewa Falls

Minneapolis

ST. PAUL

Eau Claire

**Chapter 1
TWIN CITIES
METRO AREA
Page 24**

Hastings

Lakeville

**Chapter 4
MINNESOTA RIVER VALLEY
AND SOUTHERN MINNESOTA
page 214**

Faribault

Mississippi River

Mankato

Owatonna

Rochester

Winona

Onalaska

La Crosse

Caledonia

Albert Lea

Austin

Fairmont

**MINNESOTA
IOWA**

Esterville

Forest City

Manly

Emmetsburg

Mason City

Algona

Clear Lake

Charles City

0   25 miles

0   50 km

© AVALON TRAVEL

Contents

How to Use This Book

ABOUT THE MAPS

This book is divided into chapters based on regions that are within close reach of the cities; an overview map of these regions precedes the table of contents. Each chapter begins with a region map that shows the locations and numbers of the trails listed in that chapter.

Each trail profile is also accompanied by a detailed trail map that shows the hike route.

Map Symbols

------.	Featured Trail	(80)	Interstate Freeway	O	City/Town
------.	Other Trail	(101)	U.S. Highway	✕ ✈	Airfield/Airport
▓▓▓	Expressway	(21)	State Highway	⚲	Golf Course
▓▓▓	Primary Road	66	County Highway	🖎	Waterfall
▓▓▓	Secondary Road	❶	Trailhead	〰	Swamp
▫▫▫	Unpaved Road	★	Point of Interest	▲	Mountain
··········	Ferry	❷	Parking Area	♠	Park
—·—·—	National Border	⋀	Campground	〕〔	Pass
—··—	State Border	▪	Other Location	✦	Unique Natural Feature

ABOUT THE TRAIL PROFILES

Each profile includes a narrative description of the trail's setting and terrain. This description also typically includes mile-by-mile hiking directions, as well as information about the trail's highlights and unique attributes.

The trails marked by the **BEST** ◖ symbol are highlighted in the author's Best Hikes list.

Options

If alternative routes are available, this section is used to provide information on side trips or note how to shorten or lengthen the hike.

Directions

This section provides detailed driving directions to the trailhead from the city center or from the intersection of major highways. When public transportation is available, instructions will be noted here.

Information and Contact

This section provides information on fees, facilities, and access restrictions for the trail. It also includes the name of the land management agency or organization that oversees the trail, as well as an address, phone number, and website if available.

ABOUT THE ICONS

The icons in this book are designed to provide at-a-glance information on special features for each trail.

- The trail climbs to a high overlook with wide views.
- The trail offers an opportunity for wildlife watching.
- The trail offers an opportunity for bird-watching
- The trail features wildflower displays in spring.
- The trail visits a beach or other recreational water site.

- The trail travels to a waterfall.
- The trail visits a historic site.
- Dogs are allowed.
- The trail is appropriate for children.
- The trail is wheelchair accessible.
- The trailhead can be accessed via public transportation.

ABOUT THE DIFFICULTY RATING

Each profile also includes a difficulty rating. The ratings are defined as follows:

Easy: Easy hikes are two hours or less round-trip and have less than 100 feet of elevation gain (nearly level). They are generally suitable for families with small children and hikers seeking a mellow stroll.

Easy/Moderate: Easy/Moderate hikes are between two and three hours round-trip and have less than 100 feet of elevation gain. They are generally suitable for families with active children above the age of six and hikers who are reasonably fit.

Moderate: Moderate hikes are between two and four hours round-trip and have between 100 and 200 feet of elevation gain. They are generally suitable for adults and children who are fit.

Moderate/Strenuous: Moderate/strenuous hikes are between two and four hours round-trip and have between 200 and 300 feet of elevation gain. These hikes are suitable for hikers who are very physically fit.

Strenuous: Strenuous hikes are four or more hours round-trip and have more than 300 feet of elevation gain. They are suitable for very fit hikers who are seeking a workout.

The level of difficulty for any trail can change considerably due to weather or trail conditions. Always phone ahead to check on current trail and weather conditions.

INTRODUCTION

Author's Note

Simply put, I'm a hiker. Because I'm from north-central Minnesota, my life has been framed around the outdoors since before I could tie my own hiking boots. Striding through majestic pine forests, swinging from gnarled oak branches, and swimming in north country rivers is what I do best.

Even though I was raised outside of the city, I've lived most of my adult life in the Twin Cities metro area. How do I cope? I've spent much of that time with my feet strapped into a pair of hiking boots, and I hardly let the dust settle on a trail before I come back for another visit.

St. Paul and Minneapolis boast more than 300 parks and open spaces with trail systems that total more than 200 miles. So despite living in a large metropolitan area, Twin Cities residents have their pick of places to get away from all the urban trappings.

Even though Minnesota's most well-known outdoor destinations are in the internationally renowned Boundary Waters Canoe Area Wilderness (BWCAW) and along Lake Superior and its rugged north shore, the areas within two hours of Minneapolis and St. Paul offer hikers some of the most scenic and peaceful trails in the country. The landscape, carved by the monolithic glaciers of the last ice age, is a mix of lakes, rivers, expansive wetlands, evergreen forests, and grassy prairies. The natural beauty of the region, combined with a sense of stewardship that prevails in Minnesotan culture, means that many areas around the state, and even within the Twin Cities themselves, are preserved as undeveloped parks with amazingly serene hiking areas.

If you like vast tallgrass prairies rife with blooming wildflowers, craggy cliffsides along rushing river ravines, and high blufftop overlooks with expansive vistas of the mighty Mississippi River, then you'll love the hikes in this book. From the rolling prairie lands of southwestern Minnesota to the major bird migratory corridor along the sloughs of the Minnesota River Valley south of the Twin Cities, a two-hour drive in any direction will reveal more peaceful natural spaces than you can shake a walking stick at. Try hopping over the glacial potholes along the St. Croix River Dalles. Climb the hundreds of wooden steps up the ravine walls along the Whitewater River. Watch a flock of hundreds of great blue heron come to nest in the cottonwood tree rookery just south of Minneapolis. You will come to view our great northern state in an entirely different light.

Best Hikes

(Best Historical Hikes

St. Anthony Falls Heritage Trail and Pillsbury Islands, Twin Cities Metro Area, page 29.

Mille Lacs Loop, Brainerd Lakes and the Mississippi River Valley, page 92.

Grand Portage Trail, St. Croix River Valley, page 154.

Pike Island Loop, Minnesota River Valley and Southern Minnesota, page 219.

Sugar Camp Hollow and Big Spring Trail, Minnesota River Valley and Southern Minnesota, page 267.

(Best River Hikes

Two Bridges Loop, Twin Cities Metro Area, page 59.

Crow Wing Confluence Trail, Brainerd Lakes and the Mississippi River Valley, page 86.

Swinging Bridge and Summer Trail Loop, St. Croix River Valley, page 157.

Quarry Loop to High Bluff Trail, St. Croix River Valley, page 165.

Kinni Canyon Trail, St. Croix River Valley, page 187.

Pike Island Loop, Minnesota River Valley and Southern Minnesota, page 219.

(Best for Viewing Wildlife

Crow Wing Confluence Trail, Brainerd Lakes and the Mississippi River Valley, page 86.

Lake Rebecca Loop, Brainerd Lakes and the Mississippi River Valley, page 109.

Swinging Bridge and Summer Trail Loop, St. Croix River Valley, page 157.

Riverbend Trail, St. Croix River Valley, page 198.

Big Woods Loop to Timber Doodle Trail, Minnesota River Valley and Southern Minnesota, page 252.

(Best Views

Crosby Farm Loop, Twin Cities Metro Area, page 67.

Lake Pepin Overlook Hiking Club Trail, St. Croix River Valley, page 195.

Dakota and Trout Run Creek Trails, St. Croix River Valley, page 201.

Riverview Trail to Blufftop Trail, St. Croix River Valley, page 204.

King's and Queen's Bluff Trail, St. Croix River Valley, page 207.

◖ Best for Waterfalls

St. Anthony Falls Heritage Trail and Pillsbury Islands, Twin Cities Metro Area, page 29.

Minnehaha Falls, Twin Cities Metro Area, page 56.

Two Bridges Loop, Twin Cities Metro Area, page 59.

Hidden Falls Shoreline Trail, Twin Cities Metro Area, page 64.

Hidden Falls to Hope Trail Loop, Minnesota River Valley and Southern Minnesota, page 255.

◖ Best for Wildflowers

Belle Lake Trail, Brainerd Lakes and the Mississippi River Valley, page 104.

Crow River Loop, Brainerd Lakes and the Mississippi River Valley, page 120.

Theodore Wirth Wildflower Trail, Brainerd Lakes and the Mississippi River Valley, page 145.

Seppman Windmill Trail, Minnesota River Valley and Southern Minnesota, page 249.

Hidden Falls to Hope Trail Loop, Minnesota River Valley and Southern Minnesota, page 255.

Hiking Tips

HIKING ESSENTIALS
Clothing

The reason Minnesotans talk about the weather so much is because there is a lot of it here in the Upper Midwest. Sunshine in the morning doesn't necessarily mean sunshine in the afternoon. Hikers need to prepare for changing weather conditions, especially on longer hikes. The seasons also play a large factor in what you need to wear on the trail. A sturdy pair of tennis shoes might serve you well on the steep river-bluff trails in the dry summer, but come spring you'll want ankle-supporting hiking boots with a thick tread to get you up the muddy inclines.

Paying attention to the type of fabric your clothing is made of is also important. Cotton absorbs and holds moisture, whereas polyester and polyester-blend fabrics dry faster. More advanced fabrics are designed to wick moisture away from your skin and release it through evaporation. Wool is always a safe bet for staying warm. Even if it gets wet, wool holds body heat. Weaving technology is very advanced today and provides several non-itchy wool items, including socks, shirts, and pants. Gore-Tex is my favorite waterproof fabric. It lasts long and is quite durable. If you plan on spending a lot of time on the trail, it is a good idea to spend some money on a few items of good clothing that will keep you comfortable.

I also always recommend wearing a hat and carrying a rain poncho or lightweight jacket. On shorter hikes during the summer this may not always be necessary, but if rain strikes or the bugs get bad in the middle of the woods, having a head covering and a rain jacket can make the difference between a memorable storm encounter and a miserable and dangerous trudge back to the car.

A hat can also be useful for protecting your eyes from the sun and/or keeping

HIKING GEAR ESSENTIALS CHECKLIST

Make your list and check it twice. It has always been helpful for me to have a small hiking bag that is always packed with these items. That way, if the chance to get outside comes up spontaneously, I can just grab my bag and head out the door.

It is important to carry with you what you need, both for comfort and for safety. Here is what I always have on hand:

• First-aid kit and insect repellent

• Flashlight

• Food and water

• Rain jacket and hat

• Sunglasses

• Trail map

• Warm hat, gloves, and long underwear in the cold seasons

your head warm during cold weather. In the late fall and winter always wear waterproof boots and carry gloves and a warm jacket. Long underwear can be your best friend when the temperature drops while you are hiking.

Food and Water

Your car needs fuel to get you to the trailhead, and your body needs fuel to get you through the hike. Being hungry or not having enough water while you are on the trail is a nasty way to spend the day. Always plan on having some extra food and water with you before you leave for a hike. You can easily carry what you need in a small day pack or waist pack. I usually sling a small messenger bag over my shoulder and keep a water bottle and a bag of trail mix in it. Simple foods like nuts and dried fruit will provide you with plenty of energy.

If you decide not to carry your own water, make sure you have some kind of water filtration system with you. I would never recommend drinking from any kind of untreated urban water source, whether you filter it or not. Out in the field, the threat of the waterborne parasite *Giardia lamblia* is a serious one, and giardiasis can cause you great discomfort, including diarrhea, stomach pain, and nausea. Simple water filtration systems are available at outdoor outfitting stores for reasonable prices and will ensure that your drinking water is safe. For hikes of less than three miles, I carry a Nalgene bottle of water (1 quart) with me. For longer hikes, I bring my water filter and Nalgene bottle so I can refill it as I go. As a general guideline, this translates to having a little more than 1 cup of water per mile.

Navigational Tools
Trail Maps

Maps are essential for getting the most out of your hiking experience. Taking the extra time to print or purchase a trail map can save you hours of grief and embarrassment if you get lost on the trail. Keep in mind that current maps are important. Parks often change their trail routes or close trails due to unsafe conditions. Maps are available at every state park office and website, and most other county and regional parks offer their maps online. If you can't find a current map, call the park office for information about how to get one.

Trail Ducks and Blazes

Most of the hikes in this book are well-trod paths, but you can't always count on seeing the route. Finding your way can be difficult in low-light conditions, when leaves cover the ground, or when it is raining or snowing. Many trails are marked with tree blazes, usually of white or blue paint, which indicate you are on the trail.

By standing next to a tree blaze you can look ahead to the next and thus find your way. Blazes are usually at eye level and rectangular in shape.

COMPASS AND GPS SYSTEMS

A map and compass go together like peas and carrots. With a good map it is unlikely that you will get lost, but with a map and compass, you make the chances even slimmer. Just knowing which direction is north can make all the difference when you are trying to get back on track. Make sure you know how to use the compass before you take it on the trail!

Many hikers also use GPS devices to navigate through the woods. These handheld devices track your location via satellite. They can be programmed to tell you the distance you have traveled and the direction you are heading. GPS devices also give you your exact latitude and longitude, which you can give to a rescue worker in the event of an emergency.

BOB RACE

To keep from getting lost (above tree line or in sparse vegetation), mark your route with **trail ducks,** small piles of rock that act as directional signs for the return trip.

First-Aid and Emergency Supplies

You don't need to tote a first responder kit with you, but you should have the basics, including Band-Aids, a flashlight, moleskin for blisters, aspirin, and a small bandage or two. During the summer, sunscreen and sunglasses are essentials that will keep you comfortable and prevent skin damage from the sun. I also carry a pocketknife and a pack of waterproof matches, just in case.

When you are hiking, especially in unfamiliar territory, it is important to be prepared for mishaps. In more remote areas it isn't a bad idea to carry a lightweight sleeping bag or blanket or a small tarp with you to keep you dry and safe should you need to spend the night on the trail. A whistle can also help draw attention if you are hurt or lost.

ON THE TRAIL
Wildlife, Plants, and Insects

It is a virtual guarantee that you will encounter all manner of wildlife, plants, and

STOPPING BLISTERS BEFORE THEY START

There are few things more annoying than getting a painful blister while you are out hiking on an otherwise perfect day. Blisters can happen to even the most trail-ready hikers. It doesn't matter if you've hiked one or one hundred miles – your feet are susceptible. Whether you rub your toe the wrong way when stepping over a boulder, get your feet wet while crossing a stream, or are wearing new hiking boots that haven't been broken in, getting a blister can cut your hike short or make it an extremely unpleasant experience.

The best way to treat a blister is to prevent it from happening in the first place. Try to keep your feet dry at all times, wear boots or shoes that you have gradually worn in and that fit you properly along with snug-fitting socks, and don't get too adventurous with twisting and turning your feet, especially if you haven't hiked for a while.

If you do start to feel a blister forming, stop immediately, remove your shoe and sock, and apply a Band-Aid or moleskin to the red area. If your sock has a hole in it, change it or mend it the best you can. If you don't have any blister first aid items with you, rest awhile and consider returning to your vehicle if you are close enough to get to your first-aid kit.

insects on any given Minnesota trail during every season of the year. Knowing about what is out there can help prepare you for these encounters and even enjoy the wide variety of flora and fauna Minnesota is home to.

BEARS

The thick forests, wide open grasslands, and sweeping wetlands that surround the Twin Cities are rife with wildlife. Most animals that you will encounter are small and nonthreatening. The ubiquitous whitetail deer, for example, lives all over the state in all types of habitat and would rather run into a lake than come close to a human. The hikes in the northernmost areas that this book covers are in black bear territory, however. Although bear encounters are extremely rare, it is important to know what to do and what not to do in the unlikely event that you come across a bear.

Here are some tips to prevent bear encounters:
• Avoid carrying odorous foods.
• Make noise. Bears hate to be surprised, so let them know you are coming by singing, whistling, or talking with your hiking partner(s).
• Travel with someone else or in a group.
• Bears are most active during dawn and dusk. Plan your hikes during the day and stay on marked trails.

If you encounter a bear on your hike:
- Remain calm and avoid sudden movements.
- Do not approach the bear. Give it plenty of space.
- Let the bear know that you are human. Talk to it and wave your arms. Bears have bad eyesight, and if one is unable to identify you, it may come closer for a better look.
- Never run from a bear. Running can elicit a chase.
- If the bear approaches you, distract it by throwing something on the ground near it. If this deters the bear's attention, walk away while it is distracted.
- If you carry pepper spray, make sure you are trained in its use and can trust it if a bear attacks you.
- Never feed a bear.

BIRDS

The migration seasons are always very exciting in Minnesota. Hundreds of thousands of birds move through one of the continent's major bird migration corridors on their way to their spring and winter feeding grounds. Flocks of pelicans take over Pig's Eye Lake near downtown St. Paul, belted kingfishers and black-billed magpies rest in the forests and wetlands of Rice Lake National Wildlife Refuge, and herons from the great blue to green and white hunt and nest in the sloughs and marshes of the Minnesota River Valley National Wildlife Refuge.

I strongly encourage you to walk the trails in this book during the spring and fall migration seasons. Not only will the beauty of the birds astound you, but you will get a deeper understanding of why nature conservation efforts in this state are so important. Thousands of birds and animal species are dependent on Minnesota's critical habitat areas for food, nesting, and shelter. Without places like the lush Minnesota River Valley, the dense forests north of the metro area, and the numerous freshwater lakes and rivers that blanket our landscape, these animals would quickly become endangered.

RARE WILDLIFE

Where can you hear the shake of a timber rattlesnake, see the hard shell of the rare Blanding's turtle, or glimpse the tinted wings of a green heron? All right here in Minnesota. The major bird migration corridor that sweeps vertically through the state, the vast acreage of protected prairie, and the stands of thick forests in the state are the last refuges of some of the country's rarest animals. If you're on a mission to spot some, you probably will. Look for the long-legged fisher and the pine marten while in the woods. Bring binoculars to see the common tern, loon, and rare heron that populate the wetlands, and watch your step on the prairie, where timber rattlers, bull snakes, and Blanding's turtles roam.

Flora

Minnesota is a cornucopia of trees, flowers, grasses, and shrubs. You name it, and it probably grows here. From the rare pink lady's slipper orchid, which grows in the boggy north, to the ever-present white yarrow flowers lining the grassy trails of the south, having knowledge of the plants that surround you can make your hike more enjoyable and more comfortable.

Wildflowers abound in the plush forests and grasslands that surround the Twin Cities. Indian paintbrush, butterfly weed, blooming milkweed, wild daisies, purple coneflowers, wild asters, and lupines race across the grasslands, covering the rolling hills with color and fragrance. In shadier areas near water, wild irises, pitcher plants, and orchids take light root in the wet soil. Amongst the trees, spring ephemerals like the rare dwarf trout lily, bloodroot, and snow trillium poke their blossoming heads into the sun for a few weeks. The Eloise Butler Wildflower Garden in Theodore Wirth Park is regionally renowned for its spring ephemeral collection.

While most of the flora in Minnesota is beautiful and useful, some plants should be avoided: namely, poison ivy. My dad taught me the saying, "Leaves of three, let it be," which is still a good way of identifying and avoiding this itchy weed. Usually in small patches and low to the ground, its distinctive three-leafed arrangement makes it hard to miss. Other irritating plants include purple fireweed and stinging nettle, which cause painful itching, skin irritation, and rashes. Wearing long pants and keeping your ankles covered can prevent contact with these buggers.

Insects

Insects are an unavoidable part of the Minnesota outdoors. Whether it is the mosquitoes of the woods, the flies of the fields, the ticks in the grass, or all three, you will probably emerge from your hike with an itchy bite or two. The best insect repellent is covered skin. Wearing a broad-rimmed hat, covering your neck and arms, and wearing high socks or pants will keep most mosquitoes and flies away, but ticks are another story.

Minnesota is home to 13 different types of ticks, including the black-legged tick, which can carry Lyme disease. If you notice a tick on you, remove it immediately, identify it when you get home, and watch for symptoms. Most Lyme disease symptoms occur one to three weeks after a tick bite and can include flu-like symptoms such as nausea, headaches, muscle soreness, fever, neck stiffness, and rashes. See a doctor immediately if you suspect that you have Lyme disease.

LOCAL NATIVE AMERICAN HISTORY

Minnesota has a rich Native American history. The abundant wild game, vegetation, and fresh water have provided nourishment, shelter, and meaning to indigenous societies. Much of their culture still remains in Minnesota, manifested in the wild-rice harvesting, protected fishing waters, and historic village sites throughout the state.

In Mille Lacs Kathio State Park, evidence of Native American villages dates back more than 9,000 years; the Dakota and Ojibwe Indian tribes both recognized this area for its abundant natural wealth. Ancient village walls, shoreline rice pits, and tool artifacts have drawn national attention. Several areas in the state, including the Mille Lacs Kathio site, have been recognized as national historical sites by the federal government.

Several of the trails in this book pass through or near lands that Native Americans consider sacred. Pike Island, Lake Ogechie, and Big Island (to name just a few) were the sites of early Native American settlements and gathering places. The Stone Arch Bridge, on the St. Anthony Falls Heritage Trail in downtown Minneapolis, marks a spot where tribes from all over the region gathered to trade and practice rituals.

Take some time to educate yourself about the historical significance of these areas. You may find that knowing about the villages, survival tactics, rituals, and myths that came from the Native Americans will enrich your hiking experience. The Minnesota Historical Society (www .mnhs.org) is a wonderful resource for Native American history and information.

Trail Etiquette

HIKING WITH DOGS

Dogs are sensational companions, always enthusiastic about being outside. Having a four-legged friend along for a hike can turn regular dog walking into a truly enjoyable outdoors experience. They are nosy little buggers, though, and if they aren't chasing or barking at wildlife, they are getting into animal droppings or leaving their own. Make sure you keep your dog on a leash and carry the proper waste disposal equipment to keep trails clean and safe.

Most of the trails in this book allow dogs, but many do not. Make sure you check with parks and recreation offices before bringing your dog on the trail. All Minnesota state parks allow leashed dogs on trails, as does the Minnesota Valley National Wildlife Refuge, but several county parks and some city parks do not. And when they do, they always require a dog to be kept on a leash no longer than six feet.

Just because your dog is an animal, it doesn't mean that it will get along with the wildlife. Keep your dog away from porcupines, raccoons, and skunks, and always check for ticks when you return home.

PROTECTING THE OUTDOORS

The land of 10,000 lakes is world famous for its pristine wilderness, its towering

LEAVE NO TRACE

Natural spaces are an increasingly valuable commodity in today's overdeveloped world. By practicing the following Leave No Trace guidelines, we can help to preserve the integrity and beauty of our local natural settings. Use the following list to get an idea of what it means to leave no trace. The more time you spend in nature, the better you will become at minimizing your impact.

The basic rules of Leave No Trace are as follows:

• Preserve the past: Examine, but do not touch, cultural or historic structures and artifacts.

• Leave rocks, plants, and other natural objects as you find them.

• Avoid introducing or transporting non-native species.

• Do not build structures or furniture, or dig trenches.

• Pack it in, pack it out. Inspect your campsite and rest areas for trash or spilled food. Pack out all trash and leftover food.

• Observe wildlife from a distance. Do not follow or approach animals.

• Never feed animals. Feeding wildlife damages their health, alters natural behaviors, and exposes them to predators and other dangers.

• Control pets at all times, or leave them at home.

trees, and its beautiful sky-blue waters. You can help keep it that way by practicing a little respect each time you use the outdoors—simply leave no trace on the trails and in the parks that you visit. Don't leave your mark with knife, pen, or paint on any rocks, cliffsides, or trees. Other people want to enjoy nature without having to see "John + Marsha = True Love 4 Ever" scrawled on a towering red pine or chipped into a sandstone cliff face. You can also do your part by picking up rubbish you see along the trail. Carrying a small trash bag and hauling out a few items you may find can make a world of difference.

Many parks to the south and west of the Twin Cities and within the metro area are taking part in prairie restoration projects. Tallgrass prairie once covered more than one-third of the state. Today many of the wildflowers, native grasses, prairie shrubs, and grassland wildlife that once thrived here are endangered. Respect these restoration efforts by remaining on established trails and leaving wildflowers in the field. Their natural bouquets will look better under the open sky than on your kitchen counter.

TWIN CITIES METRO AREA

© JAKE KULJU

BEST HIKES

For most hikers, Minnesota usually conjures images

of northwoods Lake Superior National Forest hiking trails and rugged canoe portage paths burrowing through the remote Boundary Waters Canoe Area Wilderness (BWCAW). It's easy to see why those exciting areas garner the attention they do. However, one part of the state that outdoor adventurers often overlook is the rich trail system of the Twin Cities.

Thought of by locals as one of the United States' best-kept secrets, the Minneapolis and St. Paul metro area is a hidden treasure largely because of the close ties it has kept with nature. The two cities boast more than 300 parks and open spaces — an almost unheard of number in modern urban areas. The hiking and walking trails that are woven throughout the cities create a system with a combined length that totals more than 200 miles, touring recreational lakes such as the ever-popular Lake Harriet, the epic Mississippi River, babbling Minnehaha Creek and its famous waterfall, and a world-renowned public rose garden created by Theodore Wirth. Amazingly, every mile is contained within the city limits. With the exceptions of Villa Park, Reservoir Woods, and Battle Creek Regional Park, the 20 hikes in this chapter are part of the St. Paul and Minneapolis park systems.

From the protected shores of the Mississippi River, which runs through the downtowns of both cities to the hilltops of each neighborhood, hiking and city dwelling find a happy marriage here. Whether scrambling along the banks of the challenging Mississippi River Gorge or walking through the serene goldfish ponds of St. Paul's Como Park Japanese Garden, the Twin Cities region is as hiker friendly as they come.

The hikes in this chapter will take you through vast floodplain forests, switchbacking up limestone bluffsides, meandering through the only true gorge and the highest waterfall along the 2,200-mile Mississippi River, and through some of the most historic neighborhoods in the city. While most major U.S. cities have park and trail systems, few have as many large, natural open spaces in their urban cores as Minneapolis and St. Paul have. Parklands have protected the majority of the Mississippi River shoreline that runs between the cities since the 1800s.

Although the skyscrapers of St. Paul and Minneapolis are never more than a few miles away, in the right places it is hard to tell you are in the largest city of the Upper Midwest. Travelers come to the Twin Cities for exposure to culture, art, commerce, and the city life, yet they often find that the transition to the urban environment is less dramatic than they anticipated – especially when walking through clouds of monarch butterflies in the bottomlands of Crosby Farm Regional Park or walking silently through the red pine groves of Reservoir Woods.

The trails you will find in this chapter give new meaning to urban adventuring, as some semblance of wilderness is actually maintained here. Take time to explore the vast parklands that make Minneapolis and St. Paul two of the most hikable cities in the country, and you will see city life in an entirely different light.

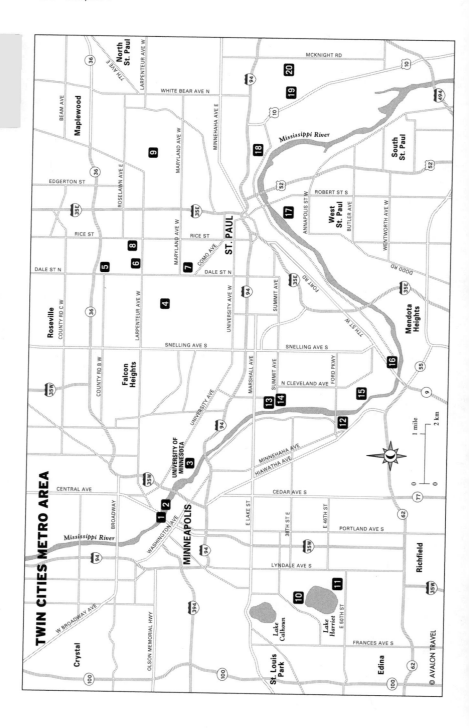

TRAIL NAME	LEVEL	DISTANCE	TIME	ELEVATION	FEATURES	PAGE
1 Nicollet and Boom Islands	Easy	1.6 mi rt	1 hr	Negligible		26
2 St. Anthony Falls Heritage Trail and Pillsbury Islands	Easy	2.25 mi rt	1.5 hr	100 ft		29
3 East River Flats to Old Wagon Road Trail	Easy	3.75 mi rt	2 hr	50 ft		31
4 Como Lake	Easy	1.67 mi rt	45 min	Negligible		34
5 Villa Park Trail	Easy	1.5 mi rt	45 min	Negligible		37
6 Reservoir Woods Trail	Easy	2.9 mi rt	1.75 hr	60 ft		40
7 Loeb Lake Loop	Easy	1 mile rt	0.5 hr	Negligible		43
8 Trout Brook Regional Trail	Easy	2 mi rt	1 hr	Negligible		45
9 Lake Phalen	Easy	3.2 mi rt	1.5 hr	Negligible		47
10 Lake Harriet	Easy	2.75 mi rt	1.25 hr	Negligible		50
11 Minnehaha Creek from Lake Harriet to Minnehaha Falls	Moderate	10 mi rt	5 hr	Negligible		53
12 Minnehaha Falls	Easy	2 mi rt	1 hr	50 ft		56
13 Two Bridges Loop	Moderate/strenuous	7.1 mi rt	3.5–4 hr	200 ft		59
14 Summit Avenue Boulevard	Easy/moderate	9 mi rt	4 hr	50 ft		62
15 Hidden Falls Shoreline Trail	Easy	3.75 mi rt	2 hr	40 ft		64
16 Crosby Farm Loop	Easy/moderate	4.2 mi rt	2.25 hr	50 ft		67
17 Harriet Island to Cherokee Bluffs	Moderate/strenuous	4.25 mi rt	2.5–3 hr	200 ft		70
18 Indian Mounds Loop	Easy	1.75 mi rt	1 hr	75 ft		74
19 Point Douglas Trail	Easy	3.5 mi rt	2 hr	Negligible		77
20 Battle Creek Loop	Easy	1.5 mi rt	1 hr	80 ft		79

■ NICOLLET AND BOOM ISLANDS

Nicollet Island Park, Minneapolis

Level: Easy

Hiking Time: 1 hour

Total Distance: 1.6 miles round-trip

Elevation Gain: Negligible

Summary: View the top of St. Anthony Falls and get one of the best views of the Minneapolis skyline.

Although these two islands are not wilderness areas by any stretch of the imagination, they do provide excellent urban hiking trails and a great view of the Minneapolis skyline. Both of the islands are just north of downtown Minneapolis in the Mississippi River.

Nicollet Island connects historic northeast Minneapolis to downtown via the Hennepin Avenue Bridge. The park and the island are named after cartographer Joseph Nicollet.

Walk from the parking lot straight through the park to the southern end of the island. From the promenade on the lower end of the island you can view the 1858 horseshoe dam just above St.

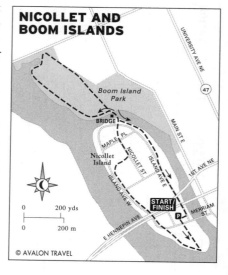

Anthony Falls—the first ever built on the Mississippi. Take a right and follow the paved trail along the island's western end.

This section of the park features the historic Nicollet Island Pavilion, built in 1893 as the William Bros. Boiler Works. The upper end of the island is a 19th-century residential district of 43 homes of architectural styles dating from the 1860s to the 1890s, when Minneapolis was rapidly growing into a boomtown. The path follows Island Avenue and gives a spectacular view of the river and downtown Minneapolis. The fringes of the island are lined with some oak and maple trees, though most of the land is developed.

One-fifth of a mile from the parking lot, a paved walking trail leads through the park area at the upper end of the island. Follow the trail to Nicollet Street and take a left. You will cross Maple Place and continue on the trail until you reach the water. Take a left here and cross the old railroad bridge, which has

© JAKE KULJU

The southern shore of Nicollet Island lies just above St. Anthony Falls.

been converted into a walking path bridge. This bridge connects Nicollet Island to Boom Island.

Boom Island is a leisurely park with a spacious atmosphere. Full of 25 acres of open grassy areas, a large prairie restoration meadow with wild roses and daisies, a picnic area and shelter, boat launch, and riverside promenade, Boom Island is an urban paradise. While the skyscrapers of Minneapolis jut into the sky just a mile away, this breezy open field is a wonderful respite from city life. A channel once separated Boom Island from the riverbank, but over time the area was filled, Boom Island was absorbed into the mainland, and prairie restoration efforts began.

After crossing the old railroad bridge, follow the trail to your left. This takes you near the water and along the riverside promenade. The paved path loops around Boom Island and returns you to the bridge. As you approach the bridge, the last 0.25 mile borders a large meadow of wildflowers and prairie grasses. Take a moment to look at the many butterflies, birds, and bumblebees that give color and music to this beautiful area.

Hop back onto Nicollet Island and follow the gravel trail below Island Avenue along the shore that leads to a set of railroad tracks. The trail merges with Island Avenue here and leads back to Nicollet Island Park and the parking lot.

Options

From Nicollet Island Park you can take a left and cross the Hennepin Avenue Bridge toward downtown and take a right onto West River Parkway for 0.75 mile. Cross the river again on the Plymouth Avenue Bridge and take a right into Boom Island Park for more views of the river and to turn this hike into a 1.5-mile loop.

Directions

From Minneapolis head north across the Hennepin Avenue Bridge and exit right into the Nicollet Island parking lot.

Public Transportation: Bus route 61 stops at Hennepin Avenue and Wilder Street.

Information and Contact

There is no fee. Dogs are allowed. Picnic tables, a playground, and restrooms are available. For more information, contact the Minneapolis Park & Recreation Board, 2117 West River Road, Minneapolis, MN 55411, 612/230-6400, www .minneapolisparks.org.

2 ST. ANTHONY FALLS HERITAGE TRAIL AND PILLSBURY ISLANDS BEST 【

Stone Arch Bridge and Mill Ruins Park, Minneapolis

Level: Easy

Hiking Time: 1.5 hours

Total Distance: 2.25 miles round-trip

Elevation Gain: 100 feet

Summary: View the largest waterfall on the Mississippi, explore the islands under the Pillsbury factory, and see historic Main St. Park.

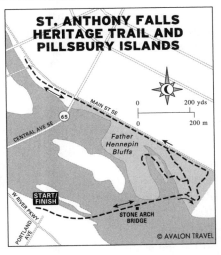

The history of downtown Minneapolis reads like a Hollywood blockbuster script. In the late 17th century an adventurous Catholic priest sought out the storied falls of the Upper Mississippi River. World-famous explorers later portaged and traded at the site, which countless generations of Native Americans had used as a ritual ground and trading hub. After 200 years of development that rapidly turned the city into a boomtown, the world's wealthiest railroad tycoon built an immovable stone arch bridge across the continent's largest river. The railroad industry faded over the next century and a half, and the city that once drew its lifeblood from rail traffic revitalizes the defunct bridge and adopts it as a symbol of its once great heritage.

All you have to do is drive to Mill Ruins Park and start hiking! From the parking lot, walk along the bench-lined paved path up to the entrance to the Stone Arch Bridge. It is a Historic Civil Engineering Landmark, added to the National Register of Historic Places in 1971 as part of the Saint Anthony Falls Historic District. The bridge is just short of being 0.5 mile long and will give you the city's best view of St. Anthony Falls. The cataract at your left is the largest on the entire 2,200-mile Mississippi River. When you cross the bridge, keep to your right.

A railing and informative plaque give a bit of history about the area, and a small wildflower garden is planted at the site. The garden blooms with Indian paintbrush and blazing stars, memorializing the site where it is believed that Father Hennepin first viewed the Falls of St. Anthony in 1680. Just beyond the garden a sidewalk path curves west through the open picnic and amphitheater area atop Father Hennepin Bluffs. Follow the path through the oak and maple trees to the walkway that leads along historic Main Street in Main St. Park. Lined with restaurants, the historic Pillsbury factory, and architecture from Minneapolis's boomtown days, historic Main Street leads to the Hennepin Avenue Bridge. Turn around here and cross the street if you wish to take in the other side of the thoroughfare. This river path and the Stone Arch Bridge are part of the longer St. Anthony Falls Heritage Trail, which loops through downtown.

When you return to the bluffs, veer to the right on the sidewalk path that leads to the yellow bandstand. Keep walking toward the river on your right and look for the set of wooden steps that lead down to the islands of Pillsbury Park. The steps are steep, so make sure to use the handrail. At the bottom, take a right and follow the rocky trail bridged with wooden steps and footbridges through a small set of islands at the foot of the falls and under the historic Pillsbury factory. You will more than likely see grebes and great blue herons wading in the backwater of the falls amidst the islands.

Take the stairs back up to the bluffs. The bridge entrance is about 100 feet ahead of you on your right. Walk back to the parking lot while taking another look at St. Anthony Falls. Just beyond the falls lie Nicollet Island and the Hennepin Avenue Bridge. Ahead of you on the return trip you will be able to see the world-famous Guthrie Theater, the Mill City Museum, and the ruins of Mill Ruins Park to your left.

Options

At the end of the bridge on the return trip, take a left on West River Parkway to see the ruins of Mill Ruins Park and the Mill City Museum along a planked boardwalk. This venture will add 0.25 mile to your hike.

Directions

From Minneapolis take West River Parkway to Mill Ruins Park at the intersection of Portland Avenue. Parking is under the bridge in the park.

Public Transportation: Bus route 22H stops at 5th Avenue and Washington Avenue.

Information and Contact

There is no fee. Dogs are allowed. Picnic tables and a bandstand are available. For more information, contact the Minneapolis Park & Recreation Board, 2117 West River Road, 612/230-6400, www.minneapolisparks.org.

3 EAST RIVER FLATS TO OLD WAGON ROAD TRAIL

East River Flats Park, Minneapolis

Level: Easy

Hiking Time: 2 hours

Total Distance: 3.75 miles round-trip

Elevation Gain: 50 feet

Summary: Enjoy a beautiful bluff walk on the Mississippi, from East River Flats to the old Meeker Island Lock and Dam.

East River Flats Park is one of the easiest accesses to the Mississippi River Gorge and waterfront on the east side of the river. The limestone bluffs here rise only 25 feet, which made it a choice spot to put a parking lot and paved walking path. The park is a 26-acre stretch of land that lies upon the flat deposits formed by the inner side of a large bend in the river. Just below the University of Minnesota's Minneapolis campus, this open, grassy park has a sand beach and wide-open recreation field that is almost always in use.

Start this hike by following the 0.5-mile loop around the flats from the parking lot. A paved walkway takes you along the river's shore and right to the foot of the bluffs. Some remnants of floodplain forest, mostly manifested by oak trees that line the face of the bluff and the riverbank, are still present on the flats and the bluff face.

Once you return to the parking lot, walk away from the river onto Mississippi River Boulevard. Take a right onto the paved path that leads southeast. This trail follows the top of the bluff along the eastern edge of the Mississippi River Gorge. This is a well-maintained area that has benches, drinking fountains, informational plaques, and kiosks interspersed throughout the park pathway.

From East River Flats Park, walk away from the river following the path to the right as it leaves the park. To get to the Old Wagon Road Trail you will walk for 1.25 miles along East River Parkway. Due to its close proximity to the University of Minnesota, this portion of the hike is a shared trail area. Bicyclists and inline

The Old Wagon Road Trail near Meeker Island is a national historic site.

skaters frequent this path in the summer, and many people walk their dogs or sunbathe in the area.

Approximately 0.5 mile from the flats you will cross the Franklin Avenue bridge. Continue along the trail, taking time to look at the opposite shore from your height on the bluffs. Several unmarked trails lead down to the riverside along this portion of the hike. You can take some time to explore these offshoot trails and enjoy the shade of the trees that grow on the steep slopes leading to the water. Large oak and maple trees line the bluffsides here and create cool, shady areas on either side of the river. Squirrels and rabbits abound here, and occasionally you may see a raccoon or a shy fox. Deer are rare in the city but can sometimes be seen at dawn or dusk feeding along the tree line.

Shortly after passing under a large railroad bridge you will come to the Old Wagon Road Trail on your right at the site of the former Meeker Island Lock and Dam. Meeker Island was the site of the first lock and dam facility on the Upper Mississippi River, built in 1912. A decade later, a hydroelectric dam was built downstream, which negated the need for the Meeker Island facility. The dam was demolished, although some ruins of the lock remain. Tops of the old lock walls are sometimes visible during low water periods. The Meeker Island Lock and Dam ruins were added to the National Register of Historic Places in 2003, and a St. Paul Parks & Recreation project recently developed the Old Wagon Road Trail that leads to the site. The switchback trail is just short of a quarter mile long and leads to a shady riverfront viewing area across from the old lock.

When you are ready to head back, climb up the switchback and retrace your steps to the flats. The return trip will treat you to views of the Minneapolis skyline and the artful architecture of the University of Minnesota campus.

Options

At the top of the Old Wagon Road Trail, continue southeast along the river bluff for 0.75 mile to see the Shadow Falls viewing area at the end of Summit Avenue. This extra stretch will add 1.25 miles to your hike. Shadow Falls is a 40-foot trickling waterfall in a ravine that leads to the river.

Directions

From St. Paul head west on I-94 for 6.2 miles. Exit onto Huron Boulevard and take a left on Fulton Street East for three blocks. Turn right onto East River Parkway just past the University of Minnesota Cancer Center. Turn left into the East River Flats parking lot.

Public Transportation: Bus route 144 stops at the Huron Station.

Information and Contact

There is no fee. Dogs are allowed. Picnic tables are available. For more information, contact the Minneapolis Park & Recreation Board, 2117 West River Road, Minneapolis, MN 55411, 612/230-6400, www.minneapolisparks.org.

4 COMO LAKE

Como Park, St. Paul

Level: Easy

Hiking Time: 45 minutes

Total Distance: 1.67 miles round-trip

Elevation Gain: Negligible

Summary: This easy walk rambles through the shady oaks, native tallgrass, and open fields surrounding Como Lake in picturesque Como Park.

The land surrounding Como Lake was set aside in 1891 to preserve open wilderness areas for city-dwelling St. Paulites. One of the metro area's most popular parks, Como Park includes the lake, a theme park, the Como Zoo, the Como Conservatory, and the Japanese Garden with goldfish ponds. Full of open fields, majestic oak trees, and "Oz"-like buildings, the park hearkens back to the early boomtown days of St. Paul and is a favorite for students looking for a quiet study spot and for people unwinding after work.

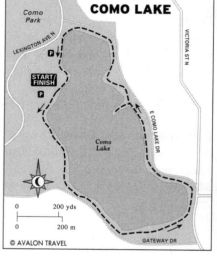

Start at the parking lot of the architecturally striking Grand Como Pavilion, which is situated on the western side of the lake, and head counterclockwise around the water. The wide paved path is shared with bicyclists, so make sure to stay on the designated walking area. The walkway curves around the southern bend of the lake for the first 0.25 mile. A portion of the southern shore is part of St. Paul's natural habitat restoration program. In the summer months, you will find yourself amidst lakeshore grasses and bright prairie flowers like asters, milkweed, and wild daisies waving in the breeze.

As the trail arcs over to the east side of the lake, it winds beneath gnarled oak trees, which provide a decent amount of refreshing shade. This stretch is a popular spot for anglers. At the 0.75-mile mark there is a memorial bench that looks across the water at the pavilion and beyond to the wide open grassy fields that stretch out from the lake. With the shore restoration project and the pine grove of the southern shore to your left and the sweep of the blue lake at your feet, this is one of the best panoramas of the park. A half mile farther

These gnarled pine trees provide shade on the southern end of Como Lake.

up the trail, a small peninsula called Duck Point juts out into the lake, just wide enough for the path. If an angler isn't stationed there with fishing pole in hand, this little nook makes for a great resting spot amidst the soft lapping of the waves. A trip along this same stretch in autumn treats hikers to rich fall colors, from the browns of the oak leaves to the golden yellows of the maple leaves that are scattered throughout the western fields of the park.

The northern bend of the lake is closer to the more populated areas of the park and the traffic of Lexington Parkway. Zoo and conservatory visitors, dog walkers, and brown-bag lunchers frequent this stretch of the trail. Here, near the golf course, the path oxbows through manicured lawns and brightly colored flower beds maintained by the park service in the spring and summer. As the arc of the walkway straightens out toward the south, it branches out in several directions leading toward the zoo, conservatory, and picnic area. Keep to the left and finish the final 0.25 mile to end up back at the pavilion.

Options

Visit the impressive Como Conservatory, Japanese Garden, or Como Zoo just 0.5 mile away to turn this hike into an entire afternoon or day trip. After circling the lake, take a right at the stone waterfall and follow the sidewalk path through the oak trees toward the conservatory. Signs will direct you to the Japanese Garden. Look for the huge goldfish the park keeps in the garden pond.

Directions

From St. Paul head west on I-94 for 3.5 miles, exit onto Lexington Parkway, and drive north for approximately 1.5 miles (30 blocks). Turn right on Nusbaumer Drive into the Grand Como Pavilion parking lot.

Public Transportation: Bus route 3 has a stop at Como Avenue and Lexington Parkway.

Information and Contact

Dogs are allowed. There is no fee. Maps are available on the park website. For more information, contact St. Paul Parks & Recreation, 50 West Kellogg Boulevard, Suite 840, St. Paul, MN 55102, 651/266-6400, www.stpaul.gov (click on *Government, Parks and Recreation,* and then *Parks*).

⑤ VILLA PARK TRAIL
Villa Park, Roseville

Level: Easy

Total Distance: 1.5 miles round-trip

Hiking Time: 45 minutes

Elevation Gain: Negligible

Summary: One of Roseville's most rural-feeling parks, Villa Park lines a pond and stream system that flows to nearby McCarrons Lake.

Villa Park provides a little taste of a pond and stream wetland system, just north of St. Paul. The park encompasses a low marshy area of small ponds and a stream that runs toward nearby McCarrons Lake. The park offers visitors a nice array of amenities, most notably the lush acreage, a ball field, two play areas, a hockey rink, a basketball court, and a small picnic shelter. One unique amenity is the bocce ball court in the western portion of the park near the B-Dale club.

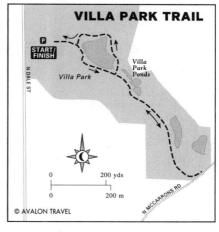

A park sign near a set of stairs marks the entrance to Villa Park from the parking lot. Walk down the stairs and follow the paved walking path toward the pond. At the trail T, take a right around the water.

Much of the beauty of Villa Park lies in its unmanicured, natural appearance. The stream that connects the small ponds of the park is laden with cattails, reeds, and tall grasses. Ducks, Canada geese, wild turkey, and frogs and salamanders love Villa Park and can almost always be spotted. Look for turtles sunning themselves on rocks and logs as well as rabbits scurrying into the underbrush.

At the far end of the pond, continue straight along the stream past the playground. You will enter a shady oak and maple tree-lined area. This 0.25-mile section of the trail leads to North McCarrons Road. When you reach the road, turn to your left and walk on the viewing platform on the edge of the pond that the stream widens into. Here at the bottom of the park you can look up the entire length of the stream through the willow, oak, and maple tree-lined mini stream valley.

After you've taken in the scenery, walk back through the tree-lined portion of

Wild turkeys roam around Villa Park in early spring looking for something to eat.

the trail. When you reach the larger pond closer to the parking lot, take a right and cross the footbridge on the southern end of the water. This paved trail leads around the eastern side of the pond. Approximately 500 feet from the bridge, veer off on the branch of the trail that leads away from the water. This detour takes you through a grassy, open area that is more residential than the rest of the park. Turn around at County Road B. When you reach the pond once more, take a right. You will cross a smaller bridge very near the set of steps that lead to the parking lot.

Options

Make Villa Park a starting point for a longer hike around McCarrons Lake. At the southern end of the park, cross North McCarrons Boulevard and take a left. This sidewalk walkway leads to the beach at Lake McCarrons County Park, and eventually loops for 1.75 miles around the entire lake. Large, overhanging willow trees line several shore areas of the lake, and the large open water is a welcome sight in the city.

Directions

From St. Paul head north on I-35 East for 4.1 miles. Exit onto MN-36 West for 1.8 miles and take the Dale Street exit. Take a left on Dale Street and another left on County Road B. The parking lot is just behind the B-Dale Club on County Road B.

Information and Contact

There is no fee. Dogs are allowed. A playground and picnic tables are available. Maps are available on the park website. For more information, contact the City of Roseville Parks & Recreation, 2660 Civic Center Drive, Roseville, MN 55113, 651/792-7006, www.ci.roseville.mn.us (click on *Departments, Parks and Recreation,* and then *Parks and Facilities*).

6 RESERVOIR WOODS TRAIL

Reservoir Woods, Roseville

Level: Easy

Hiking Time: 1.75 hours

Total Distance: 2.9 miles round-trip

Elevation Gain: 60 feet

Summary: This large park, heavily wooded with groves of red pine trees, is preserved as a natural area and open space.

If you want to get buried in the woods without leaving the city, take a hike through Reservoir Woods, a 52-acre park containing some of the highest ground in Roseville. Right on the St. Paul city limits, this heavily wooded area is reserved as a Ramsey County Open Space site. The area houses a 30-million-gallon underground reservoir that was operated by the city of St. Paul until 1997.

With Larpenteur Avenue to your back, take the trail on the right side of the parking lot near the map kiosk. The paved trail goes downhill into a wetland area past the fenced dog park. At the bottom of the hill, the trail enters a pine grove and takes on the feel of a large, remote outdoors area. The thick forest and lower elevation of the park make it a quiet and peaceful place removed from most of the sounds of traffic.

Orange mileage markers are positioned every tenth of a mile along the paved walkway. Stands of red (Norway) pine are periodically marked with signs that explain their scientific name and their role in the native habitat.

At the 0.3-mile marker, a sheltered bench offers shaded seating, and an information area features a large map that shows the trail you are on in relation to the surrounding area.

Take a left at the rest area and follow the trail through a lighted tunnel under the Dale Street road bridge. The trail winds through the quiet forest for another 0.5 mile. Look for the whitetail deer that love this secluded forest oasis. You may also see skunks, rabbits, and raccoons. At the 0.8-mile marker a planked walkway leads to a small overlook with railings and benches. Enjoy the view of a thick stand of red pine and a seasonal stream. You will no doubt hear the chirping of birds and rat-tat-tatting of woodpeckers before moving on. This quiet glen is also a favorite visiting spot for whitetail deer.

This heavily wooded city park is an urban refuge for raccoons, groundhogs, nesting songbirds, and swans. When the city of Roseville created Reservoir Woods Park, the land was intentionally left in a very forest-like state. Very little development has been done other than building a paved trail through the park and maintaining various natural-surface trails.

At the 1-mile marker the trail curves right and up a ridge to a more open area near another grove of pine trees. A portable restroom is usually available here. One-fifth mile later, just past a signal tower, the trail opens up to a meadowland of grasses and flowers. Violets, clover, and

These majestic pine trees sway in the breeze along the Reservoir Woods Trail.

some Indian paintbrush can be seen here. The wooden birdhouses that dot the field and the tall grasses are a nice contrast to the thicker forested portion of the trail.

The pavement ends at the 1.4-mile marker at Victoria Street near the Roselawn Cemetery. Take a left and walk through the red gate onto a gravel path. The gravel leads to the right and will take you through the meadowland you saw just 0.2 mile back on the paved trail. Walk through the meadow and follow the dirt trail until it loops back to the paved trail. Follow the path back through the woods to your starting point.

Options

The park's paved trail connects to the McCarrons Lake path and Trout Brook Regional trails to the east, side paths along Roselawn Avenue and Lexington Avenue to the west, a side path along Dale Street to the north, and the parking area off of Lexington to the south. These options can add anywhere from 0.5 to 2 miles to your hike.

Directions

From St. Paul head north on Rice Street for 3 miles. Take a left on Larpenteur Avenue for 0.7 mile and take a right into the Reservoir Woods parking lot across from Mackubin Street; it's marked with a large wooded sign and map kiosk.

Public Transportation: Bus route 65 stops at Dale Street and Larpenteur Avenue.

Information and Contact

The park offers two off-leash dog areas, a sheltered bench, and an information kiosk. There is no fee. Maps are available on the park website. For more information, contact the City of Roseville Parks & Recreation, 2660 Civic Center Drive, Roseville, MN 55113, 651/792-7006, www.ci.roseville.mn.us (click on *Departments, Parks and Recreation,* and then *Parks and Facilities*).

7 LOEB LAKE LOOP
Marydale Park, St. Paul

Level: Easy

Hiking Time: 0.5 hour

Total Distance: 1 mile round-trip

Elevation Gain: Negligible

Summary: In St. Paul's residential North End, Marydale Park is a refreshing splash of green amidst the urban landscape.

Great things come in small packages, and Marydale Park embodies that saying more than any other St. Paul park. With beautiful Loeb Lake, a wealth of picnic areas, a playground, fishing pier, restrooms, and barbecue grills, Marydale Park is an oasis of relaxation and open space in the city's North End. Cottontail rabbits, raccoons, and plenty of mallards frequent this peaceful park.

The park was established in 1974 after North End community organizations and citizens worked to reclaim the area around Loeb Lake. Loeb Lake has since been designated as a children's fishing pond by the Minnesota Department of Natural Resources. It is stocked each spring with crappies and bluegills. Anglers might also find the occasional bullhead or bass within its waters.

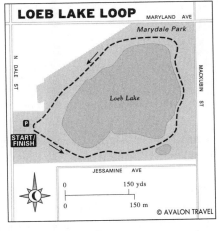

From the circular parking lot, walk toward the brick restroom building. Descend a set of wooden steps and follow the paved path with the lake to your left. About a third of the way around the lake, and 0.2 mile from the parking lot, a fishing pier and walkway juts into the water. Walk onto the platform and cast your line, or just take a look at the water and shoreline.

Willow trees, wild daisies, and shoreline grasses abound around the lake thanks to one of the city's ambitious shore reclamation projects. The projects suit Loeb Lake well, giving this well kept park a uniquely inviting feel reminiscent of lakes in more remote areas.

Continue around the lake and enjoy the shade of the large oak trees that grow throughout the open areas of the park. In the summer, Marydale is full of the laughter of children, the smell of barbecue pits, and bright Minnesota sunshine.

The natural shoreline of Loeb Lake is a welcome dash of wilderness in the city.

When you have looped back to the parking lot, take another go around the lake, or turn around and head counterclockwise to take in the trail from another angle.

Options

If 1 mile isn't enough for you, follow the sidewalk path that leads southeast away from the lake on the opposite end of the parking lot. This walkway leads out of the park and connects to the adjacent city block. The neighborhood surrounding Loeb Lake is a peaceful community that is a delight to walk through. Take a series of three right turns to return to the park, adding up to another mile to your hike.

Directions

From St. Paul take Rice Street north to Como Avenue. Turn left and drive 1 mile to Dale Street. Follow Dale Street for 0.5 mile and turn left into the park entrance parking lot.

Public Transportation: Bus route 65 stops at the entrance of the park.

Information and Contact

There is no fee. Dogs are allowed. Picnic tables and a restroom are available. Maps are available on the park website. For more information, contact Marydale Park, 542 Maryland Avenue West, St. Paul, MN 55117, 651/632-5111, www.stpaul.gov (click on *Government, Parks and Recreation,* and then *Parks*).

8 TROUT BROOK REGIONAL TRAIL

Lake McCarrons County Park, St. Paul

Level: Easy

Hiking Time: 1 hour

Total Distance: 2 miles round-trip

Elevation Gain: Negligible

Summary: The Trout Brook Trail leads through the undeveloped wetlands surrounding the waterway and through part of St. Paul's Eastside.

This hike is geared more toward the urban adventurer. Known mostly by bikers taking a divergent route from the popular Gateway State biking trail, Trout Brook Regional Trail is a nicely paved path that follows a set of railroad tracks, skirts a city pond, slips past housing developments, and cuts through an industrial district on St. Paul's North End.

From Lake McCarrons County Park, take a right on Rice Street to the crosswalk. Pick up the trail on the other side of the road and follow it across a set of railroad tracks. The trail makes a sharp right-hand turn here and runs between the brook on the left and the railroad tracks on the right.

For the next 0.25 mile you will walk along the brook and through the open grass and wetland areas that surround the waterway. Wild daisies, violets, and clover poke through the grass until the path reaches Larpenteur Avenue. Cross the street at the crosswalk into the trees and resume along the paved path.

Over the next 0.5 mile you walk through a shady wooded area of maple trees, following the reedy shores of the brook. You will walk under the Wheelock Parkway bridge, and shortly thereafter (approximately 0.25 mile after crossing Larpenteur Avenue) the brook widens after passing through a culvert bridge. The trail skirts around small ponds here in a low, wetland area that slows the brook. Ducks, geese, and the occasional swan frequent this area. You may also see redwing blackbirds, raccoons, and wood ducks. Although deer aren't frequently seen in the city, you have a much greater chance of seeing one here than almost anywhere else. Look to the tree line and watch for their tracks along the trail.

On the far side of the largest of these ponds the trail crosses to the opposite side of the brook. You walk along the edge of a residential area on the edge of a vast wetland area full of cattails and reeds. This low field is full of chirping frogs, flitting birds, and brightly colored buzzing dragonflies. You will almost certainly see deer tracks along the edge of this wet area, especially near that large pond.

The paved path eventually emerges from the cattails and deposits you on Jackson Street. The last 0.25-mile stretch to the turnaround point is through a more urbanized area. Take a right on Jackson Street to the intersection of Arlington Avenue. Cross the street and take a left on Arlington. In 500 feet, turn right on L'Orient Street for another 400 feet until the trail meets the paved Gateway State bike trail.

Follow the path back to Lake McCarrons County Park, this time headed upstream along the brook. Keep your eyes open for deer and other wildlife that may be grazing around the cattail and pond area.

Options

Take a right on the Gateway State trail at the end of L'Orient Street to walk past the large pond and walking bridge to Cayuga Park to add an extra 0.5 mile to your hike. This trail is more exposed than the Trout Brook walkway, but if you don't mind the city walk, give it a try.

Directions

From St. Paul head north on Rice Street for 3 miles. Turn left into the Lake McCarrons Beach park entrance and parking lot.

Public Transportation: Bus route 62 stops at Rice Street and Roselawn Avenue.

Information and Contact

There is no fee. Dogs are allowed. Restrooms, picnic tables, and a beach are available at Lake McCarrons County Park. Maps are available on the park website. For more information, contact Lake McCarrons County Park, 1765 North Rice Street, Roseville 55113, 651/748-2500, www.co.ramsey.mn.us (click on *Parks and Recreation*).

9 LAKE PHALEN
Phalen Regional Park, St. Paul

Level: Easy

Hiking Time: 1.5 hours

Total Distance: 3.2 miles round-trip

Elevation Gain: Negligible

Summary: Serene Lake Phalen gives views of oak savanna, shoreline restoration, and a sense of openness in picturesque Phalen Regional Park.

Lake Phalen is at once the most charming and most mysterious lake in the Twin Cities. The lake and the creek that flows from it to the Mississippi played large roles in St. Paul's history. The small delta at the creek's mouth is thought to be the place at which Father Louis Hennepin landed on his journey to discover the falls of St. Anthony in 1680. In the mid-1800s, the creek flowed southwest through Swede Hollow, a crowded, ramshackle low-rent area filled with early Swedish and Scandinavian immigrants.

Lake Phalen and Swede Hollow have since become city parks, and the creek that flows from the lake to the river was entombed underground at the turn of the 20th century by the railroad companies. The creek is now contained in a cavernous 22-foot-high drainage tunnel, and the low delta that once spread into the Mississippi was filled in and used as a rail yard.

Phalen Regional Park has a popular golf course, a beach house, shore restoration areas, picnic and outdoor amphitheater areas, a fishing pier, a playground, and a tennis court. Mallards, swans, and grebes can be seen among the reeds near the shoreline.

From the beach house parking lot, walk down to the water and take a right at the beach. The southwestern side of the lake is lined with rustic wooden fencing protecting shore restoration areas along the lake. Willow trees hug the water, and the grassy open areas narrow as the trail soon merges with Wheelock Parkway. Wrap around the southern edge of the lake and follow the trail north along East Shore Drive. When you cross the large stone culvert bridge you can see the beach

The southeastern shore of Lake Phalen is part of a shoreline renovation project led by the St. Paul Parks & Recreation Department.

house and grassy fields full of thick oak trees, clover flowers, and wild daisies at the trailhead.

The creek once cut a large ravine through the area and is rumored to have been lined with several caves. Some say that Lake Phalen itself is rife with underwater caves. Whether it is or not, Phalen is easily one of the deepest lakes in the area, which adds to its mystery.

For the next mile, the trail hugs East Shore Drive between the lake and the road. At the north end of the lake the trail enters the more open park grounds. As you curve toward the south you will walk between Lake Phalen to your left and the smaller Round Lake to your right. Stay on the walkway closest to Lake Phalen and you will cross Keller Creek, which connects the two bodies of water. Just on the other side of the bridge is the fishing pier. Lake Phalen is one of the most heavily fished metro area lakes.

The last 0.5 mile of the hike takes you through the picnic pavilion and playground and past the Lakeside Activities Center. From there, the beach house parking lot is just 0.25 mile ahead.

Options

At the northern end of the lake, veer right at the parking lot and take the walkway around adjoining Round Lake to take in more of the aquatic plants and waterfowl of the park. The diversion will add 0.5 mile to your hike.

Directions

From St. Paul head north on I-35 East. Exit right on Larpenteur Avenue East. Turn right at Arcade. Turn left onto Wheelock Parkway. Turn left onto Phalen Drive East. Park in the beach house parking lot on your right.

Public Transportation: Bus route 64 stops at Wheelock Parkway and Maryland Avenue.

Information and Contact

There is no fee. Dogs are allowed. A restroom, picnic areas, playground, and beach are available at the park. Maps are available on the park website. For more information, contact St. Paul Parks & Recreation, 50 West Kellogg Boulevard, Suite 840, St. Paul MN 55102, 651/266-6400, www.stpaul.gov (click on *Government, Parks and Recreation,* and then *Parks*).

10 LAKE HARRIET

Lake Harriet, Minneapolis

Level: Easy

Total Distance: 2.75 miles round-trip

Hiking Time: 1.25 hours

Elevation Gain: Negligible

Summary: Lake Harriet is a beautiful urban lake with swimming beaches, hiking trails, a bandstand, and a park-like shoreline.

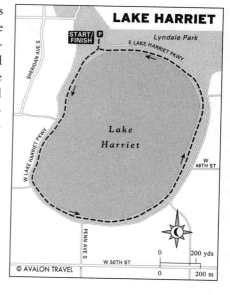

Lake Harriet is one of Minneapolis's most popular lakes. A staple of the Chain of Lakes system, Lake Harriet is bordered by Lyndale Park and its rose garden and features a park-like path along its entire shoreline. A trail at the northwest end leads to Lake Calhoun, and another at the southeast corner connects the trail system to Minnehaha Creek. Lake Harriet was named for Harriet Lovejoy, wife of Colonel Leavenworth, who in 1819 founded what was later renamed Fort Snelling. Shoreline was donated in the 1880s by local landowners. The land north of the parkway, which is now Lyndale Park and Lakewood Cemetery, was donated around 1890.

From the parking lot, walk toward the band shell. The walking path starts between the lake and band shell. Move counterclockwise around the lake with the water to your left. On the lake side of the band shell is a marina where canoes and sailboats can be rented or stored for use. A nearby dock allows canoeists to access the water. Sailboats are on the lake virtually every day during the summer.

Continue walking along the western shore of the lake, making sure you are utilizing the walking path and not the biking path. Lake Harriet is part of the Grand Rounds bike trail system, which runs through the Twin Cities and is used by thousands of cyclists each year. A mile into the hike you reach the southern edge of the lake directly across from the band shell. For the rest of the loop around the lake the striking band shell is visible.

A mile farther up the trail you near Lyndale Park and the Lyndale Park Rose

The beautiful bandshell on Lake Harriet can be seen from all points along the trail that circles the lake.

Garden. The garden is the second-oldest public rose garden in the nation. Constructed in 1908, the 1.5-acre garden was designed by the "father of rose gardens," Theodore Wirth. In 1946, it was designated an official All America Rose Selections (AARS) test rose garden. The majestic Heffelfinger Fountain is on display on the patio amidst the roses.

Lyndale Park also has gently rolling hills that feature beautiful oak savanna. Take a minute to walk in the shade of the beautiful trees and rest on soft slopes overlooking the lake. The last 0.25 mile back to the band shell is a breeze. You walk past the popular north beach and get a full view of the entire lake from north to south.

Options

After returning to the band shell, take a right on Lake Harriet Parkway and follow it through William Berry Park to add a view of glimmering Lake Calhoun and an additional 0.75 mile to your hike.

Directions

From Minneapolis take I-35 West south for 1 mile to the 35th/36th Street exit. Turn right at 35th Street East and left on Nicollet Avenue. Turn right on 36th Street West for 1.3 miles. At East Calhoun Parkway turn left. Take another left on William Berry Parkway and drive into the East Lake Harriet Parkway parking lot.

Information and Contact

Parking is $0.50 per hour. The park is open from dawn until dusk. Dogs are allowed. Picnic tables, restrooms, and refreshments are available. Maps are available on the park website. For more information, contact the Minneapolis Park & Recreation Board, 2117 West River Road, Minneapolis, MN 55411, 612/230-6400, www.minneapolisparks.org.

11 MINNEHAHA CREEK FROM LAKE HARRIET TO MINNEHAHA FALLS

Minnehaha Parkway, Minneapolis

Level: Moderate

Hiking Time: 5 hours

Total Distance: 10 miles round-trip

Elevation Gain: Negligible

Summary: Walk along Minnehaha Creek from Lake Harriet all the way to the famous 53-foot Minnehaha Falls near the Mississippi River.

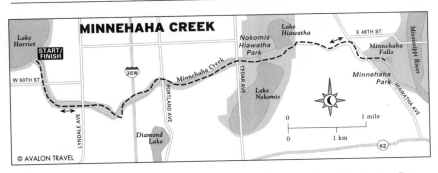

Minnehaha Creek is a playful and picturesque tributary of the Mississippi River. The most popular section of the creek runs for 5 miles from Lake Harriet to Minnehaha Falls. The entire creek is more than 22 miles long, originating at Lake Minnetonka and traveling through several suburbs and most of south Minneapolis before reaching the Mississippi River.

As beautiful as its waters are, the most notable part of the creek is the 53-foot waterfall at the center of Minnehaha Park near its confluence with the Mississippi River. The tributary site is not far from historic Fort Snelling—one of the region's earliest settlements.

From Lake Harriet Parkway, take a right at the intersection of Minnehaha Parkway. A paved path veers to the right of the parkway and leads along a small wooded waterway toward Minnehaha Creek itself. Like the Lake Harriet trail, the Minnehaha Parkway trail has a bike path and a walking path. Make sure you stay on the pedestrian-only trail. Violets grow in this shady area, and rabbits, squirrels, and sparrows all love the cover provided by these urban trees.

The trail meets the creek near 50th Street next to Lynnhurst Field. Follow the creek trail as it bends eastward. The creek's depth and speed vary depending on the time of year and the amount of recent rainfall. During long bouts of dryness in the summer the creek can literally be reduced to a trickle, and the falls can nearly

Wooden footbridges like this one cross Minnehaha Creek intermittently on the way to the falls.

disappear. But during robust rains in the spring and summer the creek quickly becomes a fast-moving and fairly deep channel that has surprising force.

About a mile from Lake Harriet, the trail dips under the Lyndale Avenue bridge—a particularly picturesque spot on the creek, with a wooden boardwalk that winds under the stone arch of the old bridge. There are some steps along the boardwalk that emerge on the other side of Lyndale Avenue, but nothing too serious. This hike has hardly any noticeable elevation change. Wheelchair users can use the paved bike path that crosses Lyndale Avenue above the creek. Half a mile from the Lyndale bridge the trail passes under the I-35 West overpass and follows the creek northwest past Portland Avenue. As the creek nears Lake Nokomis, beautifully crafted bridges connect paths across the water at various points along the creek.

At Bloomington Avenue, stay on the walkway adjacent to Minnehaha Parkway. You are not immediately next to the creek here, but you will soon walk through Lake Nokomis park and rejoin the creek near Lake Hiawatha as it flows from one lake to the other. Lake Nokomis may entice you to leave the trail to view the willow tree-lined lake and its beach. The trail and the creek cross Minnehaha Parkway on the northern side of Lake Nokomis and wind through a rolling oak savanna. A larger bridge takes you across the mouth of the creek at Lake Hiawatha and leads you to the crossing at 28th Avenue. Use the crosswalk here and descend the slope back to the creekside.

From here to the falls the creek makes four large bends on its way downstream.

Stay on the northern side of the creek during the next 0.5 mile and take a right at Hiawatha Avenue where the trail meets a T. This path brings you to the Longfellow Gardens adjacent to Minnehaha Park. Cross Minnehaha Avenue and continue to follow the creek to the falls viewing area.

You may want to rest here and enjoy the sights and sounds of the waterfall. Take the same path back to Lake Harriet, following the creek upstream this time.

Options

You can park a car at Minnehaha Park and shuttle back to your starting point to cut your hiking time in half. The falls is a great ending point and this option still gives you a great 2–3-hour hike through this beautiful natural setting that runs through the city.

Directions

From Minneapolis take I-35 West south for 2.2 miles to the 46th Street exit. Turn right on 46th Street East for 1 mile. Turn left at Humbolt Avenue South and right onto Minnehaha Parkway.

Information and Contact

Free curbside parking can be found on Lake Harriet Parkway and on nearby side streets. Dogs are allowed. Picnic tables and benches are interspersed along the entire length of the creek. Minnehaha Park has restrooms, refreshments, and sheltered picnic areas. Maps are available online at www.melchert.org/Minnehaha%20Creek%20Map.htm. For more information, contact the Minneapolis Park & Recreation Board, 2117 West River Road, Minneapolis, MN 55411, 612/230-6400.

12 MINNEHAHA FALLS

BEST ◖

Minnehaha Park, Minneapolis

Level: Easy

Total Distance: 2 miles round-trip

Hiking Time: 1 hour

Elevation Gain: 50 feet

Summary: View the state's most famous waterfall in one of Minneapolis's oldest parks.

Minnehaha Park is Minneapolis's most well-rounded hiking area. Walking paths vary from packed dirt to forest floor to pavement. Scenery includes a dazzling waterfall, a babbling creek, native wildflowers, and the Mississippi River. The park was established in 1889 by the City of Minneapolis and has served millions of visitors since.

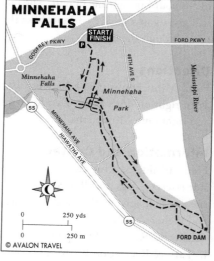

Follow the paved path through the park gates near the drinking fountain. The trail heads 0.25 mile through an oak savanna picnic area toward the creek. In the summer, this portion of the park is usually full of people throwing Frisbees, walking their dogs, and barbecuing. As you near the creek you walk past the bandstand and come to the stone wall and railing that leads to the viewing area for the falls.

You will hear the falls before you see them. Minnehaha means "laughing waters," and you'll soon hear why. When they do come into sight it is through silver birch trees that line the rim of the basin the creek falls into. Henry W. Longfellow wrote the poem "Song of Hiawatha" about these very falls, and the footprints of President Lyndon Johnson commemorate the spot he viewed the falls from on a visit to Minnesota.

Take the stone stairway to your left that leads below the falls, and soak in the spectacular view from a footbridge that crosses the creek just under the waterfall. When you are ready to move on, cross the bridge and follow the trail downstream as it runs adjacent to the creek. The trail leads through the small ravine cut by the creek and swings through an open grassy area. Turn left in a few hundred feet downstream from the falls and follow a second stone bridge over the creek. Turn right and keep following the trail, with the water to your

© JAKE KULJU

The famous Minnehaha Falls is a 53-foot cataract near the terminus of Minnehaha Creek.

right. After a bend in the creek, the path joins a wider gravel walkway that leads farther downstream. Stay on this path as it narrows into a packed dirt trail. This route takes you through the floodplain forest floor, through grassy creekside flower beds of wild daisies and creeping bellflowers to the rocky mouth of Minnehaha Creek as it becomes a tributary of the Mississippi River. This spot, just below Ford Dam, is a popular fishing hole for local anglers. All season long you are sure to find people in waders or casting from shore.

Cross the bridge at the river's mouth and head upstream on the opposite bank. You can see the shoreline and the trail on the other side of the creek that you previously traveled. Take your time to spot the native wildflowers and the diverse trees in this portion of the park, including oak, silver maple, basswood, birch, elm, and cottonwood.

When you return to the bend in the creek that led you to the gravel path, cross over the water on the stone bridge at the mouth of the small ravine. Walk 0.2 mile across the open grassy area and up a gravel path to the sidewalk. Follow this path to your left back to the parking lot.

Options

Cross Minnehaha Park Drive on the western edge of the park to enter the Longfellow Gardens. The garden area is a land bridge that traverses Hiawatha Avenue. The formal garden features a sundial, flowers planted in paisley patterns, and a pergola. Prairie flowers and grasses line the creek and outer edges of the garden. This will add an extra 0.25 mile to your hike.

Directions

From Minneapolis drive east on Washington Avenue. Turn right onto Hiawatha Avenue/Highway 55 for 3.5 miles. Turn left at 46th Street East and right again onto Minnehaha Avenue. After the traffic circle take the third exit and drive west on Godfrey Parkway. Turn right into Minnehaha Park parking lot just before 46th Avenue South.

Public Transportation: Bus route 27 stops at 46th Street and Minnehaha Avenue.

Information and Contact

There is no fee. Dogs are allowed. A restroom, picnic shelter, bandstand, and refreshments stand are all in the park. Maps are available on the park website. For more information, contact the Minneapolis Park & Recreation Board, 2117 West River Road, Minneapolis, MN 55411, 612/230-6400, www.minneapolisparks.org.

13 TWO BRIDGES LOOP

Mississippi Parkway, St. Paul

BEST ☾

Level: Moderate/strenuous

Total Distance: 7.1 miles round-trip

Hiking Time: 3.5-4 hours

Elevation Gain: 200 feet

Summary: Follow the Mississippi River gorge as it clings to the edges of the bluffs and descends into the bottomlands along the river's shore.

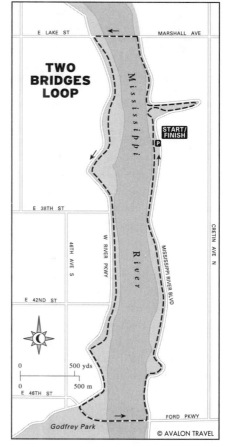

As far as urban wilderness exploration goes, this is as good as it gets. More than 7 miles of Mississippi River gorge trail fishtails through the floodplain forest and low bluffs along one of the most scenic portions of the river between St. Paul and Minneapolis.

Start by walking behind the railing at the western edge of the parking area and taking a right. The path leads out to a rock outcropping that overlooks the river and the skyline of Minneapolis. Take in the scenery and keep moving to your right. A packed dirt trail follows a stone wall for about 100 feet and then veers to the left and through the shady oak trees that surround a small ravine cut by Shadow Falls. The path leads to the top of the fall where you can watch the small stream that feeds it tumble into the gorge. Turn right here and follow the path as it merges with the paved walking trail along Mississippi River Boulevard at Cretin Avenue. Take a left on this walking path as it follows the river.

The path winds along the edge of the bluffs for 0.5 mile, leading to a stairway at the base of the Lake Street bridge. Climb the stairs and walk over the river. Upstream, to the north you will see the University of Minnesota's Minneapolis campus. To the south you will see the Ford Parkway bridge—the second bridge

This overlook from the trailhead gives a clear view of the Lake Street bridge.

of the loop. Once you reach the Minneapolis side of the river, take a left and walk down to West River Parkway. Cross the street and take a right. In a few hundred feet you will come to a set of stairs that leads down to the river. At the foot of the stairs, join up with the packed dirt trail that leads along the shoreline forest at the base of the low rising bluffs. From here you will be able to see the rock formation at your starting point across the river.

Follow the trail as it moves through shady oaks, wild daisies, violets, and blooming milkweed flowers amidst the river grasses that cover the area. Keep your eyes peeled for urban wildlife like rabbits, groundhogs and raccoons that live near the river. About a third of the way to the second bridge (near 38th Street) the bluffs move closer to the riverbank, and the trail ascends along the bluff walls as they come flush with the water. This part of the hike can be challenging and will require some light climbing. Make sure you have good ankle support and are willing to hold on to trees for balance along the narrow parts of the trail on the edge of the bluff.

This river gorge area you are passing through is part of Mississippi Park, which merges with Godfrey Park and Minnehaha Park to the south. On both sides of the river you will encounter great blue herons, whitetail deer, painted turtles, and possibly raccoons. Urban wildlife love the lush, shady river gorge and often have small dens and nests among the rocks and trees.

Around 44th Avenue, the trail leads out of the gorge and up to a small grassy area along West River Parkway. Turn to the right, away from the river, and follow the paved walking path on the parkway. The path will lead you past the Lock & Dam #1 site near 46th Street. Follow the walkway as it curves to your right. Approximately 400 feet from the lock, climb the steep slope at the base of the 46th Street bridge. You will emerge in Godfrey Park on 46th Street as it crosses the Mississippi River. Walk over the bridge and take a left onto Mississippi River Boulevard. The paved path leads 1.75 miles along the bluff back to the parking area and lookout point that you started from. This last section of the loop gives you great lookout points to the opposite bank and the bottomlands you were just climbing through a few miles back.

Options

The brave of heart can descend the gorge on the St. Paul side of the river as well. After taking a left onto Mississippi River Boulevard off of the Ford Parkway bridge, find a footpath that descends the bluff. This part of the bluff is extremely steep and difficult to descend. Practice extreme caution. A packed dirt trail at the bottom of the gorge twists its way back to the parking lot and lookout point.

Directions

From St. Paul head west on Summit Avenue for 4.5 miles. Park in the Mississippi River Boulevard parking lot at the end of the avenue by the river.

Public Transportation: Bus route 63 bus stops at Summit Avenue and Cretin Avenue. Bus route 134 stops at Summit Avenue and Cretin Avenue.

Information and Contact

The parking lot is open from dawn until dusk. Dogs are allowed. There is no fee. For more information contact St. Paul Parks & Recreation, 50 West Kellogg Boulevard, Suite 840, St. Paul, MN 55102, 651/266-6400, www.stpaul.gov (click on *Government, Parks and Recreation,* and then *Parks*), or the Minneapolis Park & Recreation Board, 2117 West River Road, Minneapolis, MN 55411, 612/230-6400, www.minneapolisparks.org.

🔢 SUMMIT AVENUE BOULEVARD

Summit Avenue, St. Paul

🔭 👓 🐕 👪 🚌

Level: Easy/moderate

Total Distance: 9 miles round-trip

Hiking Time: 4 hours

Elevation Gain: 50 feet

Summary: Historic Summit Avenue passes the opulent mansions of Victorian-era St. Paul and treats you to views from the bluffs.

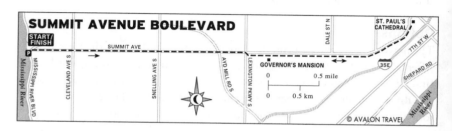

For a walk along one of the best-known urban parks in the Twin Cities, look no further than famous Summit Avenue. Jam-packed full of Victorian mansions of the 1850s, Summit Avenue is 4.5 miles of history and charming open park boulevard that runs like a green lifeline through the heart of St. Paul. This entertaining hike will take you past the opulent mansions of railroad tycoon James J. Hill, one of F. Scott Fitzgerald's early St. Paul residences, and the classy Governor's Mansion. If those historical sites aren't enough, Summit Avenue starts at the brilliant century-old St. Paul Cathedral and ends on the high bluffs of the Mississippi River's eastern shore.

You can start the hike at either end of the avenue, but a starting point at the river lets you begin and end in more of a park setting, and parking is more readily available on the river end.

From the parking lot, cross Mississippi River Boulevard and walk through the tree-lined boulevard running down the middle of Summit Avenue and separating the two lanes of traffic for 2.5 miles, until Summit Avenue intersects with Lexington Parkway. Use caution at road crossings along the route. After crossing Mississippi River Boulevard, the path climbs a slope adjacent to the University of St. Thomas's South Campus and the St. Paul Cemetery. This open area is full of stately oak trees and on a clear day gives a view of the Minneapolis skyline from the river bluff lookout point. Joggers and dog walkers frequent this stretch of the avenue, and bikers use the bicycle-only lanes on either side of the boulevard. Evergreen and deciduous trees, flower beds, and park benches make this a lovely path to stroll down, especially on weekends during the summer, when the city is full of people who are out and about.

At Lexington Parkway, use the crosswalk and move to the right side of Summit Avenue. Approximately 500 feet after crossing, you come upon the Governor's Mansion. From here to the cathedral, the majority of the Victorian houses that Summit Avenue is famous for are on display. Summit Avenue is currently part of two National Historic Districts and two City of Saint Paul Heritage Preservation Districts; 373 of the original 440 1800s residences are preserved here.

At Dale Street, ascend a small incline and veer left shortly after Arundel Street. At the top of the hill, the historic University Club and a small park overlooking downtown St. Paul are on your right. From here the avenue curves northeast and ends at the majestic St. Paul Cathedral. The cathedral is surrounded by an open grassy area where you can enjoy a picnic or rest before heading back toward the river.

A grassy, tree-lined boulevard runs down the middle of Summit Avenue for nearly three miles.

Options

The small park at the start of this hike is home to Shadow Falls. The surrounding neighborhood was once named after the small falls. From the parking lot take a left on Mississippi River Boulevard and follow the paved path around the small ravine cut by the falls and back to add another 0.5 mile to your hike.

Directions

From St. Paul head west on Summit Avenue for 4.5 miles. Park in the Mississippi River Boulevard parking lot at the end of the avenue by the river.

Public Transportation: Bus route 134 stops at Summit Avenue and Cretin Avenue.

Information and Contact

The parking lot is open from dawn until dusk. Dogs are allowed. There is no fee. For more information, contact St. Paul Parks & Recreation, 50 West Kellogg Boulevard, Suite 840, St. Paul MN 55102, 651/266-6400, www.cathedral saintpaul.org/.

15 HIDDEN FALLS SHORELINE TRAIL BEST (

Hidden Falls Regional Park, St. Paul

Level: Easy

Hiking Time: 2 hours

Total Distance: 3.75 miles round-trip

Elevation Gain: 40 feet

Summary: Enjoy a quiet riverside hike through the floodplain forest of the Mississippi near the confluence of the Minnesota River.

Hidden Falls Regional Park dates back to 1887, when it was set aside by the famous landscape architect Horace Cleveland as one of St. Paul's four major park sites. The park remained virtually unmodified until the mid-1930s, when the Works Progress Administration (WPA) did a fair amount of work on it, installing a stone stairway and viewing area for the falls.

The spring-fed waterfall that gives the park its name is tucked into a small ravine on the northern side of the park approximately 0.25 mile from the picnic pavilion. The falls feed a beautiful little creek that empties into the nearby Mississippi River.

As wonderful as this park is, it is rarely crowded, even during the summer. This shady walk is a cool and quiet way to escape the city without leaving the city limits.

Walk toward the picnic pavilion and across an open grassy area toward Hidden Falls Creek. Follow the stream up to the falls and you will see the stonework of the WPA, which was laid in 1936 and 1937. A large stone stairway leads up to a lookout point over the falls. Two large stone fire rings sit in the ravine to the left of the trail.

Retrace your steps out of the ravine and take a right on the packed dirt path that follows the bottom of the gorge. The trail is level and wide enough for a wheelchair, but a little bumpy in places. The path loops 1.25 miles back to the parking lot, swinging through the floodplain forest, following a stretch of Mississippi shoreline, and crossing the creek as it empties into the river. Whitetail deer, groundhogs, and raccoons call this area home. As in many of the parks and natural areas along the shores of the Mississippi River in the metro area, oak

© JAKE KULJU

These stone steps lead to the top of the river bluffs.

savanna and bottomland forests cluster along the flats at the base of the river bluffs, providing shade and habitat for songbirds and other wildlife.

When you return to the parking lot, cross the driveway and take a right on the paved trail that leads farther into the park. You will walk past the boat landing, and will more than likely see a few anglers. Hidden Falls Regional Park is just below the Ford Plant Dam and is a congregating point for local anglers.

From the boat landing, the trail leads south and follows the shore of the Mississippi for another 1.25 miles along a stretch of some of the oldest protected shoreline in the city. The gorge area is home to the serene and shady floodplain forest that characterizes this portion of the river.

You eventually come to the Highway 5 bridge. Shortly after crossing under the bridge, the trail enters Crosby Farm Regional Park. Turn around at the bridge and return along the trail to the parking lot. This area of the park has many small packed dirt and natural turf trails that run parallel to the paved trail. If you're in the mood, branch off of the pavement and explore some of the side paths that winnow through the woods.

Options

You can climb out of the bottomlands to get a better view of the opposite shore and the bluff line. Just continue following the paved trail under the Highway 5 bridge and walk up the driveway on your left to Mississippi River Boulevard. Return to the park entrance on the trail high above the river gorge with occasional glimpses of the opposite shore and limestone formations along the face of the bluffs.

Directions

From St. Paul head west on Shepard Road/Mississippi River Boulevard for 6.5 miles. Take a sharp left down the steep driveway to the north park entrance and parking lot.

Public Transportation: Bus route 46 stops at Cleveland Avenue and Magoffin Avenue.

Information and Contact

There is no fee. The park is open from dawn until dusk. Dogs are allowed. A rest-room and a picnic shelter facility are provided for public use. Maps are available on the park website. For more information, contact St. Paul Parks & Recreation, 50 West Kellogg Boulevard, Suite 840, 651/266-6400, www.stpaul.gov (click on *Government, Parks and Recreation,* and then *Parks*).

16 CROSBY FARM LOOP

Crosby Farm Regional Park, St. Paul

BEST C

🏕 🦌 🐾 🌲 🏊 🐕 🐾 ♿ 🚌

Level: Easy/moderate

Hiking Time: 2.25 hours

Total Distance: 4.2 miles round-trip

Elevation Gain: 50 feet

Summary: St. Paul's largest natural park, Crosby Farm is full of wildflowers, floodplain forest, river vistas, and limestone bluffs.

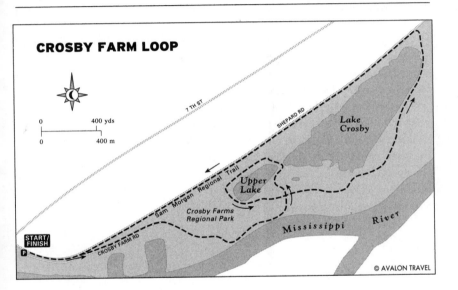

It is a requirement for any Twin City resident who calls him- or herself a hiker to explore the trails of St. Paul's Crosby Farm Regional Park. Clocking in at 500 acres, Crosby Farm is the largest natural park within the city. It is also one of the state's significant natural areas along the State of Minnesota Mississippi River Critical Area Corridor and the Mississippi National River and Recreation Area.

Named after the English immigrant farmer Thomas Crosby, who worked the land more than 150 years ago, the natural area became a park in 1962. Today, the park includes two lakes, shares nearly 7 miles of hiking trails with adjacent Hidden Falls Regional Park, has a sheltered picnic area with restrooms, and displays some of the best-preserved pre-settlement habitat along the river in the metro area. The park is sandwiched between the Mississippi River and Mississippi River Boulevard/ Shepard Road, which run along the bluff that rises from the floodplain.

From the parking lot at the Two Rivers Overlook, take a moment and walk to the viewing area. From the bluff, you can see portions of Fort Snelling State Park, including Pike Island. The overlook shows the confluence of the Minnesota and Mississippi Rivers, where the Minnesota River Valley merges into the larger Mississippi River Valley. From the overlook, walk down Crosby Farm Road to your left. The road leads to the picnic shelter and open recreation field. A paved trail leads from the shelter toward the river. Follow this path through the floodplain forest and along the banks of the river on the southern end of the park. It is just short of a mile from the overlook to the point where the trail borders the river. This portion of the trail is flush with the water. Anglers commonly fish here at the water's edge.

Crosby Farm is a plush, shady natural park. You will find that the paved trail is excellently maintained, but the rest of the park is mostly natural area with little structural interference. Whitetail deer and great blue herons are commonly found in this expansive floodplain area.

The trail hugs the shore for 0.25 mile then turns north toward Upper Lake. As you walk north, you cross over another paved path that leads east and west. Keep walking straight ahead and loop counterclockwise around Upper Lake, crossing the floating boardwalk near the fishing pier. Keep your eyes open for spring ephemeral flowers like bloodroot and trout lily. A recent study conducted by city officials revealed that more than 300 plant species grow in the park. Fishing is also mildly popular here. The lakes provide some pan fish and northern pike.

The wetlands of Crosby Farm Regional Park extend for 500 acres along the shore of the Mississippi River.

As the trail winds around the lake, it eventually becomes the path that you previously crossed. From the crossing point, continue east for another mile along the shore of Lake Crosby. Here the trail runs along the shade-filled wooded bottomlands between the lake and the river. As the trail draws closer to the lake, the marshes and low wetlands near the water dominate the scenery. Here you may see some of the huge original cottonwoods that once enjoyed larger numbers along this stretch of the river.

At the northeast end of Lake Crosby, the trail emerges at Mississippi River Boulevard/Shepard Road. Take a left here along the paved trail that runs along the upper edge of the bluff. The bluff line outlines the northern edge of the entire park for 1.75 miles, revealing beautiful vistas of the opposite shore and the Minnesota and Mississippi River confluence. The trail eventually merges with Crosby Farm Road and leads back to the Two Rivers Overlook point and parking lot.

Options

After returning to the Two Rivers Overlook, continue ahead on the paved walkway along Mississippi River Boulevard; 200 feet to your left the South Entrance to Hidden Falls Regional Park leads down into the floodplain. Follow the road down and take a left onto the paved trail at the bottom of the drive for more riverfront views. The trail leads to the pavilion in Crosby Farm Regional Park. From there, turn left and climb the road that leads back up to the Two Rivers Overlook parking area. This adds 0.25 mile to your hike.

Directions

From St. Paul head west on Shepard Road/Mississippi River Boulevard for 5.1 miles. Turn left at Gannon Road onto Crosby Farm Road and Two Rivers Overlook parking area.

Public Transportation: Bus route 54 stops at West 7th Street and Davern Street.

Information and Contact

There is no fee. Dogs are allowed. The park is open from dawn until dusk. For more information, contact St. Paul Parks & Recreation, 50 West Kellogg Boulevard, Suite 840, St. Paul, MN 55102, 651/266-6400, www.stpaul.gov (click on *Government, Parks and Recreation,* and then *Parks*).

17 HARRIET ISLAND TO CHEROKEE BLUFFS

Harriet Island Park, St. Paul

Level: Moderate/strenuous

Hiking Time: 2.5-3 hours

Total Distance: 4.25 miles round-trip

Elevation Gain: 200 feet

Summary: This challenging hike includes climbing the bluffs to Cherokee Heights, viewing fossil beds in Lilydale Park, and circling Harriet Island Park.

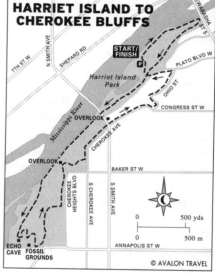

Harriet Island is one of the best known islands on the Mississippi River, and certainly the one best known to Twin Cities residents. The island is named after the pioneer teacher Harriet Bishop, St. Paul's first public school teacher. Bishop moved to Minnesota in 1847 and was a champion of education and women's suffrage in the state. Harriet Island was a true island until 1950, when the channel separating it from the riverbank was filled in. Since then the city has used it as a public park and annual summer concert grounds.

From the West Entrance parking lot, follow the paved path in a clockwise direction around the island toward the nearby pavilion. On the way there, you will see the shell of a replica of Bishop's schoolhouse near the Harriet Bishop Playground on your right. This stretch of trail leads along the waterfront toward the riverboats docked at Lower Harbor. Halfway to the harbor, an overlook gives the best river-level view of downtown St. Paul in the city. At the harbor you will walk near the Wabasha Street Bridge, get a view of Raspberry Island, and get up close to the historic riverboats, including the *Minnesota Centennial Riverboat.*

Just to the right of the harbor is the base of the Wabasha Street Bridge. Walk along the path as it leads away from the bridge. The open oak savanna of the park will be to your right as you walk along Water Street past the band shell and the pedestrian gateway entrance of the park on your way back toward the West Entrance. At the entrance, keep heading west along Water Street. You will pass near Upper Harbor and follow near the base of the river bluffs that quickly rise on your left.

© JAKE KULJU

Water trickles over hanging moss at the foot of a bluff in Lilydale Park.

The paved walkway follows the riverside for 1.5 miles, passing under the Smith Avenue High Bridge and entering Lilydale Park. The area is an undeveloped floodplain on the inner curve of a river bend. Marsh and wooded areas mix in this bottomland park, creating a haven for herons, whitetail deer, and wildflowers. You will undoubtedly see signs of these and other wildlife, especially during the late spring and summer seasons.

Lilydale Park is also the site where the former Twin City Brick Co. operated. The company mined the bluff for clay for almost 100 years. The mining operations have exposed an impressive set of fossil beds, which has made the area well known to urban adventurers and paleontologists alike. At the entrance to Lilydale, Water Street becomes Lilydale Road and veers right. Stay to the left and follow the trail to the fossil beds parking lot on the eastern end of Pickerel Lake. The trail becomes a crushed limestone path that meanders along the base of the bluff on the eastern edge of the park. This trail leads through the floodplain to the foot of the bluff that rises to Cherokee Park. The limestone path winds through three switchbacks up the bluff, approximately 150 feet above.

As you near the bluff you will see several offshoots of the main trail. These lead into the fossil beds. After you make your first sharp left on the limestone path, an offshoot branches to the right. This path leads 20 feet to Echo Cave, a manmade cave once used for mushroom growing and cheese making. The cave entrance is blocked off and is used as a hibernating place for brown bats. Do not attempt to enter Echo Cave, but take time to look at the fossil grounds around it.

After you return to the main trail, start climbing and look for more offshoots—virtually all of them lead to fossil beds and clay pits. In the low areas around these trails, standing water can attract herons and gulls. Also be alert for rabbits and occasional whitetail deer.

After climbing the switchbacks, you will encounter a T in the trail on top of the bluff. Take a right to see the Bruce Vento Overlook just 50 feet away, and return to take a left into Cherokee Regional Park. The gravel trail soon emerges from the wooded area to a paved road. Take a left on Cherokee Heights Boulevard. The road is lined with parkland on either side. Keep the road on your right and walk approximately 500 feet through the grassy field to a parking lot. From here, a paved path leads east through Cherokee Regional Park.

Cherokee Park was set aside as park land in the early 1900s with money given predominantly by railroad baron James J. Hill. The area has always been cherished for its spectacular views of downtown and the Mississippi River. The best views are from the picnic grounds 0.25 mile east of the parking lot. Cherokee Park was a campground for tourists until the 1920s, when it was transformed into more of the public park and picnic area that it is today.

Many natural-turf and packed-dirt paths lead off of the paved walkway toward the edge of the bluff. Explore some of these to get a beautiful vista of the Mississippi River and downtown St. Paul from the blufftop. You will hike the entire length of the park for 1.5 miles, crossing the Smith Avenue High Bridge and winding down the bluff slope along Ohio Street. At the bottom of the hill cross Plato Boulevard to the entrance to Harriet Island Park, where you started.

Options

To put another mile into this hike you can cross the Mississippi River along the Smith Avenue High Bridge. The bridge has pedestrian walkways on either side and gives a great view of the river as it winds through downtown. Return on the opposite side of the bridge and continue to Harriet Island.

Directions

From St. Paul head 0.25 mile south across the Wabasha Street Bridge. Take a right on Water Street and another right into Harriet Island Park at the West Entrance into the parking lot.

Public Transportation: The 75F bus route stops at Wabasha Street and Water Street.

Information and Contact

There is no fee. Dogs are allowed. Restrooms and a picnic shelter are available in Harriet Island Park and Cherokee Park. Maps are available on the park website. For more information, contact St. Paul Parks & Recreation, 50 West Kellogg Boulevard, Suite 840, St. Paul, MN 55102, 651/266-6400, www.stpaul.gov (click on *Government, Parks and Recreation,* and then *Parks*).

18 INDIAN MOUNDS LOOP

Indian Mounds Park, St. Paul

🏛 🦌 🚲 🐕 🚻 🚌

Level: Easy

Total Distance: 1.75 miles round-trip

Hiking Time: 1 hour

Elevation Gain: 75 feet

Summary: This woodsy walk takes you near ancient Indian burial mounds on the bluffs surrounding the Mississippi River.

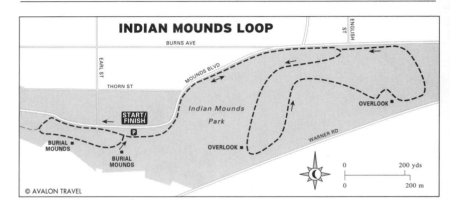

Even if you've seen them a hundred times, the ancient Indian burial mounds at Indian Mounds Park on St. Paul's Eastside are always impressive. This peaceful parcel of land is part of the larger Battle Creek Regional Park and sits atop the quiet bluffs of the Mississippi River. As it leaves the Twin Cities via Pig's Eye Lake, the Mississippi has left large limestone cliffs and bluffs that characterize much of the river valley in southern Minnesota.

From the Mounds Boulevard parking lot, head toward the pavilion on the paved path and follow the boulevard for about 700 feet, then veer left toward the river and the edge of the bluff. Stay left at the next two forks in the trail until you come upon the first set of burial mounds.

The Minnesota Historical Society has identified six distinct remaining burial mounds and speculates that as many as 37 may have once existed. Approximately 2,000 years old, these mounds are believed to have been left by members of the Hopewell culture. The Native American tribe buried their dead with artifacts and ashes from their bodies. Later during the 1600s, 1700s, and early 1800s when the Dakota Indians occupied the area, the site was used to bury their dead wrapped in animal skins.

This section of the park is an open, grassy field with good visibility. The

St. Paul skyline is easily spotted, and benches along the way make this a wonderful spot to take in a summer day.

About 200 feet from the site, you will come upon another group of mounds on your right. Follow the trail to the left back toward the parking lot and follow the paved path east along Mounds Boulevard. When you get to English Street, turn right and leave the pavement, walking toward the tree line and seven large rocks that mark a trail into the woods. A narrow oak-lined path leads past seasonal streams and ponds. In the summer, the plush oaks create a shady canopy over the trail. Wood ducks can be seen here, nesting in houses near the wet areas. You will also see deer tracks, and if you are lucky you might see a deer.

This steep trail leads to the blufftop that overlooks the Mississippi River.

The path eventually veers left up a 30-foot incline to a jutting outlook over Pig's Eye Lake and the river valley. Flocks of pelicans, Canada geese, and trumpeter swans often congregate in the open water during migratory periods. A steep, gravelly slope leads down to a trail on the edge of the bluff near Warner Road. Turn left at the bottom of the slope and follow the trail along the bottom of a horseshoe-shaped ridge. Take the path near the water. Some fallen trees and branches will be across the trail but can be easily stepped over. Whitetail deer and great blue herons are common sightings here.

At the opposite point of the horseshoe, the path climbs back up to the ridgeline and another lookout point. Take the path as it leads to the left and up another slope into a grouping of Norway pine trees. The trail meets a wider path; take it to the right and follow it back to the paved path. Take this left to Burns Avenue and it will loop back to the seven large stones. Continue on the paved walkway to the parking lot.

Options

You can nearly double the length of this hike by walking west on Mounds Boulevard on the edge of the park to the new Bruce Vento Nature Sanctuary and back. The area is a wildlife and native habitat restoration area near the mouth of Lower Phalen Creek.

Directions

From St. Paul head east on Kellogg Boulevard for 1.3 miles. Turn left on Mounds Boulevard and follow it for 1 mile to the park entrance and Mounds Boulevard parking lot.

Public Transportation: Bus route 70 stops at Burns Avenue and Johnson Parkway.

Information and Contact

There is no fee. Dogs are allowed. A playground, a picnic shelter, and a restroom facility are near the parking lot. Maps are available on the park website. For more information, contact St. Paul Parks & Recreation, 50 West Kellogg Boulevard, Suite 840, St. Paul MN 55102, 651/266-6400, www.stpaul.gov (click on *Government, Parks and Recreation,* and then *Parks*).

19 POINT DOUGLAS TRAIL
Battle Creek Regional Park, St. Paul

Level: Easy

Hiking Time: 2 hours

Total Distance: 3.5 miles round-trip

Elevation Gain: Negligible

Summary: Follow playful Battle Creek from the Point Douglas ravine to the upper ponds of the eastern parcel of the park.

One of the most picturesque and peaceful hikes in the city, the Battle Creek trail starting at Point Douglas is a beautiful tour of a Mississippi River creek valley tributary.

Headed south of St. Paul on Highway 61/10 amidst the wrecked car recycling factory and the expansive train yard, you wouldn't think one of the city's most peaceful hikes was nearby. But right off of the highway, Point Douglas Road leads to just that. The

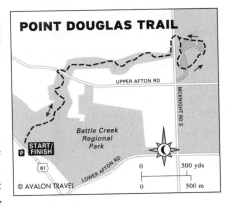

POINT DOUGLAS TRAIL

short road ends at a small parking lot set between the bright exposed limestone cliffs the creek has cut through on its way to Pig's Eye Lake and the Mississippi.

From the parking lot, walk through the ravine with the creek on your right. The soft limestone walls are a bright contrast to the dark trees that line the low bluffs of this area. The paved trail follows the creek upstream past a series of ten three-tiered waterfalls and as many footbridges that crisscross the open water. Benches are placed intermittently along the trail, and open grassy areas invite picnickers and sunbathers, as well as groups of wild turkeys.

As the trail leads away from the parking lot, the limestone cliffs meld into pine and oak woodland and some wetland grass near the creek. In 0.75 mile, the path rises to cross Upper Afton Road/Battle Creek Road. When you reach the road, take a right and cross on the other side of the creek where the paved trail dips back down to the creek. A third of a mile later after the seventh waterfall and a grove of pine trees, cross Ruth Street.

The creek widens here, slightly, and the footbridges become larger. After the tenth waterfall, the path makes a large S curve and emerges at McKnight Road. Cross the road and take a left onto the sidewalk. The paved path will be on your right in 100 yards and will circle through a large portion of the park with three distinct bodies of water. Make a loop around the ponds and the sheltered area. This section of the park is bisected by Upper Afton Road. The area is dominated by majestic oak savanna that provides acres of shaded ground. After walking through the trees and around the ponds retrace your steps downstream from the shelter, across McKnight Road and back to Point Douglas. Since you travel from higher to lower ground on the return trip, there are areas along the trail where you can see far downstream and take in several of the small waterfalls at once. Bring your camera on this hike, as it is one of St. Paul's most picturesque walking trails.

These tiered waterfalls line the creek all the way along the Point Douglas Trail.

Options

If you feel like going all out, continue following the path to your right after crossing McKnight Road. You will cross Upper Afton Road and enter the southern portion of the park. Another mile of trail loops through several more ponds and returns you to the shelter near McKnight Road.

Directions

From St. Paul head east on Shepard Road/Warner Road for 2.4 miles. Veer right onto US-10 East for 1.5 miles. Turn left at Lower Afton Road and take an immediate left onto Point Douglas Road. Continue to the Point Douglas parking lot.

Public Transportation: Bus routes 361, 364, and 365 stop at Lower Afton Road.

Information and Contact

There is no fee. The park is open from dawn till dusk. Dogs are allowed. Maps are available on the park website. For more information, call Ramsey County Parks at 651/266-8500 or visit online at www.co.ramsey.mn.us/parks.

20 BATTLE CREEK LOOP

Battle Creek Regional Park, St. Paul

Level: Easy

Hiking Time: 1 hour

Total Distance: 1.5 miles round-trip

Elevation Gain: 80 feet

Summary: This hike explores the eastern section of Battle Creek Regional Park. The trails meander through oak, birch, and maple trees.

Battle Creek Regional Park is one of the largest open areas in the metro. Consisting of Battle Creek Lake, the westward flowing Battle Creek itself, Indian Mounds Park, and Pig's Eye Lake, the area is an important 1,840-acre Mississippi River Watershed area.

BATTLE CREEK LOOP

© AVALON TRAVEL

Located near the eastern city limits of St. Paul adjacent to the town of Woodbury, Battle Creek Regional Park preserves open and wild areas between the highly developed urban landscape of St. Paul and the suburban community of Woodbury.

Parking is easy to find—the recreation center has a large parking lot and excellent facilities. Facing the center, take a left to the trailhead, marked by a white sign. A grassy trail leads you to the right of a small pond. Wooded areas, grasslands, and wetlands characterize this portion of the park. The beginning of the trail is spotted with pine and large oak trees.

Fifty yards from the trailhead, slant right up a steep hill. This open grassy area is used for cross-country skiing in the winter. The trail turns left at the top of the hill, but take a moment to turn around and look at the sweeping view of the pond and lower portion of the park.

At the top of the hill, the trail moves into a wooded area. Keep your eyes open for whitetail deer, foxes, herons, egrets, and hawks, all of which can be seen in the park. Removed from the highway and bordered by low traffic roads, this portion of the park is very quiet and forest-like.

Entering an oak canopy, the trail bends left into a stand of birch trees. Take a right up a small 20-foot slope and take another right at the top. Another 30 feet later, turn left, following the orange marker arrow. This is a ridgeline trail above an oak-filled

© JAKE KULJU

Natural turf trails run throughout Battle Creek Regional Park.

gully. The trail breaks to an open view of the floodplain to the west. Advance to the next orange marker on the other side of a grassy meadow. Take a left at the marker onto a narrow tree root trail down into the gully. When a wider trail merges with yours, stay straight to the next orange marker and take a left into scattered birch trees and a gradual uphill slant.

This portion of the trail borders Lower Afton Road. Take a right at the next orange marker and another right onto a wide gravel path. During the spring and summer, the frogs from the ponds will be audible from this point on the trail. You can almost follow their sound back to the trailhead. Take a left at a small gate and a right at the next orange marker to leave the woods and reenter the open grass and pond area near the recreation center. Move to the right along the tree line back to the parking lot.

Options

To add another mile to your hike, cross Battle Creek Road at the bottom of the slope you descend after taking a left at the grassy meadow. A trail loops through a smaller wooded section of the park and returns to the same crossing point on the road.

Directions

From St. Paul head east on I-94 East for 3 miles. Exit on White Bear Avenue and take a right. Turn left at Upper Afton Road for 0.8 mile. Turn right at Winthrop Street and right into the Battle Creek Regional Park entrance and parking lot.

Public Transportation: Bus routes 361, 364 and 365 stop at Lower Afton Road.

Information and Contact

There is no fee. The park is open from dawn until dusk. Restrooms and a drinking fountain are available in the recreation center by the parking lot. Dogs are allowed. Maps are available on the park website. For more information, contact Battle Creek Regional Park, 2300 Upper Afton Road, Maplewood, MN 55119, 651/266-8500, www.co.ramsey.mn.us/parks.

BRAINERD LAKES AND THE MISSISSIPPI RIVER VALLEY

© JAKE KULJU

BEST HIKES

Minnesota is home to the headwaters of the mighty Mississippi River. Hundreds of miles of river wind through the state on the way through the heart of the country. From the thick forests of the Brainerd Lakes area to the wide open meadows farther southwest, this diverse area northwest of the metro region is rich in history and habitat.

Although much of the land along the river and in the western part of Minnesota has been converted to farmland, many miles of undeveloped shoreline, oases of forest, and remnant and restored prairie fields can easily be found. The shady Big Woods forests of Lake Maria State Park are a woodsy Eden on hot summer days, and the wide wetlands surrounding Lake Katrina in Baker Park Reserve are a testament to environmental conservation. One of the last nesting places of the rare common tern is found in Father Hennepin State Park on the southern shore of Mille Lacs Lake.

The hikes in this chapter are a comprehensive tour of river walks, forest paths, and prairie tracks northwest of Minneapolis and St. Paul. Hiking terrain in this region of the state can be separated into three sections, moving from hardwood and evergreen forests and marshy wetlands in the north, to the open, rolling prairie lands that extend west toward the Dakotas, to the floodplain forests north of Minneapolis.

Like most of the protected hiking areas in Minnesota, this region is full of historical significance. Many Dakota villages and early European settlements took root along the river and surrounding plains and forests, taking advantage of the abundance of food, water, and ease of travel that it provided them.

Archaeological digs in Mille Lacs Kathio State Park have revealed signs of Native American villages that are more than 9,000 years old along the wild-rice beds of Lake Ogechie. You can also see some of this Native American history firsthand along the Red River Oxcart Trail in Crow Wing State Park.

The confluence of the Crow Wing and Mississippi Rivers was once a bustling logging and trading town. The Beaulieu House mansion still stands at its original site here, commemorating the optimistic attitude the settlers of this area held. Farther down the river at Charles A. Lindbergh State Park, hikers can tour the boyhood home and the practice fields of Charles Lindbergh, the famous aviator.

Farther south you will encounter the winding oxbows and floodplain forests of the Rum River and the tons of gushing water that shoot through the Coon Rapids Dam along the Mississippi just north of the Twin Cities. River trails in this area lead past abandoned barns standing in fields full of wildflowers, through canoe campsites tucked into shoreline coves, and along transitional zones between forest and field where wildlife like whitetail deer, red fox, and the occasional black bear seek food and shelter.

Minnesotans pay tribute to this historical and diverse region by keeping many of the forests, fields, and prairies that run throughout the greater river valley region undeveloped and accessible to hikers and canoeists.

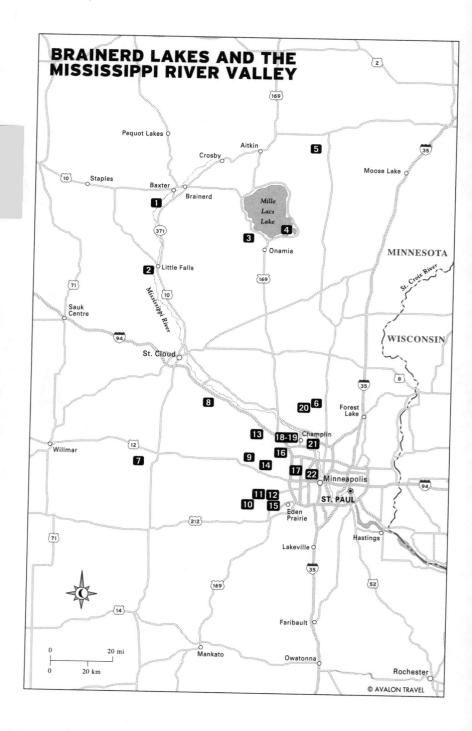

TRAIL NAME	LEVEL	DISTANCE	TIME	ELEVATION	FEATURES	PAGE
1 Crow Wing Confluence Trail	Moderate	6.2 mi rt	3.5 hr	60 ft		86
2 Charles A. Lindbergh Hiking Club Trail	Easy	3.4 mi rt	1.5–2 hr	100 ft		89
3 Mille Lacs Loop	Easy	3.1 mi rt	1.5–2 hr	30 ft		92
4 Mille Lacs Shoreline Trail	Easy	2.5 mi rt	1.5 hr	Negligible		95
5 Rice Lake Refuge Trail	Easy	3 mi rt	1.5 hr	Negligible		98
6 Mount Tom Trail	Easy/moderate	3.7 mi rt	2 hr	100 ft		101
7 Belle Lake Trail	Easy	2 mi rt	1 hr	Negligible		104
8 Big Woods Loop	Easy	3.6 mi rt	2 hr	70 ft		106
9 Lake Rebecca Loop	Easy/moderate	3.5 mi rt	2.5–3 hr	50 ft		109
10 Crosby Lake Trail	Easy/moderate	4 mi rt	2–2.5 hr	50 ft		112
11 Lundsten Lake Loop	Easy/moderate	4.8 mi rt	2.5 hr	Negligible		115
12 Minnetonka Trail	Easy	1 mi rt	0.5–1 hr	Negligible		118
13 Crow River Loop	Moderate	5.7 mi rt	3 hr	50 ft		120
14 Lake Katrina Loop	Easy/moderate	5.5 mi rt	2.5–3 hr	Negligible		123
15 Lake Minnewashta Lake and Woodland Loop Trails	Easy	2.65 mi rt	2 hr	30 ft		126
16 Fish Lake Trail	Easy	2.6 mi rt	1.5 hr	30 ft		128
17 Medicine Lake Trail	Easy	1.5 mi rt	1 hr	40 ft		131
18 Elm Creek Trail	Easy/moderate	4.75 mi rt	3 hr	Negligible		133
19 Mud Lake Loop	Easy/moderate	4.5 mi rt	2.5–3 hr	Negligible		136
20 Rum River Trail	Easy	3.25 mi rt	1.5 hr	50 ft		139
21 Coon Rapids Dam Trail	Easy	2.7 mi rt	1–1.5 hr	Negligible		142
22 Theodore Wirth Wildflower Trail	Easy	2.8 mi rt	1.5–2 hr	Negligible		145

1 CROW WING CONFLUENCE TRAIL BEST ☾

Crow Wing State Park, Brainerd

Level: Moderate

Hiking Time: 3.5 hours

Total Distance: 6.2 miles round-trip

Elevation Gain: 60 feet

Summary: View the historic sites of Native Americans and early settlers as well as the confluence of the Mississippi and Crow Wing Rivers.

A historic Native American battle, an abandoned pioneer-era town, a rich fur trader's mansion, and a century-old cemetery are all packed into this northwoods hike. Just south of Brainerd, Crow Wing State Park is on the northern edge of the Mississippi River Sand Plains region, which was formed by the outwash from the giant glacial Lake Grantsburg. For more than a century this fur and logging town was the northernmost settlement of European-Americans on the Mississippi River. When the railroad chose to cross the river at Brainerd, the town dwindled and eventually faded away.

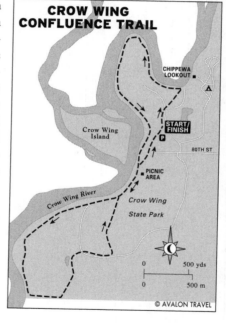

The trail begins directly west of the parking lot near the missionary chapel. Take a right onto the path and head north for 0.3 mile toward the boat landing. As you approach the river, towering red and white pines dominate the riverbank forest. Red squirrels will chatter at you as you walk by, and your footsteps will be softened by the forest turf and pine needles that characterize this rustic northwoods trail. When you reach the boat landing, take a hard left at the parking lot along the southern shore of the river's oxbow. Look for bald eagles soaring above the river channel. Some of them may be nesting nearby in the tops of dead pines. With a pair of binoculars and a little patience you can probably find a nest or two.

At the next trail intersection 0.2 mile ahead, stay to the right and follow a portion of the Red River Oxcart Trail as it drops 30 feet into the floodplain and arcs around the peninsula of land that juts into the oxbow. The trees are broken into clusters where patches of meadow have taken hold here. This once-famous trail was a very important supply route for oxcart traffic in the 1800s between St. Paul and the Red River Settlements. Stay to the right at the next two trail intersections before reaching the Beaulieu House historic site. A merchant named Beaulieu took over the American Fur Company at Crow Wing in 1847 and built a stately Greek Revival mansion at the site. It still stands and is a testament to how promising this area once was for early settlers.

Continue south for 0.2 mile back into the thick pine, maple, oak, and aspen forest to the picnic area parking lot, staying to the right as the trail continues south up the riverbank and through the picnic area; 0.3 mile from the picnic area stay to the right at the trail intersection. Just ahead are the legendary rifle pits. Historians claim that in 1768 the rifle pits were the scene of a major battle between the Ojibwe and Dakota tribes.

Continue west along the riverside trail past the canoe camp. Stay right at the next trail intersection and walk past the G1 group campsite. Continue south for 1.5 miles to the southern border of the park, where the trail makes a 90-degree bend to the east. The trees become less dense once more, with swaths of meadow brushed on the landscape. Some prairie flowers may line the trail here in the spring. Look for columbine and harebell, as well as wild daisies. This forest and meadow mixture is also a haven for wildlife. Whitetail deer, badgers, raccoons, foxes, and even coyotes live here. Porcupines also love the tall pine trees. If you

© JAKE KULJU

An alert chipmunk holds stock-still on a fallen tree branch.

see bark and droppings at the base of a tree, look to the upper branches and you will more than likely see a prickly porcupine busy stuffing its cheeks.

Veer left at the next two trail intersections. The trail makes a small eastern arc for 0.1 mile and then meets a T. Turn right and then left in 0.2 mile to walk north to the intersection just north of the rifle pits. Take a right at the end of the 0.6-mile stretch of trail and retrace your steps back through the picnic area. Take a right at the picnic area parking lot to the chapel at the trailhead and parking lot.

Options

At the boat landing, take a right and climb 40 feet to Chippewa Lookout, a pine-tree-clad hill above the shores of the Mississippi that gives a stunning view of the waterway. This short diversion adds only 0.2 mile to your hike. The overlook point presides over the large oxbow the river makes before it reaches Crow Wing Island. This is also an excellent viewing point for eagles and hawks. On sunny days you can see for miles.

Directions

From Minneapolis take I-94 West for 63 miles. Exit onto MN-15 North toward St. Cloud for another 9 miles. Take US-10 West for 29 miles, then merge onto MN-371 North for 20 miles. Turn left at Koering Road for 0.2 mile and continue straight onto County Road 27. Go straight past the park office to the parking lot by the picnic area.

Information and Contact

There is a $5 daily vehicle permit fee. Restrooms and drinking fountains are available in the picnic areas and at the park office. Dogs are allowed. Maps are available at the park office and on the park website. For more information, contact Crow Wing State Park, 3124 State Park Road, Brainerd, MN 56401, 218/825-3075, www.dnr.state.mn.us.

2 CHARLES A. LINDBERGH HIKING CLUB TRAIL

Charles A. Lindbergh State Park, Little Falls

Level: Easy

Hiking Time: 1.5-2 hours

Total Distance: 3.4 miles round-trip

Elevation Gain: 100 feet

Summary: Visit the boyhood home of the famous pilot Charles Lindbergh while taking in beautiful views of the upper Mississippi River.

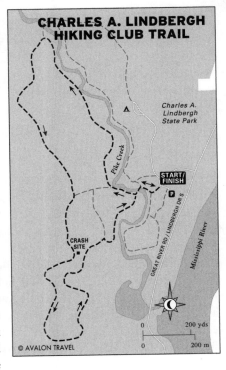

Everyone knows that Charles Lindbergh made the first solo trans-Atlantic flight, but not everyone knows that he grew up right here in Minnesota. Near Little Falls, Lindbergh's childhood home is on the banks of the Upper Mississippi River. The rising river bluffs and grassland prairie that blanket the area provided plenty of practice for Little Lindy. Before he went to college in 1920, he managed this farmland for two years. The family home and a few other original buildings remain on the property and are managed by the Minnesota Historical Society.

From the picnic area parking lot follow the Hiking Club trail west toward Pike Creek. This park is known for its massive red pine trees, and you'll soon see why. The stately pines hearken back to the time when much of this area and the entire northeast section of the state were covered in thick pine forest. The path crosses the creek in 0.1 mile and then splits. Turn right and make the ascent up the creek valley to start the counterclockwise Hiking Club trail loop; 0.2 mile from the creek take a right at the trail intersection. Just a few hundred feet ahead is an overlook point above the vista of the creek valley. Keep walking north through the thick red pine and oak forest landscape for 0.5 mile as the trail parallels Pike Creek and makes a gentle descent.

Norway pine groves cover much of Charles A. Lindbergh State Park.

This northern arc of the trail is across the creek from the campground in the thick forest. Look for whitetail deer amid the trees, as well as foxes and raccoons.

The top of the trail meets an intersecting path that forms a T. Take a left and head south 0.6 mile away from the creek through the wide meadow. Wild daisies, coneflowers, and creeping bellflowers bloom here, as do small patches of Indian paintbrush and prairie smoke flowers. Keep to the right at the next trail intersection. The trail dives back into the forest here as it moves south; 0.2 mile from the last intersection, the trail passes the crash landing site of Lindbergh's Jenny plane. A small spur trail leads to the clearing in the trees, memorialized by a plaque. Return to the main trail and take a right along the 1-mile arc that leads up and over a small ridge and back north to the overlook point. The southern end of this arc is the most secluded part of the park—the area where you are most likely to encounter wildlife. This is a potential black bear area, but you are much more likely to see more whitetail deer, foxes, owls, and rabbits.

At the end of the 1-mile arc take a right and follow the Hiking Club trail 0.3 mile northeast back to the Pike Creek bridge. Take a right after crossing the bridge back to the park road that leads to the trailhead and picnic area parking lot.

Options

A trail at the upper end of the Hiking Club trail loop crosses back over Pike Creek and passes through the camping area. This option shortens the hike to a more peaceful 1.6-mile creekside walk. After walking to the creek, take a right before crossing and follow the trail north through the Pike Creek valley to the campground. Take a left at the group camp driveway and take a right 0.2 mile later at the next trail intersection. The trail arcs south to the eastern edge of the campground and then follows the park road south back to the parking lot and trailhead.

Directions

From Minneapolis take I-94 West for 63 miles. Exit onto MN-15 North toward St. Cloud for another 9 miles. Take US-10 West for 25 miles, then exit onto County Road 76 North toward Little Falls for 2.8 miles. Turn left at MN-27 and left again onto County Road 52 for 1.5 miles. Take a right at the park entrance and follow signs to the Charles A. Lindbergh State Park parking lot near the picnic area.

Information and Contact

There is a $5 daily vehicle permit fee. Dogs are allowed. Restrooms and drinking fountains are available in the picnic areas and at the park office. Maps are available at the park office and on the park website. For more information contact Charles A. Lindbergh State Park, 1615 Lindbergh Drive South, Little Falls, MN 56345, 320/616-2525, www.dnr.state.mn.us.

3 MILLE LACS LOOP

BEST ☾

Mille Lacs Kathio State Park, Onamia

🦌 🌲 🎿 🐕 👫

Level: Easy

Total Distance: 3.1 miles round-trip

Hiking Time: 1.5-2 hours

Elevation Gain: 30 feet

Summary: View some of the 30 sites of ancient Native American villages and learn about the lives of the Dakota people.

Regaled as one of the most culturally and historically significant areas in Minnesota, Mille Lacs Kathio State Park is home to some of the earliest known Native American villages in the Midwest. Evidence of Native American villages here dates back more than 9,000 years, as several federally funded archaeological projects have revealed. You can actually see signs of where and how people have lived here for more than 9,000 years—first the Dakota and

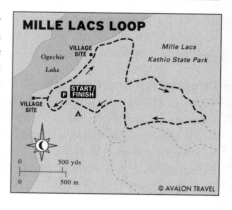

then the Ojibwe tribes, who both recognized it for its abundant natural wealth. The archaeological dig sites have revealed artifacts and the foundations of village walls, which can be seen at the village sites.

Hugging the southwestern shores of Mille Lacs Lake, the park encompasses the beginning of the Rum River as it slithers toward the Mississippi. The trailhead is just south of the parking lot. A large map and information kiosk give historical and natural background information, as well as show sketches of what the early villages on the trail may have once looked like. Follow the packed dirt trail as it makes a quick northward hook and comes to a T about 0.2 mile from the trailhead. Turn left onto a branch trail that leads you through an archaeological dig site that is believed to be a semipermanent Native American village, complete with ancient ricing beds and log wall foundations. The village area is near the midsection of Ogechie Lake, now peppered with tall oak trees and reed beds. The shore of the lake once held dozens of wild-rice beds that Native Americans cultivated.

Return to the main trail and take a left. The next village site is about 0.5 mile to the north. On the way there you will walk alongside the cattails, sedge grasses, reeds, and wild lilies that grow in the thick sedge lining Ogechie Lake. Wild lilies and daisies bloom here all summer long and are a beautiful setting for the

© JAKE KULJU

Native Americans have lived on or near Ogechie Lake for more than 9,000 years.

harmonious whistling of the redwing blackbirds that inhabit this marshy lake-shore area of the park.

Veer left down to the lakeshore at the second village site. A smaller archaeological dig area, this was believed to be a seasonal village that housed only five or six Native American families during the summer months. Colorful dragonflies flit among the bright harebell and wild columbine flowers that call this wetland shore home. Continue north and climb 15 feet or so back up to the trail. In another 0.1 mile the trail hooks south and enters the wooded, hilly portion of this hike. Wild ferns blanket the shady forest floor and chipmunks scoot between fallen trees. Wildflowers take advantage of the treeless trail edges, with more harebells, columbines, and blooming milkweed lining your path.

As you move away from Ogechie Lake, you become connected to a network of hiking trails that crisscross throughout this rich, wooded area of the park. You will no doubt see whitetail deer, chipmunks, and a hawk or two in the openings of the lush tree canopy. Keep your eyes open for colorful frogs, butterflies, raccoons, and foxes as well. Continue following the Hiking Club signs, which point you in the right direction at each trail intersection. This thick-canopied oak and maple forest area is characterized by gently rolling hills and pockets of marshy wetland areas in the low places.

About 1 mile from Ogechie Lake at numbered post 14, make a sharp right and head west along the Hiking Club trail toward the parking lot. You are just past the halfway point of the hike. The forest turf trail continues through thick woods until it emerges on the road that leads to the parking lot. Take a right and follow the gravel road north. From here you have 0.2 mile to the trailhead.

Options

Mille Lacs Kathio is full of trails and historic sites. Drive and park at the picnic area at the southern end of Lake Ogechie to get access to several more miles of hiking trails, the Ogechie dam, and another historic Native American site near the park's interpretive center. From the parking lot, follow the trail that leads west from the picnic area to the historic marker at the dam. Return to the parking lot and walk north, then turn right onto the hiking trail that leads east for 0.5 mile past the camper cabins and arcs north to another trail loop in the center of the park. From here you can take a right toward the lookout tower, a left to Ogechie Campground, or turn around and walk back to the picnic area parking lot.

Directions

From Minneapolis, drive north on I-35 West for 3 miles. Merge onto US-10 West for 23 miles. Exit onto US-169 North for 63 miles. Turn left at Shakopee Lake Road and take a right onto Kathio State Park Road. Drive another 2 miles past the park entrance to the Ogechie Campground and Landmark Trail parking lot.

Information and Contact

There is a $5 daily vehicle permit fee. Restrooms and drinking fountains are available in the picnic areas and at the park office. Dogs are allowed. Maps are available at the park office and on the park website. For more information, contact Mille Lacs Kathio State Park, 15066 Kathio State Park Road, Onamia, MN 56359, 320/532-3523, www.dnr.state.mn.us.

4 MILLE LACS SHORELINE TRAIL

Father Hennepin State Park, Isle

Level: Easy

Hiking Time: 1.5 hours

Total Distance: 2.5 miles round-trip

Elevation Gain: Negligible

Summary: Explore the southern shore of Mille Lacs Lake and see one of the last nesting places of the common tern.

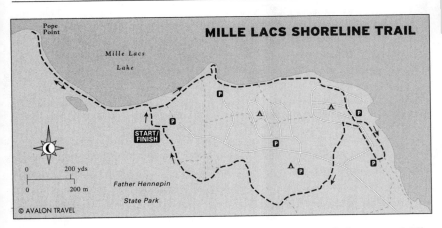

MILLE LACS SHORELINE TRAIL

You can use US-169 for more than going to Anoka—drive all the way to Mille Lacs Lake and bury yourself in the pine forests, oak groves, and rocky lakeshores in Father Hennepin State Park. This quiet lakeshore hike along one of Minnesota's largest bodies of water is just over an hour and a half from Minneapolis.

The trailhead begins on the western edge of the parking lot. The gravel path arcs north to a picnic area on the southern shore of the lake. Take a left here toward Pope Point. The 0.5 mile path to the point hugs the rocky shore of Mille Lacs Lake and treats you to beautiful vistas of the water and distant shore, all from a shady canopy of maple and basswood trees. When you reach Pope Point, an information kiosk provides information about the uncommon common tern. The unique boulder habitat of Mille Lacs Lake supplies the specific nesting and feeding habitat this rare bird needs to survive. Backtrack to the picnic area where you turned left and continue following the shoreline east. This 0.1 mile leads past the beach and picnic areas of the park. Just before the boat launch a spur trail to your left makes a quick loop on a small point. Venture out to the point for another view of mighty Mille Lacs.

When you rejoin the trail you will enter a thick maple grove. The tall, dark

Maple and birch trees provide a shady path along the rocky shore of Mille Lacs Lake.

trunks of these strong trees hold a high canopy of maple leaves, creating a shady, almost enchanted forest feeling. A campground nestles among the trees, though on quiet days you would never even know it. Whitetail deer, raccoons, and smaller creatures like painted turtles and salamanders seek the shade of this maple grove. Walking quietly through the woods will almost ensure a wildlife encounter.

A short 0.2 mile from the maple grove you come upon Lakeview Campground. The trail follows the campground road for 0.1 mile. Take a right before reaching the boat landing and walk past the playground and parking area. Walk past the first sign on your left for the Hiking Club trail and take the next right. About 500 feet down this path take a left into red and white pine forest. This forest turf trail leads south, away from the lake, and is lined with tall and whispering pine trees. Red squirrels, foxes, and shy porcupines can be seen here, or at least signs of them. The path crosses the park road and arcs east; 0.4 mile from the campground a map kiosk near a stand of birch trees gives some natural and geological information. Continue east, remaining to the right at the next trail intersection in 0.1 mile. At the third map kiosk, veer left on the Hiking Club trail, staying to your left at each of the next two intersections. From the fourth map kiosk, the trailhead is 0.1 mile away. From here, make a short right turn back to the parking lot.

Options

Instead of doubling back at the eastern picnic area on the Hiking Club trail, you can continue straight on a 0.5-mile trail that links to the Hiking Club trail about

0.5 mile before returning to the trailhead. While this detour doesn't add significant distance to your hike, it does take you deeper into the quiet pine woods of this peaceful park and increases your chances of seeing wildlife.

Directions

From Minneapolis, drive north on I-35 West for 3 miles. Merge onto US-10 West for 23 miles. Exit onto US-169 North for 63 miles. Turn left following the state park sign for 0.3 mile. Take a right into the park entrance. Follow signs to the beach area parking lot.

Information and Contact

There is a $5 daily vehicle permit fee. Restrooms and drinking fountains are available in the picnic areas and at the park office. Dogs are allowed. Maps are available at the park office and on the park website. For more information, contact Father Hennepin State Park, 41294 Father Hennepin Park Road, Isle, MN 56342, 320/676-8763, www.dnr.state.mn.us.

5 RICE LAKE REFUGE TRAIL

Rice Lake National Wildlife Refuge, McGregor

Level: Easy

Hiking Time: 1.5 hours

Total Distance: 3 miles round-trip

Elevation Gain: Negligible

Summary: Enjoy a hike amid north-central Minnesota lakes in the heart of one of the continent's major bird migration corridors.

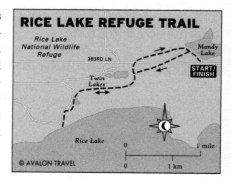

Minnesota's wetlands are some of its most important habitat. The wild-rice-bearing lakes, shoreline nesting areas, and insect-filled marshes are critical habitat for literally millions of migratory birds. The Rice Lake National Wildlife Refuge (RLNWR) is one of the most important stops for birds along North America's central bird migration corridor. Just under two hours from the Twin Cities, this refuge is a must visit in the spring and fall months when birds like the American coot, ruby-throated hummingbird, and belted kingfisher are on the move.

Follow the south shore of Mandy Lake as the trail leads you west toward North Bog Road; 0.5 mile from the trailhead veer left at the intersection. After walking through the red pine and oak forest, you will shortly break into an open field just before the CCC Camp parking lot. A few red squirrels may scold you for disturbing their peaceful forest. Watch for chipmunks at your feet, as well. To the south is a wide bog area. The underbrush and berry patches in this area make it attractive to bears, though they are rarely seen. This set of trails west of Mandy Lake lies in a wooded area between two bog systems and is full of whitetail deer, minks, otters, raccoons, porcupines, and foxes. You might not see them all, but rest assured they are there. This refuge is known for its wildlife and even has a designated wildlife drive.

Continue east from the parking lot for 0.25 mile to the next open field and trail intersection. Take a left here onto the Rice Lake Pool trail. This path leads through the tallgrass and wetland areas surrounding Rice Lake and ends at the observation tower on the reedy northern shore. This area is rich with nesting and feeding waterfowl, especially during the migratory seasons. Make sure to bring a pair of binoculars with you. The observation tower gives you a full view of the

© JAKE KULJU

Wild mushrooms grow on the forest floor in Rice Lake National Wildlife Refuge.

lake, often swarming with throngs of migratory birds in the spring and fall months. Look for pelicans, kestrels, coots, grebes, mergansers, and great blue herons. If you're lucky you may even catch a glimpse of the rare yellow rail, which has been spotted nesting in the tall grasses of the refuge.

Follow the Rice Lake Pool trail back to the CCC Camp parking lot and take a left, returning to Mandy Lake on the northern arm of the small loop. After taking a right at the trail intersection near the water, the trailhead and parking lot are 0.5 mile ahead.

Options

On the return trip from the Rice Lake observation tower, take a left at the first trail intersection. This detour takes you past the Twin Lakes and along the northern edge of the grassy area near the trailhead, reconnecting at Mandy Lake and adding 0.75 mile to your hike.

Directions

From St. Paul head north on I-35 East for 87 miles. Exit on MN-73 toward Moose Lake. Turn left at MN-73 for 2.5 miles, and left again onto MN-27/MN-73 for another 5 miles. Stay left on MN-27 for 19 miles and turn right onto MN-65; 5 miles north, take a left into the Rice Lake National Wildlife Refuge. Drive 2 miles past the headquarters building and park at the Mandy Lake parking lot.

Information and Contact

There is no fee. Dogs are allowed. Restrooms and a drinking fountain are available in the recreation center by the parking lot. Maps are available at the park headquarters and on the park website. For more information, contact Rice Lake National Wildlife Refuge, 36298 State Highway 65, McGregor, MN 55760, 218/768-2402, www.fws.gov/midwest/ricelake.

6 MOUNT TOM TRAIL
Sibley State Park, New London

Level: Easy/moderate

Hiking Time: 2 hours

Total Distance: 3.7 miles round-trip

Elevation Gain: 100 feet

Summary: View the rolling hills, lush hardwood forests, and hilltop prairies from atop Mount Tom and surrounding high points.

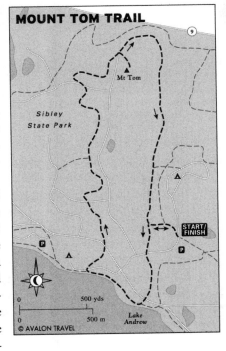

MOUNT TOM TRAIL

Popular in the 1930s as a swimming and hiking destination (and for the views from the park's high point, Mount Tom), Sibley State Park is still one of western Minnesota's prime outdoor areas. Like most of Minnesota's landscape, the Sibley State Park area was sculpted by retreating glaciers during the last ice age. Rolling hills, tallgrass prairie, and small, lush, leafy-treed valleys abound.

Facing the Trail Center, you will find the trailhead to your left. Keep to the left at the first intersection, just 0.2 mile up the trail along the edge of the oak forest. The trail navigates through a transitional zone between grassland and oak forest, giving you an early opportunity to spot wildlife that love these transitional areas. Look for deer at the edge of the trees, especially. At the second junction, take another left onto the Mount Tom Trail. This path makes a loop that visits Mount Tom to the north, but taking a left here brings you south to Lake Andrew first.

On its way to Lake Andrew the trail crosses a park road and a paved bike path as well as a shared-use hiker-biker path. Stay on the turf trail and turn right at the lakeshore, following the water for 0.3 mile. Look to the west along the northern shore of Lake Andrew; large expanses of hardstem bulrush and cattails provide habitat for fish and birds alike. Kingfishers may linger in the trees, as well as owls and great blue herons. The lakeside trail merges with the paved biking trail and

The stone observation deck atop Mount Tom gives sweeping views of the surrounding grasslands and forests.

shared-use trail but shortly breaks off to the right. Follow this turf trail north for 0.3 mile through the maple, oak, and aspen trees, then take a left to continue on the Mount Tom Trail. From the lake the trail ascends 140 feet to grassy Badger Hill. Take a left on the short spur trail that leads to the Badger Hill overlook 0.4 mile from the last trail intersection.

Return to the Mount Tom Trail and take a left back down the hill and through the forest. Turn right at the next intersection and walk 0.4 mile to the park road. Take a left and follow the road west for a few hundred feet, then turn right at the sign pointing to the Mount Tom Trail. Little Mount Tom lies just 0.1 mile northeast in an elevated forest clearing. Keep going for 0.2 mile to the gravel parking lot at the foot of Mount Tom. Walk to the eastern end of the parking lot and take a right at the trail intersection. This path leads up 60 feet to the stone tower atop the hill. Climb the several dozen steps to the top of the overlook tower for a sweeping view on all sides of the rolling hills, forests, farmland, and meadows of the area. Look for circling hawks, eagles, and turkey vultures.

Return to the parking lot and take a right on the trail that leads north through the trees. As the trail arcs south it rolls up and down with the undulating wooded hills. Wild turkeys may huddle in the clearings between the trees, and you are sure to scare up a whitetail deer or two on your way south. Take a left at the trail intersection 1.2 miles from Mount Tom that leads back to the trailhead. Keep to the right at the next one as well, just 0.1 mile east. The parking lot lies 0.2 mile away along the oak and grassland transitional zone where you started the hike.

Options

If 3.7 miles isn't enough for you, take a left at the first intersection 0.9 mile after Mount Tom. A trail makes a 1.1-mile circle through the thick forest that surrounds the campground area. A shady oak forest blankets this ridge trail. You may see an occasional grouse here, especially in the autumn. Foxes and raccoons are more common sights, as well as the ubiquitous whitetail deer. After passing the overlook point 1 mile from the trail intersection, turn right to return to the parking lot and trailhead at the Trail Center.

Directions

From Minneapolis head west on I-94 for 2.3 miles. Take the I-394 West exit and keep right at the fork. I-394 merges with US-12 West in 8 miles. Continue west on US-12 for 81.7 miles. Turn right onto the US-71 East ramp and merge onto US-71 for 13 miles. Turn left at Sibley Park Road for 1.2 miles to the park entrance. Take the next two right turns after the park office for 0.3 mile, following signs to the Trail Center parking lot.

Information and Contact

There is a $5 state park vehicle permit fee. Restrooms and a drinking fountain are available at the Trail Center. Dogs are allowed. Maps are available at the park headquarters and on the park website. For more information, contact Sibley State Park, 800 Sibley Park Road Northeast, New London, MN 56273, 320/354-2055, www.dnr.state.mn.us.

7 BELLE LAKE TRAIL

BEST ◖

Piepenburg County Park, Hutchinson

🦌 🌲 🏊 🐎 👫

Level: Easy

Total Distance: 2 miles round-trip

Hiking Time: 1 hour

Elevation Gain: Negligible

Summary: Walk through lilac-lined fields, lush maple and basswood forests, and clusters of wildflowers near peaceful Belle Lake.

Just north of Hutchinson on Belle Lake, Piepenburg County Park isn't known as a hiking destination, though it should be. Used by locals for its beach and public boat access, it is also home to rich maple and basswood forests, a bird-filled wetland, and sweeping tallgrass fields.

Facing the beach, take a left onto the forest turf trail along the lake. You are a good 15 feet above the water here, able to look down onto the rocky and boulder-lined shore interspersed with cedar and maple trees. The trail leads to the boat launch, then jackknifes north again, veering gently away from the lake. About 200 feet from the boat launch the trail begins to follow a low, slough-like wetland area. Redwing blackbirds, sandhill cranes, great blue herons, and several species of ducks frequent this large area. The path is also lined with honeysuckle, wild columbine, and harebell flowers—so much so that on midsummer days you can literally sniff your way down the trail. Wild asters, daisies, and purple coneflowers also make a strong showing. The density of flowers here is truly amazing, one of the strong points of this small park.

After 600 feet of this wetland walk, the trail slips briefly back into the maple trees and emerges behind the park caretaker's home. The trail hugs the tree line and crosses the park road. The path blends into the grass for a while and can be hard to follow; just make sure you cross the gravel road onto the field ahead. If you lose the trail, make your way to the parallel rows of trees that lead to the forest. Ahead of you will be an open field with two rows of flowering trees on the southern end. The hiking trail threads between the rows for 0.2 mile. If you come here in the spring you'll be treated to the sight and smell of thousands of fragrant tree blossoms.

At the end of the tree rows the trail dives into the woods. This forested path of towering maple and basswood trees cuts an arc through a thick skirt of ferns that grow in the heavy shade of the forest canopy. Whitetail deer and raccoons are commonly seen here, as well as rabbits, foxes, and the occasional wild turkey. When you emerge from the woods, the trail wraps around the edge of another wetland area. A narrow line of cedar trees and lilac bushes borders the left side of the path. In the springtime these lilacs are heavy with intoxicatingly aromatic purple flowers. Herons and redwing blackbirds find cover in this marshy area. The trail turns right at the end of the line of trees and follows the northern border of the wetland, once again entering a thickly wooded area.

Continue 0.1 mile through the forest and you'll be back in the field. With the trees at your back, the whole sweep of the tallgrass field lies ahead of you. Take a right and follow the lilac-lined tree line toward the lake. The path curves left and traces a small inlet near the campground. Stay close to the water, as the path is not so easily seen here. It soon turns to a gravel path along the lakeshore and leads back to the beach and the parking lot.

Options

If you'd like to spend some more time among the trees but not add any distance, follow a path from the boat launch parking lot toward the camping area through the wooded area between the slough and the beach. Take a right when the path emerges at the gravel drive and a left onto the main trail beginning at the blossoming tree line.

Directions

From Minneapolis take I-394 West to I-494 South. Go south for 3.5 miles and exit right onto MN-7 West for 47 miles. Turn right onto MN-15 and make an almost immediate left onto County Road 12 for 5.3 miles. Take a left onto County Road 60 for 1.3 miles. Drive past the boat launch parking lot and the caretaker's home to your left. Follow the gravel drive all the way to the beach parking lot past the camping area.

Information and Contact

There is no fee. Restrooms and drinking water are available in the camping area. Dogs are allowed. Maps are available at the caretaker's office. For more information, contact Piepenburg County Park, 21104 Belle Lake Road, Hutchinson, MN 55350, 320/587-2082.

8 BIG WOODS LOOP

Lake Maria State Park, Monticello

Level: Easy

Hiking Time: 2 hours

Total Distance: 3.6 miles round-trip

Elevation Gain: 70 feet

Summary: Rise over the tree canopies on Anderson Hill and dip into the thick forests and wetlands around Lake Maria.

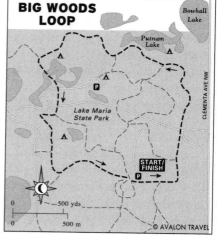

Like many of Minnesota's parklands, Lake Maria has rolling hilltop prairies, thick Big Woods forests, and vast wetlands. Few parks, however, have such dynamic examples of these habitats so close to the Twin Cities. The Big Woods Loop trail in Lake Maria State Park is a cornucopia of wilderness variety and is only a 45-minute drive northwest of Minneapolis.

The Trail Center is about 300 feet west of the parking lot. Start here and take a left onto the Big Woods Loop trail. Wooden signs with arrows are placed at most trail intersections, including the Trail Center. A quarter mile into the hike, the trail makes a sharp left into open grassland. Walk straight ahead on the mowed pathway and across the road you drove on near the park entrance. This area is dotted with wooden birdhouses meant for the eastern bluebird, a strikingly blue creature that loves the open grassland areas of western Minnesota. Wildflowers are sprinkled among the grasses of this meadow as well. Indian paintbrush, prairie smoke, and purple coneflowers grow here. Some clusters of lupines can be found along the edge of the trail in early summer, and wild asters are prevalent in whites and purples.

As the trail curves to the left, it hugs the foot of Anderson Hill, one of the highest points in the park. A lone tree grows atop the hill, but it's a steep 40-foot scramble to get there. The view is worth the footwork once you look out over the canopy of old-growth oak trees and rolling hills. Scoot down the opposite side of the hill after you've caught your breath and dip into the woods. This is the beginning of the Big Woods forest the trail is named after.

The next 0.25 mile takes you past three hike-in campsites along Putnam Lake.

This is a low, wetland area, and in the spring it can be a little mucky. Just past the trail to Camper Cabin C-1 (you'll see a sign for it) there is an information sign at a trail intersection. The main trail seems to go left, but you want to stay to your right on the Big Woods Loop trail. If you enter a group campsite, you'll know you went the wrong way.

From here the forest turf trail continues to wind through large basswoods and shady maple trees. Below the forest canopy even a hot summer day feels nice and cool. This hike is a great way to beat the heat, especially when a breeze is blowing. Near the 2-mile mark the trail makes a T. A footpath to the right leads to Lake Maria; take the wider Big Woods Loop, which turns left. The following 0.5 mile leads you past the B-5 campsite, C-2 camper cabin paths, across

This gnarled maple stands out from the rest of the Big Woods forest in Lake Maria State Park.

a low-lying pond and wetland area, and then across two of the park's gravel roads. At the second crossing the trail re-enters the forest about 200 feet up the road on your left.

Shortly after leaving the road the trail meets another T. Take a right and oxbow around a small hill through the rolling forest turf trail in the thick of the Big Woods. A half mile after the T take a left following signs for the Big Woods Loop and Bjorkland Lake Trail. In just under 0.5 mile you'll be back at the Trail Center and parking lot.

Options

Just before the B-5 campsite take a right on the 0.5-mile trail that leads past Lake Maria to the Zunnbrunnen Interpretive Trail. Adding a total of 1 mile to your hike, this option gives you a view of the park's namesake lake and takes you across a boardwalk through a marsh to the interpretive trail.

Directions

From Minneapolis head west on I-94 West for 37 miles. Exit onto MN-25 toward Monticello and turn right for 0.5 mile. Turn left at West Broadway Street and left on Elm Street 0.5 mile later. Turn right onto County Road 39 for 5.5 miles and another right onto County Road 111. The park entrance is 0.5 mile on your left. Follow signs to the Trail Center parking lot.

Information and Contact

There is a $5 state park vehicle permit fee. Restrooms and a drinking fountain are available at the Trail Center. Dogs are allowed. Maps are available at the park headquarters and on the park website. For more information, contact Lake Maria State Park, 11411 Clementa Avenue Northwest, Monticello, MN 55362, 763/878-2325, www.dnr.state.mn.us.

9 LAKE REBECCA LOOP

BEST 🄲

Lake Rebecca Park Reserve, Greenfield

Level: Easy/moderate

Hiking Time: 2.5-3 hours

Total Distance: 3.5 miles round-trip

Elevation Gain: 50 feet

Summary: Come here for the peace, serenity, and challenge of the prairie hills and lakeside ridges.

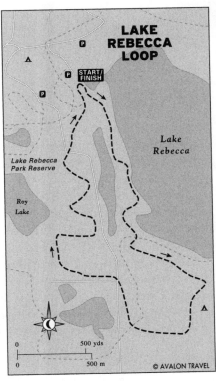

Tucked into a bend of the twisting Crow River, Lake Rebecca Park Reserve is one of the Twin Cities' must-hike areas. An undeveloped lake surrounded by Big Woods forest, flocks of trumpeter swans (the world's largest waterfowl), prairie landscape, and wetlands are all in store along the Lake Rebecca Loop hiking trail.

Facing the lake at the paved boat launch just north of the parking lot, follow the forest turf trail to your right; 500 feet from the trailhead take the trail leading to your left and climb 20 feet to the ridge above Lake Rebecca's western shore. The trail leads south along the shore and gives you glimpses of the lake's bright blue waters through the trees. A quarter mile from the intersection a scenic overlook opens to the west over a pond and low-lying area that is home to one of the state's largest flocks of trumpeter swans.

Settlers cleared the land to use for farming, but as you will see those fields are being reclaimed by the prairie landscape and remnants of the basswood and maple forest that surrounds the lake. The trail soon leaves the lake and begins carving through the undulating prairie landscape. Just before it does, it crosses a paved bike path and does so again in another 0.5 mile. Along this stretch of the loop you will encounter waist-high sweetgrass, blooming harebells, wild asters, and daisies, and wide-open spaces along the many small hills the trail climbs.

© JAKE KULJU

Grasslands cover most of the rolling hills in the Lake Rebecca Park Reserve.

Eastern bluebird houses are set amidst the wavy grasses, whitetail deer tracks pepper the trail, and painted turtles rustle through the undergrowth during the early summer. Just 500 feet after the second bike path crossing the trail follows a park service road for another 500 feet. Turn left at the intersection and turn right back onto the prairie trail. During the spring and summer you will almost certainly see and hear the trumpeter swans that congregate near the pond where the trail meets the park service road again just under 0.5 mile later—the area you saw from the overlook 1.5 miles back.

This loop shares use with mountain bikes, so keep your ears pricked for oncoming riders. It is a one-way clockwise loop for bikers, so you'll know where they will be coming from. From the pond the trailhead lies 0.3 mile to the northeast. Cross the service road and take a left at the intersection back to the paved boat landing. Straight ahead is the small hill that leads up to the ridge above the lake.

Options

For a shortcut through the prairie grasses and wildflowers, take a right on the paved biking trail that leads away from the lake 0.2 mile south of the overlook point. The trail leads west for just under 0.5 mile until it crosses the unpaved grassy hiking path again. Take a right to continue on the loop as it heads north along the maintenance road.

Directions

From Minneapolis head west on I-394 West for 9 miles. Continue for 17 miles on US-12 West. Turn right onto County Line Road Southeast for 1.5 miles. Turn right at Delano Rockford Road for 0.5 mile. Continue on Rebecca Park Trail for another 0.5 mile. Turn right at the park entrance and take an immediate left. Turn right 0.2 mile later into the Lake Rebecca boat landing parking lot.

Information and Contact

There is no fee. Dogs are allowed. Restrooms and a drinking fountain are available in the recreation center by the parking lot. Dogs are allowed. Note that the park is closed November–March each year. For more information, contact Lake Rebecca Park Reserve, 9831 County Road 50, Rockford, MN 55373, 763/694-7860, www.threeriversparkdistrict.org/parks.

10 CROSBY LAKE TRAIL

Carver Park Reserve, Victoria

Level: Easy/moderate

Hiking Time: 2-2.5 hours

Total Distance: 4 miles round-trip

Elevation Gain: 50 feet

Summary: Get a close-up view of wetlands on extensive boardwalk trails through cattails, ponds, and old tamarack tree marshes.

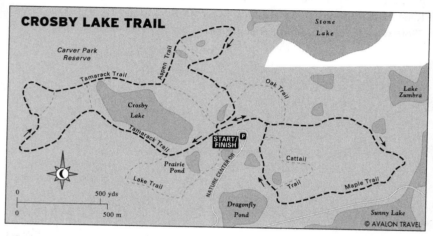

The next time you don't feel like fighting traffic heading west out of Minneapolis on Highway 7, pull off into Carver Park Reserve's Crosby Lake trail area. This park is large enough to block out the sounds and sights of traffic, and by the time you've got 4 miles under your belt, traffic will have melted away. Peaceful Crosby Lake and its surrounding wetlands and prairie meadows are a world away from the highway.

From the parking lot, walk behind the nature center and take a right on the path bedded with wood chips. The Lowry Nature Center trail system is divided into small loops, each named after a tree that dominates the park's wooded areas. This portion of the trail is called Maple. Stay left at the first trail intersection, but take a right at the second one 200 feet up the trail. About 600 feet into the Maple loop an overlook gives you a sweeping view of the wide cattail pond the trail traces. A few feet from the lookout point is a wooden bridge that crosses the creek that feeds the pond; 0.25 mile ahead you will walk several hundred feet along a boardwalk among the cattails directly across the pond from the lookout point. In another 0.25 mile the Cattail trail breaks off the right. Stay to your left here and once more in another 500 feet where the Cattail trail starts. Take a left at the next intersection. The Maple trail makes an approximately 1.5-mile loop and brings you back behind the visitors center.

Keep a steady course here and walk straight through the educational play areas and small gardens surrounding the building. After passing the butterfly garden on your left, the trail becomes a mowed grass path through the prairie hills that surround Crosby Lake. As you leave the trees behind you will notice the wild asters, harebells, and coneflowers blooming in the tallgrass meadow. Look for garter snakes slithering at your feet and painted turtles making their way through the grass.

Just beyond Crosby Rock (a monument dedicated to the area's late landowner) follow the trail to the right along the ridge above the lake. You will get views of the water and more than likely several of the waterfowl that call it home, including great blue herons, mergansers, wood ducks, and mallards. A narrow mowed path branches to the right 0.25 mile from Crosby Rock. Keep to your left on the main path. Another 0.25 mile through the grassy hills brings you to another intersection. Make a hard right turn onto the wooded ridgeline trail. You leave the grassland behind here and enter the oak and maple forest that borders the northern edge of the lake; 500 feet from the intersection the Tamarack boardwalk trail dips down from the wooded ridge into the marsh. Take a left down the hill to the boardwalk.

Most of the land here just north of Crosby Lake and west of Stone Lake is a vast wetland marsh. The Tamarack trail boardwalk puts you right in the heart of it, looping through the silent, swampy stands of dead tamarack trees. Redwing blackbirds thrive here, as well as marsh wrens. The boardwalk can become wet and slippery in places, so watch your step. After 600 feet of boardwalk, the trail climbs back up the ridge. Look for ospreys and eagles perched high in the dead trees, and herons standing among the reeds.

At the top of the ridge, take a left and

Bluebird houses like this one are helping the eastern bluebird thrive near Crosby Lake.

© JAKE KULJU

walk 0.25 mile along the northern shore of Crosby Lake. At the next intersection take a left onto the Aspen trail. The path leads through—you guessed it—aspen trees. You will cross the third boardwalk of this hike, and a floating one at that. Use caution when crossing, as the boards can get wet. An overlook 0.25 mile from the end of the boardwalk gives another view of the expansive wetland on the western shore of Stone Lake.

Choose the middle path at the trail intersection 0.1 mile from the overlook point. You are hooking on to part of the Oak trail here on your way back to the trailhead. Take another left a few hundred feet later and then one more. This brings you near the butterfly garden area at the beginning of the Tamarack trail. The visitors center is in sight and the trail leads you to your starting point at the trailhead parking lot.

Options

To dip back into another wetland area after finishing this hike, take the Lake trail past Prairie Pond after returning to the nature center. The Lake trail leads south from the butterfly garden and adds nearly 1 mile to your hike.

Directions

From Minneapolis take I-394 West for 9 miles, then turn left onto I-494 South for 3.7 miles. Exit onto MN-7 West for 13.5 miles. Turn left onto Victoria Drive for 1.2 miles and another left at Nature Center Drive for 1 mile to the Lowry Nature Center parking lot.

Information and Contact

There is no fee. Restrooms and a drinking fountain are available in the recreation center by the parking lot. Dogs are allowed. Maps are available at the nature center and on the park website. For more information, contact Carver Park Reserve, Lowry Nature Center, 7025 Victoria Drive, Victoria, MN 55386, 763/694-7650, www.threeriversparkdistrict.org/parks.

11 LUNDSTEN LAKE LOOP
Carver Park Reserve, Victoria

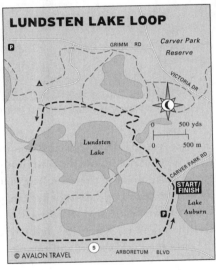

Level: Easy/moderate

Hiking Time: 2.5 hours

Total Distance: 4.8 miles round-trip

Elevation Gain: Negligible

Summary: Hike along the overlooks of Lundsten Lake's rolling prairies and wetlands, full of redwing blackbirds, wildflowers, and gently wooded areas.

Lundsten Lake is the premier waterfowl area in Carver Park Reserve. The undeveloped shores of the lake and its reedy, marshy habitat are a haven for pelicans, swans, mergansers, grebes, and almost any kind of duck you can think of. Located in the southwestern corner of Carver Park Reserve, the hiking trail that loops around the lake is shared with horse riders. More secluded than the rest of the park, this hiking loop usually plays second fiddle to the popular hiking trails near Crosby Lake and the Lowry Nature Center. Because of its low profile, this is truly one of the most peaceful hikes in this book.

From the parking lot walk north along the park road you took to get to the parking area for 0.25 mile. Small stands of oak trees dot the way, but for the most part, tallgrass, clover, and mustard line the road. The early summer may bring some lupines. Take a left on the wide dirt trail that leads northwest. Follow it for 0.7 mile across the creek that connects to Lake Auburn and to the intersection just south of the paved hiker-biker trail. If you get to the pavement you have gone too far. A wide dirt trail leads to the west just before the pavement and is easy to find.

The trail passes through a large stand of oak, maple, and basswood trees for 0.5 mile past an overlook point just prior to the next trail intersection. Stay to the left and continue hiking straight west for 0.4 mile to the group picnic and campsite parking lot. Stay to the left as the trail swings south and crosses a tree-lined land bridge along the western shore of the lake. Water approaches both sides of the strip of oak woods and is a great place to find turtles, frogs, and salamanders.

This chewed-off stump is a sure sign that beavers are close by.

After crossing the lake, a cross-country-ski-only trail veers to the left. Keep to your right and follow the trail south for 0.7 mile along the farmland and Parley Lake Road to the west. The trail curves east and borders Highway 5 for 1.25 miles along stands of oak, maple, basswood, and cottonwood trees. Look for whitetail deer that linger in this strip of forest between the lake and the highway. When the trail curves north it will lead 0.5 mile back to the park road. Take a left and complete the remaining 0.25 mile back to the parking lot.

Options

Just before the first trail intersection with the paved bike trail, the hiking path branches to the right for 1.25 miles around Lake 2. Take this route to add the extra distance and pass through a more wooded area of oak and maple forest. You will encounter wildlife like raccoon and fox here in the higher ground away from Lundsten Lake. Stay left at the two unpaved hiking trail intersections and take a right at the third to head west on the main hiking trail.

Directions

From Minneapolis take I-394 West for 9 miles, then turn left onto I-494 South for 3.7 miles. Exit onto MN-7 West for 13.5 miles. Turn left onto Victoria Drive for 1.2 miles and then right at Carver Park Road for 1 mile to the King Blind parking lot.

Information and Contact

There is no fee. Restrooms and a drinking fountain are available in the recreation center by the parking lot. Dogs are allowed. Maps are available at the nature center and on the park website. For more information, contact Carver Park Reserve, Lowry Nature Center, 7025 Victoria Drive, Victoria, MN 55386, 763/694-7650, www.threeriversparkdistrict.org/parks.

12 MINNETONKA TRAIL
Lake Minnetonka Regional Park, Minnetrista

Level: Easy

Hiking Time: 0.5-1 hour

Total Distance: 1 mile round-trip

Elevation Gain: Negligible

Summary: This shady, creek-side trail is a quick and peaceful escape from the hubbub of the city.

Whether you hike with a dog or not, the Minnetonka Trail in Lake Minnetonka Regional Park is a pleasant place to stretch your legs and get a little nature time in. The hiking trail is a shared-use dog trail and begins at the small parking area. The first 0.13 mile of the path runs parallel to a paved hiker-biker trail until shortly after crossing under the County Road 44 bridge; 0.25 mile from the parking lot the wide gravel trail transitions into a narrow forest turf path under a canopy of oak and maple trees.

A winding creek bed crisscrosses the path several times here. At some points you may need to rock hop if the water is high. For the most part, the creek is a seasonal spring waterway, occasionally filling up in the summer after heavy rains. The maple trees are not thick here, but the canopy they create is. This shady creek bed area is easily the most peaceful section of the park.

The far end of this trail makes a 0.2-mile loop through the shady forest landscape. Few people who use this trail for dog walking venture this far, and the narrow path at times blends easily into the forest floor. Whitetail deer and grey squirrels mingle in this shady paradise. You will see their tracks all along the edges of the creek and will more than likely catch sight of them. While this trail may not provide the distance or elevation changes that hardcore hikers crave, it is a nice respite from the city for anyone looking for some peace and quiet in the forest. At the end of the loop, walk back toward the parking lot and out of the woods. The waist-high grasses near the trailhead usher you back to the trailhead and parking lot.

Options

If you'd like to get a view of the park's namesake lake, cross the road after returning

© JAKE KULJU

This shady canopy of maple leaves is a great way to beat the heat at Lake Minnetonka.

to the parking lot and follow the paved hiker-biker path to your left. After curving clockwise for 0.25 mile past the picnic area and into a large parking lot, take another left onto an unpaved hiking trail. This path leads to the boat landing on the shore of Lake Minnetonka and is a great way to add 0.5 mile to this short hike. This route can turn into an extremely family-friendly hike. The path leads through two picnic areas and a playground with slides, swings, and sandboxes. You could easily spend a day here at the beach and in the cool shade of the abundant oak and maple trees.

Directions

From Minneapolis take I-394 West for 9 miles, then turn left onto I-494 South for 3.7 miles. Exit onto MN-7 West for 12 miles. Turn right on County Road 44 for 0.2 mile and then another right into the park entrance. Drive past the entry station and turn left. The hiking/dog trail parking lot is 0.1 mile ahead on your left.

Information and Contact

There is a $5 vehicle permit fee. The park is open 6 A.M.–sunset. Restrooms and a drinking fountain are available in the visitors center, and a restroom is located by the boat landing. Dogs are allowed. Maps are available at the visitors center and on the park's website. For more information, contact Lake Minnetonka Regional Park, 4610 County Road 44, Minnetrista, MN 55331, 763/694-7754, www.threeriversparkdistrict.org/parks.

13 CROW RIVER LOOP

Crow-Hassan Park Reserve, St. Michael

BEST 🌙

Level: Moderate

Hiking Time: 3 hours

Total Distance: 5.7 miles round-trip

Elevation Gain: 50 feet

Summary: Pass along the high banks of the Crow River and walk through wide prairie lands swathed in blooming wildflowers.

For a real prairie experience, there's no place like Crow-Hassan Park near St. Michael. This grassy nook in a bend of the Crow River is a paradise of rolling hills, grassy expanses, and colorful prairie flowers. Right off the bat you'll be in shoulder-high grass. Take the trail that heads north from the parking lot, staying to your right at the two intersections in the first 0.25 mile. Except for a smattering of shade trees, the next 1.5 miles pass through open prairie.

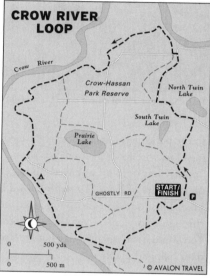

At the third trail intersection take a left as the path threads between North and South Twin Lakes. Wood duck houses stand in the grass, and redwing blackbirds trill during summer days. The trail breaks into three prongs 0.25 mile ahead. Take the rightmost path. This stretch leads slightly upward and the vastness of the prairie landscape is revealed to you on all sides. In another 0.25 mile the trail again gives you three choices. This time take the middle road, which leads farther north. As the trail curves to the left you enter the forest canopy, primarily made up of elm and maple trees. On a hot summer's day, the abundant shade is a welcome respite from the exposed grasslands behind you.

As you head west, the trail gets closer to the river; 2.25 miles into the hike you get a nice view of the wide brown waters of the Crow River. Shortly thereafter you come upon a lean-to shelter and a cross-country ski trail intersection. Stay to the right (the path to the left is usually overgrown with grass in the summer, anyway). Here the trail cuts away from the riverbank and makes a more dramatic turn to the south. After passing through a small marshland, the trail briefly

White yarrow flowers fill the grassy fields of Crow-Hassan Park Reserve.

arcs westward, then straightens out toward the Bluestem Group Camp area at the 3.5-mile mark. You'll know you're there when you see the large abandoned barn. Another view of the river awaits you after crossing the access road. In a few hundred feet you come upon Crow River Group Camp. Cross this camp's access road and you soon come upon wooden stairs that lead to the canoe access site at the water's edge.

When the trail turns to your left, you will soon break out of the woods and return to the prairie. This part of the park is especially rich in wildflowers. Most notable are the large swaths of purple prairie clover and lupine that cut colorful gashes in the grassy landscape. At the next trail intersection take a right, continuing to follow the river. In another 0.25 mile take two left turns, about 50 feet from each other, to point you in the direction of the parking lot. This last 0.5-mile stretch is alternating grassland and forest. This area of the park is home to the occasional bull snake and rare Blanding's turtle. Keep your eyes open for other prairie creatures such as groundhogs, gophers, garter snakes, foxes, and raccoons.

Options

To get more time along the river and to tack another 2 miles onto this hike, continue straight at the final turn, making a left at the second intersection onto the northward leading dog/hiking trail. The trail meets the road near the park entrance. Take a left here back to the parking lot.

Directions

From Minneapolis take I-94 West for 22 miles. Take the Rogers exit and turn left onto Main Street for 0.5 mile. Turn right at 129th Avenue for 1.8 miles. Turn right at Territorial Road for 0.5 mile. Turn left onto Hassan Parkway for 1.4 miles. Turn right at Ghostley Road for 0.5 mile. Drive past the entry station and park in the Trailhead parking lot.

Information and Contact

There is no fee. Restrooms and drinking fountains are available at the Trailhead and Bluestem Group Camp areas. Dogs are allowed on designated trails. Maps are available on the park website. For more information, contact Crow-Hassan Park Reserve, 12595 Park Drive, Hanover, MN 55341, 763/694-7860, www .threeriversparkdistrict.org/parks.

14 LAKE KATRINA LOOP

Baker Park Reserve, Maple Plain

Level: Easy/moderate

Hiking Time: 2.5-3 hours

Total Distance: 5.5 miles round-trip

Elevation Gain: Negligible

Summary: Walk through the shady forests and open wetlands that surround secluded Lake Katrina in Baker Park Reserve.

A surprising 27,000+ acres of park reserve wilderness is less than an hour's drive from Minneapolis. It is called Baker Park Reserve. Lake Katrina is nestled in the southern portion of the reserve, just southeast of the campsites, picnic areas, beaches, and boat landings on Lake Independence.

While all the hubbub is happening on Lake Independence, the serene, wide, grassy forest turf trail that loops around less-accessible Lake Katrina is a hiker's paradise. From the parking lot both the unpaved and paved hiking paths are visible. Take a right on the unpaved path and begin the counterclockwise loop around the lake. The first 0.25 mile will be through light forest cover, but the trail soon opens up to an open tallgrass prairie landscape with scattered trees and shrubs. Purple coneflowers, clover, and wild daisies all grow in abundance here. Look for whitetail deer on the forest edge, as well as garter snakes, painted turtles, and wetland birds like redwing blackbirds and great blue herons in the reeds several hundred feet to your left nearer the lake. From this slightly elevated area above the lake you can watch how the lake transitions to marsh, then sedge, prairie, and forest. Where you are standing you can see the prairie flowers increase in frequency to your left as they enter the more established prairie landscape.

At 1.3 miles you will come to a trail intersection at Oak Knoll Group Camp. Stay to your left and cross two paved hiker-biker paths about 100 feet from one another. The next mile takes you near three small ponds in the wetland system that borders the lake. As the trail swings back south after these ponds you enter another wooded area. Cottonwood, basswood, and some maple trees grow here. At the 3-mile point you will be near Highway 12 and the large cattail field on

Plumes of tallgrass sway in the breeze along Lake Katrina's grassy sides.

the southern shore of the lake. Watch for herons and cranes in the open patches of shallow water between the vegetation.

The trail borders Highway 12 for a few hundred feet, then breaks northeast. Four miles in you'll cross the road to the Katrina Group Camp. The trail continues eastward, entering more rolling prairie grassland. Stay left at the upcoming trail intersection where the path turns northward. This marks the last 0.75 mile to the trailhead. A wildlife management area lies to your left. Turtles frequently crawl from the lake to this section of the trail to lay eggs in the early summer. From here you pass through one more patch of trees before reaching the parking lot.

Options

To visit the beach at Lake Independence, take a right after the Oak Knoll Group Camp onto the paved hiker-biker trail. This trail leads to the camping area and lakeside recreation area on Lake Independence and puts an extra 0.5 mile on your hike. It is also a more family-friendly option. Children don't necessarily get a thrill from walking around a marshy lake. Lake Independence has picnic areas and a playground to treat the youngsters to.

Directions

From Minneapolis drive west on I-394 West for 9 miles. Continue on US-12 West for 7.7 miles. Turn right at Old Crystal Bay Road for 0.5 mile. Turn left at 6th

Avenue North for 0.2 mile and then right for 1.5 miles on Homestead Trail. The Horse/Hike/Bike Trail parking lot is on your left.

Information and Contact

There is no fee. Restrooms and drinking fountains are available at the trailhead and on the south end of Lake Katrina. Dogs are allowed on designated trails but not this one. Maps are available at the trailhead and on the park website. For more information, contact Baker Park Reserve, 2301 County Road 19, Maple Plain, MN 55359, 763/694-7662, www.threeriversparkdistrict.org/parks.

15 LAKE MINNEWASHTA LAKE AND WOODLAND LOOP TRAILS

Lake Minnewashta Regional Park, Chaska

Level: Easy

Hiking Time: 2 hours

Total Distance: 2.65 miles round-trip

Elevation Gain: 30 feet

Summary: Follow the shores of Lake Minnewashta, through waist-high prairie grasses and the birdsong marshes of Lake Minnewashta Regional Park.

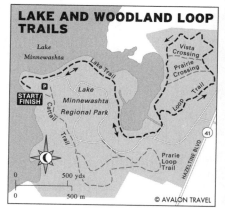

Lake, marsh, and prairie are all present in Lake Minnewashta Regional Park. The Lake and Woodland Loop Trails will take you from marshy shores to breezy fields.

From the beach parking lot, walk to your left near the vending machines. The Lake Trail begins here and wraps north around the peninsula that juts into Lake Minnewashta. Take a right past the beach and the restroom facility and along the northern edge of the parking lot through the maple trees. This low trail can be wet and muddy in the spring and after heavy rains. A half mile from the trailhead the Lake Trail nears the small marshy bay the park encompasses. The trail turns south here and leads to the boat landing. Look for herons and muskrats in the reeds, as well as painted turtles sitting on branches or rocks that protrude from the water.

You come to a small parking lot and picnic area 1.25 miles into the hike. Take a right when the trail splits and begin walking counterclockwise along the Woodland Loop Trail. The path climbs slightly to a more open area with scattered trees and fields. Wild clover, daisies, and purple coneflowers are in bloom here during the summer months. Waist-high grasses line this section of the trail. The mowed grass path often catches a breeze that you won't feel in the trees that line the lake. This loop is 1.4 miles long and has two cross trails within it. Stay to the right at each intersection to remain on the Woodland Loop Trail. Returning south on the loop trail you re-enter the wooded area that hugs the lakeshore.

As you move from tree cover to wetland to prairie, watch for the deer and

A willow tree arcs over the water in Lake Minnewashta Regional Park.

foxes that dwell in these border zones. Deer like to feed at the edges of fields, especially, and are often seen in groups of four or five. When you return to the picnic area, pick up the Lake Trail and head back through the trees to the parking lot.

Options

To get a taste of more of the park's low-lands, head down the Cattail Trail leading south from the beach parking lot. The path connects with the Prairie Loop trail and adds 1.5 miles to your hike. This low area on the western side of the peninsula holds a vast cattail field. Wetland birds like the redwing blackbird can be heard loudly calling during the summer. When the cattails release their tight clusters of seeds, this area is full of their white fluff, both blowing through the air and clinging to the grass, leaves, and cattail stalks along the trail. You'll probably even get some up your nose.

Directions

From Minneapolis take I-394 West for 9 miles, then turn left onto I-494 South for 3.7 miles. Exit onto MN-7 West for 7 miles. Turn left at MN-41 North. The park entrance is in 1 mile on your right. Follow signs to the beach parking lot.

Information and Contact

There is a $5 vehicle permit fee. Restrooms and drinking fountains are located at the beach parking lot. Dogs are allowed. Maps are available at the park entrance and on the park website. For more information, contact Lake Minnewashta Regional Park, 6900 Hazeltine Boulevard, Chanhassen, MN 55331, 952/466-5250, www.co.carver.mn.us (click on *Parks & Recreation* under *Quick Links*).

16 FISH LAKE TRAIL

Fish Lake Regional Park, Maple Grove

Level: Easy

Hiking Time: 1.5 hours

Total Distance: 2.6 miles round-trip

Elevation Gain: 30 feet

Summary: Explore the marshy southern inlet and wooded peninsula of Fish Lake.

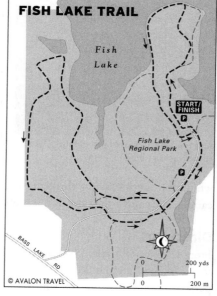

Although Fish Lake is a popular place to—you guessed it—fish, it also has an excellent trail system. Start by climbing the hill north of the pavilion. A short service road goes to the top, and a mowed grass path continues for another 200 feet. A small clearing with a fire ring sits atop the hill. If you're stealthy, there's a good chance you'll see whitetail deer grazing at the edge of the clearing. At the northern edge of the hill a small footpath leads down to the water. Take a left on the paved hiker-biker trail and arc past the beach to the parking area. The relatively undeveloped shores of the lake are a refreshing sight so close to the city. Many of Minnesota's lakes, especially near the metro area, are entirely developed and offer little or no natural lakeshore. Follow the paved hiker-biker path along the edge of the parking lot, and then turn left, crossing the park road. An unpaved path joins the trail here.

Take a right onto the unpaved path and follow it alongside the road for about 0.1 mile; 0.3 mile into the hike you will come to another paved hiker-biker path. Take a right on it and follow it for 0.1 mile as it crosses the park road and heads west. After crossing the bridge built over the creek veer right on the unpaved path. You will be heading north toward the lake on the west side of the inlet.

The thick oak and maple woods of this section of the hike are a rarity in the suburban sprawl outside of the park. This thick patch of trees treats hikers to a shady, forest turf trail that arcs for nearly a mile through the forest. If you haven't already, you will very likely see wildlife here. Turtles sunning themselves on fallen

© JAKE KULJU

A cluster of berries droops off of a branch of this young mountain ash.

trees, deer hiding in the shadows, and even the occasional marsh hawk can be seen here near the marshy inlet. Some wild daisies and asters also line this path, though this park is not known for its wildflower displays.

At 1.6 miles you meet another paved trail. Take a left on it for 0.2 mile to the maintenance facility road. Take a right to the park road just a few hundred feet away. Cross the road and veer left on the unpaved hiking trail. This leads you to a paved trail intersection 0.1 mile ahead. Cross the intersection and you will find yourself on the path you took earlier alongside the park road. Follow it back to the parking lot 0.25 mile away.

Options

To get a more woodsy experience and throw another 0.5 mile onto your hike, follow the maintenance facility road south. After reaching the main road take a short left and an unpaved hiking trail leads into the trees. After curving through the woods for 0.4 mile, take a left on the paved hiker-biker trail that leads back to the main road. Take a right here toward the parking lot.

Directions

From Minneapolis take I-94 West for 13.5 miles. Exit left onto I-494 South for 1.7 miles. Take the County Road 10 exit and turn right onto County Road 10 West for 1.3 miles. Turn right at Fish Lake Park Road. Drive past the entry station and follow the park road to the second parking lot by the picnic area.

Information and Contact

There is no fee. Public restrooms are not available. Dogs are allowed. Maps are available on the park website. For more information, contact Fish Lake Regional Park, 14900 Bass Lake Road, Maple Grove, MN 55369, 763/694-7818, www.threeriversparkdistrict.org/parks.

17 MEDICINE LAKE TRAIL
Clifton E. French Regional Park, Plymouth

Level: Easy

Hiking Time: 1 hour

Total Distance: 1.5 miles round-trip

Elevation Gain: 40 feet

Summary: Follow the winding inlet on the northern end of Medicine Lake along forest turf and gravel trails.

Commonly called French Park, this Hennepin County park is wrapped around the quiet north end of Medicine Lake. Just west of Minneapolis, Clifton E. French Regional Park is situated along the winding inlet into Medicine Lake that is home to a plethora of area wildlife. Beavers, muskrats, and snapping turtles live here, as well as great egrets, herons, and kingfishers. This park is popular in the early autumn when its maple forest colors begin to blaze with the turning leaves.

A large set of steps on the right side of the visitors center starts you off on

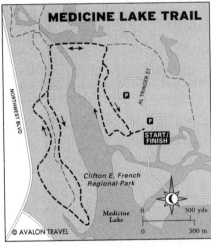

this easy hike. Climb the concrete steps and follow the handrail-lined sidewalk to the top of the hill behind the building. At the trail intersection, follow the middle of the three paths, heading downhill toward the lakeshore. The trail curves to the right and follows the reedy wetland area that surrounds the Medicine Lake inlet. At the 0.3-mile mark turn left and walk across the inlet to the other side of the water. This is where the biggest chunk of the hike begins. The maple trees that crowded the east side of the inlet grow thick here as well. Their dense canopy makes for shady hiking trails in the summer and beautiful red and yellow leaf displays in autumn.

Turn left at the bench after crossing the water and climb the small, sandy hill that rises above the lakeshore. Snapping turtles from the lake love this area for laying their eggs. If you come at the right time you might catch one in action, or at least see one of their nests dug into the soft, sandy soil. Stay to your left at all trail intersections for the next 0.5 mile until the trail makes a sharp right turn. Keep left 300 feet later as the trail traces the edge of a wetland area and pond.

The leaves of the sumac trees on Medicine Lake turn a deep burgundy in mid-autumn.

Just under 0.5 mile from the intersection, choose the middle path, which takes you to the foot of the sandy hill you climbed earlier. Veer left back to the bench and take a right to cross the inlet on your way back to the visitors center.

Options

Before crossing the inlet on your way back to the visitors center, keep walking straight on the west side of the water. Cross the footbridge and loop counter-clockwise around the pond and wetland area at the upper part of the inlet. The trail passes by the park's operations center and near Highway 61. This loop will add 0.75 mile to your hike and give you some more time in the quiet trees that surround this peaceful inlet.

Directions

From Minneapolis take I-394 West for 9.2 miles. Exit left onto I-494 North for 4.1 miles. Exit onto County Road 9 and take a right for 0.6 mile. Turn right into the park entrance and follow signs to the visitors center parking lot.

Information and Contact

There is no fee. Restrooms and a drinking fountain are available in the visitors center by the parking lot. Dogs are allowed on designated trails. Maps are available at the visitors center or on the park website. For more information, contact French Regional Park, 12605 County Road 9, Plymouth, MN 55441, 763/694-7750, www.threeriversparkdistrict.org/parks.

18 ELM CREEK TRAIL

Elm Creek Park Reserve, Maple Grove

Level: Easy/moderate

Hiking Time: 3 hours

Total Distance: 4.75 miles round-trip

Elevation Gain: Negligible

Summary: Walk near the shores of the playful creeks, cross footbridges over waterways, and traverse a marsh boardwalk.

The Eastman Nature Center in Elm Creek Park Reserve may at first glance seem like a day-care center. A large playground teeming with children greets anyone headed to the center's front door. The serenity and beauty of the hiking trails that lie beyond may not be readily apparent, but you'll soon see why this hike is featured here.

From the parking lot, facing the nature center, this trail starts behind you. The trailhead branches off of the road that leads to the nature center. Walk 100 feet on the sidewalk that borders the road and take a left onto the unpaved hiking trail that leads northwest. You are walking into a marshy area surrounding a small pond and will eventually walk right through it all on a boardwalk. The reeds, cattails, and other wetland plants dominate this area. Make the slight descent to the 307-foot-long boardwalk amid the bulrushes, reeds, and lily pads. Be careful if the boardwalk is wet; it can be slippery. Do not jump or stomp on the boardwalk, as the excess motion can disturb the plant life in the pond and soak the boardwalk with marsh water.

The trail makes a sharp left turn on the other end of the pond and heads south to the Sumac Trail. Turn right here toward the Meadowlark Trail, named after the showy grassland bird. This 1.5-mile loop starts about 0.5 mile into the hike and circles an open grassland on the western edge of the trail system. More elevated than the nearby pond and wetland area, this grassy meadow contains the beautiful pastels of blooming asters, coneflowers, harebells, and wild daisies. As the trail turns south, a spur trail leads to a group campsite. Stay to the left and continue on the Meadowlark Trail. When you return to the beginning of the loop, continue ahead and keep right where the Sumac Trail enters. Take another right at the next intersection. You have entered the Oxbow Loop and will cross a series of five wooden footbridges built over the various waterways near Rush Creek. At the bottom of the loop take a right toward the Monarch Trail. On the way you'll walk out of the trees and follow the edge of the forest adjacent to the rolling grasslands that dominate the second half of this hike.

After taking a right onto the Monarch Trail, you dip in and out of stands of maple trees on your way to Elm Creek. Look for whitetail deer at the edges of the trees and turtles rustling through the grass. Stay to your right at the next trail intersection and cross the paved hiker-biker trail near the 3.25-mile point. A few hundred feet ahead you will cross another unpaved trail and begin on the Creek Trail, which borders Elm Creek. A half mile from the last intersection take a left and arc across the prairie grasslands north of the creek. After turning south take a right at the trail intersection and cross the paved hiker-biker path to start on the Monarch Trail. The nature center lies 0.25 mile ahead.

Options

Instead of taking a left at the end of Creek Trail, take a right and follow the bridge across the creek. This path loops to the right and connects to part of a horse trail. Take a right at all intersections until you reach the paved hiker-biker trail. Take a right here and cross the creek until the unpaved path leads slightly to the right. Take a left at the second unpaved intersection after leaving the pavement and you will be on the Monarch Trail and the last leg of the hike.

Sedge grass grows on the banks of Rush Creek in Elm Creek Park Reserve.

© JAKE KULJU

Directions

From Minneapolis take I-94 West for 9.7 miles. Exit onto County Road 81 for 6.6 miles. Turn right at Fernbrook Lane North for 1 mile. Take a right at Elm Creek Road for 0.5 mile. A sign to the park entrance will be on your right. Follow this road to the Eastman Nature Center parking lot 0.3 mile from the park entrance.

Information and Contact

There is no fee. The park is open 5 A.M.–sunset. Restrooms and a drinking fountain are available in the Eastman Nature Center by the parking lot. Dogs are not allowed. Maps are available at the nature center and on the park website. For more information, contact Elm Creek Park Reserve, Eastman Nature Center, 13351 Elm Creek Road, Dayton, MN 55369, 763/694-7700, www.threerivers parkdistrict.org/parks.

19 MUD LAKE LOOP
Elm Creek Park Reserve, Maple Grove

Level: Easy/moderate

Total Distance: 4.5 miles round-trip

Hiking Time: 2.5–3 hours

Elevation Gain: Negligible

Summary: Walk along the tree-lined shores of marshy Mud Lake.

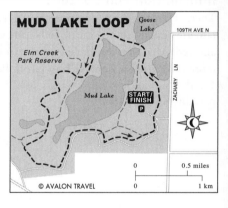

The largest lake in Elm Creek Park Reserve, Mud Lake is rife with trails. In fact, there are so many trails around Mud Lake that it can get a little confusing. I recommend staying on the paved hiker-biker trail that circumnavigates the lake. If you know the area or have a great sense of direction, you can break off onto the unpaved portions that crisscross the entire 4.5 miles of this hike. In any event, it is a good idea to have a current trail map with you as you navigate your way along this path. A large prairie and wetland area, Elm Creek Park Reserve is an amazing example of how secluded natural areas and developed urban communities can coexist.

Cross the road from the parking lot and take a left onto the paved trail heading north. Remember that this is a shared-use trail for hikers and bicyclists, so keep to the right and be alert for oncoming cyclists. In 0.25 mile the trail splits. Veer to the left as you near the northern tip of the lake. The next 2-mile section is a tangle of trail crossings through scattered stands of trees, marshland, and meadow. This transitional landscape makes for great wildlife- and bird-watching. Herons and egrets stand stock still in the marsh grasses, while whitetail deer keep close to the shelter of the trees. You may also see beaver here during the low-light times of the day. Stay true and remain on the pavement unless you're feeling adventurous and have a map with you.

At the 2-mile mark take a left at the paved trail intersection and begin heading east. The trail quickly arcs south past a stand of cottonwood and aspen trees; 0.3 mile from the last intersection the paved trail crosses Pineview Lane and then follows the road south into a dense stand of trees for 0.25 mile across Elm Creek. Look for beavers and muskrats in this muddy, marshy creek area. They love the trees, brush, and mud that characterize this soggy wetland habitat. After crossing

a transitional zone between forest and meadow near Mud Lake

Elm Creek, continue south for 0.5 mile to the next paved trail intersection. Take a left and cross another marshy creek through the open wetland. During the summer this area erupts with the sound of frogs. At sunset they are so loud you can hardly hear the traffic on Highway 81.

Stay to your left at the next two trail intersections and follow the paved path as it parallels Elm Creek Road for 1.5 miles back to the trailhead and parking lot.

Options

At the north end of Mud Lake you can get a view of Elm Creek and add 0.75 mile to your hike. At the trail intersection after Goose Lake take a right and arc past Elm Creek, staying on the unpaved hiking/mountain bike trail until it rejoins the Mud Lake trail, then take a right. This additional arc passes through open grassland that is slightly more elevated than the wetland areas surrounding Mud Lake. You will see wildflowers here in the spring and summer, including wild asters, harebells, purple coneflowers, wild daisies, and milkweed.

Directions

From Minneapolis take I-94 West for 13.1 miles. Take the County Road 81 North exit and merge onto MN-278. Drive for 1.8 miles and take a slight right to stay on MN-278 for another 3.4 miles. Turn right at Territorial Road and take another right at Elm Creek Park Road in 0.2 mile. Drive for 2 miles, veering to the right past the large parking lot and picnic area to the smaller trailhead parking lot.

Information and Contact

There is no fee. The park is open from 5 A.M.–sunset. Restrooms and a drinking fountain are available at the picnic shelter area by the larger parking lot east of the trailhead parking area. Dogs are not allowed. Maps are available on the park website. For more information, contact Elm Creek Park Reserve, Eastman Nature Center, 13351 Elm Creek Road, Dayton, MN 55369, 763/694-7700, www .threeriversparkdistrict.org/parks.

20 RUM RIVER TRAIL
Rum River Central Regional Park, Ramsey

Level: Easy

Hiking Time: 1.5 hours

Total Distance: 3.25 miles round-trip

Elevation Gain: 50 feet

Summary: Wind through the thick forests along the curvaceous Rum River.

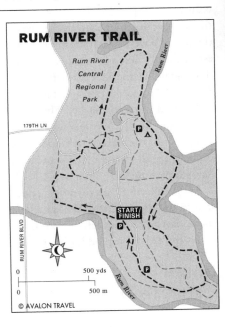

As far as rivers go, the section of the Rum River that flows 30 miles north of Minneapolis is as crooked as they come. Rum River Central Park is tucked into the curviest portion of this winding river, where the channel makes several oxbows and dramatically changes direction from southeast to northwest.

The unpaved hiking trail starts on the northern end of the parking lot and leads west. Take a left onto the path until the trail splits after a few hundred feet. Veer to the right and walk the 0.4-mile arm of trail, keeping to the right through the bottomland forest at the next trail intersection. Take a left at the following junction and head through 0.25 mile of tangled trail crossings, always staying on the wide, unpaved hiking/horse trail. At the last crossing of the pavement the trail moves straight north through thick cottonwood, basswood, and maple forest. This 0.6-mile arc follows the river south and meets the paved hiker-biker trail near the northern parking lot and boat access site. Take a left onto the pavement and continue to follow the south-flowing river for 0.5 mile to the fishing pier. There is not much variation in the vegetation in this park. The low-lying tangled river section floods frequently, keeping maple, oak, and aspen away from the water and welcoming bottomland trees like cottonwood and basswood. Some oaks and maples fill the higher regions of the park. These slightly elevated areas are where you will see the most mammalian wildlife. Whitetail deer, foxes, and raccoons dwell in the hardwood forests, while beavers and muskrats, along with herons, egrets, and mallards, take to the riverbanks. Birds of prey take advantage of this rich wetland river, as well. Barred owls and red-shouldered hawks are the most commonly sighted.

Continue following the paved path as it follows the river south. Wood duck houses jut out from the river grasses, and kingfishers hunt from the overhanging branches. The path heads southeast into the narrow pinch of land in the river's tightest oxbow, where it crosses the forest turf trail. Take a left at this intersection and follow the path further into the forest as it arcs to the northwest past the playground and picnic shelter. The canoe launch site lies 0.25 mile ahead. Take a right onto the paved path and walk slightly uphill to the Carry-in Canoe Launch parking lot.

a dry stream bed in the Rum River Valley

At 0.1 mile after you turn right, sidestep to the unpaved trail that parallels the pavement on your left. This trail continues north, following the river during its northward curve, and leads you back to the parking lot.

Options

To shorten this hike by a third and still get to the most scenic parts of the river, take a right when the paved path makes a Y after the fishing pier. At just over a mile, this trail leads through the forest back to the parking lot just under 0.1 mile away.

Directions

From Minneapolis take I-94 West for 5.3 miles. Exit onto MN-252 North for 3.8 miles. Merge onto MN-610 East for 3 miles, then exit onto MN-47 North for 1 mile. Merge onto US-10 West for 6.5 miles and take the County Road 7 exit. Turn right onto County Road 7 for 6.8 miles. Turn right at the sign for the park entrance. Drive past the gatehouse and take a right turn, following signs to the Carry-in Canoe Launch parking lot.

Information and Contact

There is a $5 vehicle permit fee. Restrooms are available at the Horse Trailer parking lot and at the picnic pavilion at the southernmost parking lot. Dogs are allowed. Maps are available on the park website. For more information, contact Rum River Central Regional Park, 17955 Roanoke Street NW, Ramsey, MN 55303, 763/767-2820, www.anokacountyparks.com (click on *Parks and Maps*).

21 COON RAPIDS DAM TRAIL

Coon Rapids Dam Regional Park, Brooklyn Park

Level: Easy

Total Distance: 2.7 miles round-trip

Hiking Time: 1–1.5 hours

Elevation Gain: Negligible

Summary: Walk over the impressive Coon Rapids Dam and watch the churning waters of the Mississippi River head downstream.

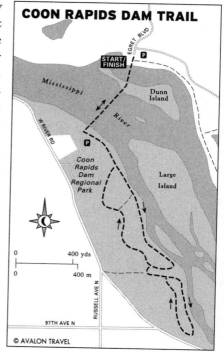

The Coon Rapids Dam was built way back in 1913 to harness hydroelectric power from the mighty river. More than 50 years later it was handed over to the Three Rivers Park District, which turned the area into public park land and has handled the maintenance and function of the dam ever since. Just 12 miles upstream from Minneapolis, this park is a unique way to view the Mississippi and a great way to get your feet on the trail.

The visitors center is adjacent to the parking lot. Start here and take a left toward the river and the dam. A paved sidewalk leads to the structure, and this portion of the hike is wheelchair accessible. You could easily find the structure with your ears as five flood gates surge with overflow water from the 6-mile reservoir the dam contains. The first section of the dam is a short jaunt to tiny Dunn Island. The second stretch is about 0.25-mile long and is the cause of the surging waters. Huge arcs of river water tumble through the dam's five chutes, creating a roaring, mist-filled experience for anyone crossing above them.

When you reach the west side of the river take a left and follow the packed dirt path that leads away from the pavement. You almost immediately come upon an open picnic area with restrooms; 200 feet ahead of this area and to your left is a narrower turf trail that holds tightly to the water's edge. This is the part of the park that really makes hiking here worthwhile. The shady cottonwood and basswood

Water gushes over the dam in Coon Rapids Dam Regional Park.

trees that overhang the banks of the river are fun for climbing on and around. Anglers frequent this area below the dam and cast their spinners from the large tree roots that dangle into the water. For the next 0.5 mile, enjoy scrambling along the riverside. Kids love this park for the air of exploration and adventure the river lends. You will probably find yourself grabbing tree roots and jumping the small tributary streams that cross this path as if you were nine years old.

When you encounter a larger stream the downstream portion of the hike is over. Follow the path to the right and cross the footbridge 500 feet ahead. Take an immediate left and follow the turf trail through a wooded area near the lower islands of the park. The oak, maple, and sumac woods are a quiet haven between the highway and the river. Whitetail deer feed in this area, and snapping turtles sometimes waddle up from the muddy river to lay their eggs along the dirt path. There is a good chance you will see a fox or the occasional skunk. The 0.5-mile loop takes you back to the footbridge you previously crossed. Instead of backtracking to your right when you get there, take a left and follow the trail along an open meadow full of waist-high sweetgrass and wild daisies. A quarter mile from the bridge a mowed path leads to your right. Stay to your left and follow the trail back to the picnic and restroom area. From here, cross back over the dam to the visitors center.

Options

To add another mile to your hike you can follow some of the paved hiking and biking trails that lead along the river's east bank. After crossing the dam on your way back to the parking lot take a right and follow the path to Cenaiko Lake. The grassy shores of this lake are a nice downstream viewpoint for watching the water that gushes forth from the massive dam. Instead of using a regular gate system, the Coon Rapids Dam operates with large inflatable rubber stoppers that water surges over before they are entirely closed.

Directions

From Minneapolis take I-94 West for 5.3 miles. Exit onto MN-610 East for 1.6 miles. Take the County Road 1 exit and turn left onto East River Road Northwest for 1 mile. Veer right onto Coon Rapids Boulevard Northwest for 0.7 mile. Turn left at Egret Boulevard Northwest for 0.5 mile. Drive past the entry station and park at the Anoka Visitor Center parking lot.

Information and Contact

There is a $5 vehicle permit fee. Restrooms and a drinking fountain are available in the visitors center by the parking lot. Dogs are allowed. Maps are available at the visitors center and on the park website. For more information, contact Coon Rapids Dam Regional Park, 9750 Egret Boulevard, Coon Rapids, MN 55433, 763/767-2820, www.anokacountyparks.com (click on *Parks and Maps*).

22 THEODORE WIRTH WILDFLOWER TRAIL

BEST ☾

Theodore Wirth Park, Golden Valley

Level: Easy

Hiking Time: 1.5–2 hours

Total Distance: 2.8 miles round-trip

Elevation Gain: Negligible

Summary: View the renowned Eloise Butler Wildflower Garden and Bird Sanctuary and take in the beautiful oak savanna of this historic park.

Theodore Wirth Park is the largest park in the Minneapolis Park System. It was established in the late 1800s by the Minneapolis Park & Recreation Board. The land was then used primarily as a nursery. Throughout the 20th century the park was developed for more recreational use. A beach was formed on Wirth Lake, as were picnic shelters and a trail system. The most notable part of the park is the stunning wildflower garden. With the Minneapolis skyline just a few miles away, this secluded little forest glen does an amazing job of blocking out the urban landscape and bringing you face to face with some of the rarest and most beautiful native wildflowers in the state.

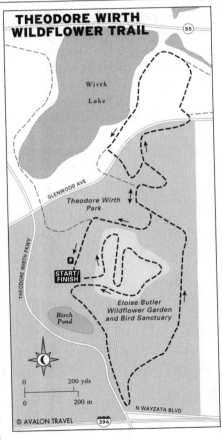

The entrance to the garden is adjacent to the parking lot. Walk through the metal gates that start the garden trail and follow the 0.5 mile of meandering wood-chip path through the displays. Each stand of flowers is identified by a small plaque. When the spring ephemerals are in bloom, this path is very popular with local flower lovers. You will see trout lilies, bloodroot, and coneflowers, along with dozens of other beautiful wildflowers. Take as many pictures as you'd like, but leave your dog behind. Pets are not allowed in the garden. After winding through the flowers the trail returns you to the metal gates at the parking lot. Cross the park road and take a left on the paved trail that leads south toward Birch Pond; 0.25 mile from the parking lot that trail crosses the park road and runs parallel to Theodore Wirth Parkway. Take a left at Wayzata Boulevard and follow the trail up the slight hill into the oak savanna portion of the park. The large, gnarled oak trees that grow here are giants compared to the other young growth on the park's outskirts. In the summer their canopy filters the sunlight and creates a shady paradise, and in the late autumn and winter their twisted, naked branches make beautiful silhouettes against the sky.

Take a left 0.5 mile north of Wayzata Boulevard as the paved trail makes its way northwest toward the picnic area. Keep to the right at the picnic tables, then take another right at the trail T. This path arcs north to another picnic area in a grassy clearing. Follow the path as it parallels Glenwood Avenue, then cross the road and veer left across the bike trail. The path makes a 0.5-mile loop around the Wirth Lake picnic area, passing the boat landing and the Beach House. Take a left at the Beach House and cross the bike trail and Glenwood Avenue toward the first picnic area. Turn right at the next two trail intersections through the oaks, then take a left 0.3 mile from the picnic area to return to the wildflower garden parking lot and trailhead.

A wild iris blooms on the forest floor in the Eloise Butler Wildflower Garden in Theodore Wirth Park.

© JAKE KULJU

Options

You can make more time near the water by taking a right just after crossing Glenwood Avenue the first time. The paved path leads east for 0.5 mile past the JD Rivers' Children's Garden, then swings northwest along Bassett's Creek for another 0.5 mile. The trail merges with the picnic area loop near Wirth Lake and brings you past the boat landing to the Beach House. This adds 1 mile to your hike and gives you some walking time along the shores of a peaceful tree-lined creek.

Directions

From Minneapolis head west on Highway 55 for 2.3 miles. Turn left onto

Theodore Wirth Parkway for 0.5 mile. After crossing Glenwood Avenue take a left into the Eloise Butler Wildflower Garden parking lot.

Information and Contact

There is no fee. Restrooms and a drinking fountain are available at the Wirth Beach parking area. Dogs are allowed, but not in the wildflower garden. Maps are available at the park website. For more information, contact Theodore Wirth Park, 1339 Theodore Wirth Parkway, Minneapolis, MN 55411, 612/230-6400, www.minneapolisparks.org.

ST. CROIX
RIVER VALLEY

© JAKE KULJU

BEST HIKES

◖ **Historical Hikes**
Grand Portage Trail, **page 154.**

◖ **River Hikes**
Swinging Bridge and Summer Trail Loop, **page 157.**
Quarry Loop to High Bluff Trail, **page 165.**
Kinni Canyon Trail, **page 187.**

◖ **Viewing Wildlife**
Swinging Bridge and
    Summer Trail Loop, **page 157.**
Riverbend Trail, **page 198.**

◖ **Views**
Lake Pepin Overlook Hiking Club Trail, **page 195.**
Dakota and Trout Run Creek Trails, **page 201.**
Riverview Trail to Blufftop Trail, **page 204.**
King's and Queen's Bluff Trail, **page 207.**

Bordering the eastern side of Minnesota, along with the Mississippi River, the St. Croix River is known for its rocky and cliff-lined shores with hard basalt and sandstone formations. Rapids and waterfalls are common along the St. Croix, drawing kayakers and canoeists to its white water. In addition, its surrounding shores and bluffs make for great hiking. St. Croix is one of the most recreational rivers in the state.

Whether you want to skip stones from a sandy beach or climb 300-foot bluffs for panoramic views, the St. Croix River Valley is a treasure trove of awesome geology. The landscape alongside the Minnesota and Wisconsin border is characterized by evergreen forests, rock formations, and, farther south, the rolling bluffs, apple orchard hills, and escarpments of the Mississippi River Valley. Wildlife, ranging from soaring bald eagles to scurrying weasels, thrives in the bluffs, valleys, and riverbanks that make up this region.

The hiking trails in this chapter will bring you to the tops of ridges and the bottoms of valleys that are like no other place in the state. Pockets of land spared by the ubiquitous glacial drift have left ravines and gorges rife with rocky overlooks and lush creek valleys. Interstate State Park is home to some of the world's rarest and largest glacial potholes. The high cliffs of the Vermillion River gorge, the seemingly endless climb to Inspiration Point along the Whitewater River, and the deep-cut river valley in Carley State Park show off some of Minnesota's most diverse landscapes.

South of the Twin Cities, the Mississippi, St. Croix, and Vermillion Rivers all meet in the city of Hastings. The Mississippi River carries these waters south as it continues the border between Minnesota and Wisconsin. This portion of the valley is true bluff country. High above Lake Pepin, the trails of Frontenac State Park overlook one of the state's most picturesque bodies of water. Forest turf trails cling to bluffsides and tall stands of red and white pine create majestic natural cathedrals. Across the border in Wisconsin, trails climb the undulating bluffs that rise helter-skelter from the ground. In Great River Bluffs State Park you can stand more than 400 feet above the Mississippi bottomlands, where the wide river channel sluices through the low-lying valley.

Working your way from the rapid-filled St. Louis River in Jay Cooke State Park to the mile-wide Mississippi River Valley in southern Minnesota is an outdoors education in the rhythm and movement of river waters. The north-flowing St. Louis feeds Lake Superior, and the Grand Portage Trail along the river is the same centuries-old voyageur portaging trail that French trappers and explorers used in the 1700s. Hikes along the Vermillion, Kinnickinnic, and Whitewater Rivers take you along the thick forests that surround tributaries to the St. Croix. And in the bluff country south of Hastings you will witness the Mississippi take on the grand width that it carries, ever-widening, more than 2,000 miles south to the Gulf of Mexico.

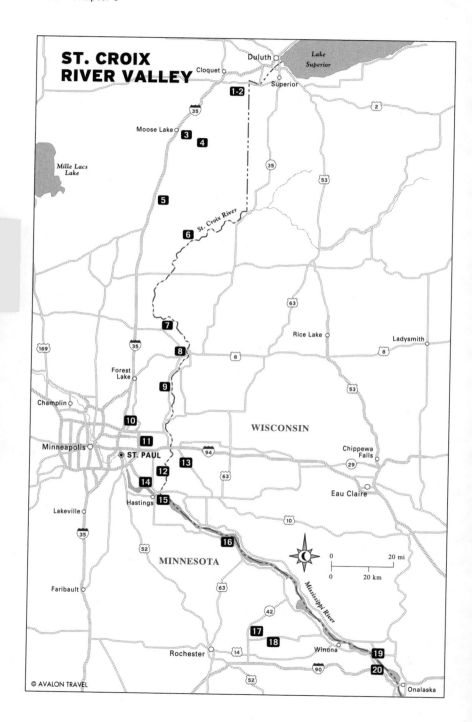

TRAIL NAME	LEVEL	DISTANCE	TIME	ELEVATION	FEATURES	PAGE
1 Grand Portage Trail	Moderate/strenuous	4.2 mi rt	2.5 hr	360 ft		154
2 Swinging Bridge and Summer Trail Loop	Moderate	3.75 mi rt	2 hr	180 ft		157
3 Rolling Hills and Echo Lake Trail	Moderate	4.7 mi rt	2.5 hr	200 ft		160
4 Christmas Tree Trail	Easy	2 mi rt	1–1.5 hr	30 ft		162
5 Quarry Loop to High Bluff Trail	Moderate	3 mi rt	1.5 hr	200 ft		165
6 Kettle River and Bear Creek Trail	Moderate	6.2 mi rt	3.5–4 hr	30 ft		168
7 Deer Creek Loop and River Trail	Moderate	7.3 mi rt	4 hr	120 ft		171
8 River Trail to Sandstone Bluffs	Moderate/strenuous	3.75 mi rt	2.5–3 hr	250 ft		174
9 Prairie Overlook and Woodland Edge Loop	Moderate	5.7 mi rt	2.5–3 hr	160 ft		177
10 Goldenrod and Fish Lake Trail Loop	Easy	3.6 mi rt	2 hr	70 ft		180
11 Eagle Point Lake Trail	Easy/moderate	4.5 mi rt	2.5–3 hr	Negligible		182
12 St. Croix River Trail	Moderate	4 mi rt	2–2.5 hr	180 ft		184
13 Kinni Canyon Trail	Moderate	3.7 mi rt	2.5–3 hr	60 ft		187
14 Cottage Grove Ravine Trails	Moderate	2.8 mi rt	2.5 hr	150 ft		190
15 Vermillion Falls Trail	Easy/moderate	4.6 mi rt	2.5 hr	Negligible		193
16 Lake Pepin Overlook Hiking Club Trail	Moderate	3.3 mi rt	2 hr	220 ft		195
17 Riverbend Trail	Moderate/strenuous	3.1 mi rt	2 hr	350 ft		198
18 Dakota and Trout Run Creek Trails	Strenuous	6.7 mi rt	4.5 hr	400 ft		201
19 Riverview Trail to Blufftop Trail	Strenuous	4.5 mi rt	3 hr	420 ft		204
20 King's and Queen's Bluff Trail	Moderate	4.5 mi rt	2.5–3 hr	220 ft		207

1 GRAND PORTAGE TRAIL

BEST C

Jay Cooke State Park, Carlton

Level: Moderate/strenuous

Hiking Time: 2.5 hours

Total Distance: 4.2 miles round-trip

Elevation Gain: 360 feet

Summary: Walk along a centuries-old path once frequented by the hardy voyageurs and Native Americans of the northwoods.

Most Minnesotans know about the voyageurs—the Frenchmen who came to precolonial America to make their living trapping and trading in the northwoods. There are museums, pictures, artifacts, and songs that all remind us of their legendary presence here. At Jay Cooke State Park you can actually walk along the same centuries-old path that the voyageurs took along the St. Louis River. If you're panting

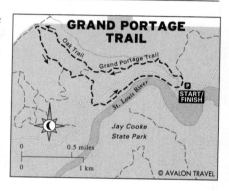

when you get through this 4.2-mile trek, imagine doing it two or three times with a canoe or 90 pounds of beaver skins strapped to your back!

The trailhead is to the left of the parking lot toward the train tracks. An information kiosk gives some history of the trail area and a picture of a 1700s voyageur. From the kiosk, take a left onto the trail as it enters the underbrush of the forest. (The first few hundred feet are also the beginning of the famous Superior Hiking Trail.) If you'd like to set foot on the bank of the St. Louis River where the original portage began, take a right and you'll get to the water in about 100 feet.

The trail almost immediately crosses the paved park road and dives back into the woods. Just south of Duluth, this area is considered north country by most Minnesotans and has the characteristic Norway pine trees that thrive here and once covered more than half of the state. A quarter mile later, the trail dips down to a small creek. The water level is usually quite low and you can rock-hop across. From here you begin a 150-foot ascent over 0.75 mile. While most of this hike is in the thick forest, this is the thickest of it. Keep your eyes open for foxes, white-tail deer, porcupines, and minks. Other critters like red squirrels and chipmunks will surely be scurrying around you as well.

One mile into the hike, at the top of the hill, you come to a wooden marker with the number 24 emblazoned on it. Take a right here onto the Oak Trail. This trail is a loop that follows the top of the ridge and has somewhat of an oak savanna, though no naturalist would call it that. Oak trees do dominate the forest here, though. The wooden 22 marker is the 2.5-mile mark from the trailhead. Take a right here and begin a steep descent toward Gill Creek. This 0.5-mile portion of the trail descends 140 feet and will definitely give your calves a workout. Cross the park road at wooden marker 23 and walk to your left to where the trail picks up again. The scenery opens up a bit here as the trail approaches the river. The trees aren't quite as thick and you are more likely to see ducks, geese, and other waterfowl.

From the park road along the river to the trailhead is the final mile of the hike. The trail bounces along the riverbank, coming right up next to the water and easing back into the trees several times before hugging the park road in the final 0.1 mile to the parking lot. This flat stretch along the river is a nice way to finish the ups and downs of this challenging northwoods hike.

Options

If you'd like to add a panoramic view to this outing you'll have to tack on a few miles, but it's worth it. Take a right at wooden marker 21 and follow the trail as it descends to Gill Creek and then climbs 150 feet to marker 19. Take a left here and another left onto the wider Horseback/Hiking trail at marker 18; a 0.5-mile walk from here will lead you to a trail shelter and a lookout point over the St. Louis River as it flows northwest. Head back the way you came and take a right

a view of the wide, clear waters of the St. Louis River on its way to Lake Superior

at marker 21 to rejoin the main hiking trail. This addition will put 2.1 more miles under your belt!

Directions

From St. Paul head north on I-35 East/I-35 for 128 miles. Exit right onto MN-210 for 7 miles. Drive 3 miles past the park entrance to the Grand Portage Trail parking area on the right.

Information and Contact

There is a $5 daily vehicle permit fee. Restrooms and drinking fountains are available at the park office. Dogs are allowed. Maps are available at the park office and on the park website. For more information contact Jay Cooke State Park, 780 Highway 210, Carlton, MN 55718, 218/384-4610, www.dnr.state.mn.us.

2 SWINGING BRIDGE AND SUMMER TRAIL LOOP
Jay Cooke State Park, Carlton

BEST ☾

Level: Moderate

Hiking Time: 2 hours

Total Distance: 3.75 miles round-trip

Elevation Gain: 180 feet

Summary: Cross the swinging footbridge over the boulder-laden St. Louis River and walk through the thick forests that surround Silver Creek.

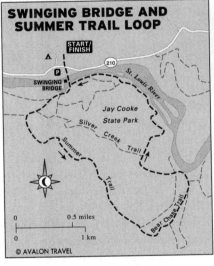

SWINGING BRIDGE AND SUMMER TRAIL LOOP

If you are afraid of heights, especially those that involve Indiana Jones-style swinging bridges over boulder-filled rivers, this hike might not be for you. Make sure to wear ankle-supported footwear and be ready for some light climbing. From the parking lot, walk to the left of the visitors center and down toward the river. A sign points to the swinging bridge, which is where this hike starts.

The first 200 feet of this hike is on wooden planks over the tumultuous St. Louis River. The swinging bridge is an area tourist attraction that draws people to the stunning views of this portion of the river. This rocky hike is an adventure and a geology lesson all wrapped into one. Large upturned slate beds jut from the earth where the swiftly moving waters have exposed them. On the other side of the bridge you'll get a taste of climbing along the sharp angles of their geometry. Gnarled red pines grow among the rocks, twining their long roots along the slate looking for footholds. This part of the hike can be tricky, as it is easy to get lost among the rocks. Stay to your right near the water as the trail moves toward a larger pool along a branch of the river off of the main channel. Veer left here onto the trail that enters the woods. As you move away from the water you will come upon three trail intersections. Turn left at the third onto the wide grassy path through the forest. This is Summer Trail and is 0.5 mile from the trailhead. It leads away from the water, south into the forest.

A gentle decline through the forest leads you to Silver Creek. Cross the little stream and continue south through the thick maple and basswood trees. You

Upturned sheets of slate and greywacke line the St. Louis River rapids.

will almost certainly see a few whitetail deer in this secluded area. Bears can be around as well, though they are rarely sighted. One-fifth mile from the creek the trail crosses the smaller south branch of Silver Creek and begins a 50-foot ascent at the Silver Creek backpacking campsite on your left. The trail turns east here, arcing back toward the river.

Half a mile from the campsite take a right at the trail intersection onto the Bear Chase Trail. You won't be chased by any bears here, but you will be treated to a beautiful view of the St. Louis River. Take three lefts over the next 0.5 mile to a quaint wooden trail shelter that sits on a high bank overlooking a sharp turn of the river. This is a good resting point and is just over the halfway point. The trail cuts west here for a few hundred feet and then meets an intersection. Keep straight ahead and take a right at the next intersection 0.25 mile away. You'll pass another wooden shelter on your right before the path begins running adjacent to the river. The thick maple, basswood, and poplar trees continue throughout this section of the trail.

A gradual 60-foot incline greets you along this river walk during the final 0.75 mile; 0.25 mile from the swinging bridge you reenter the craggy, angled rock formations. Pick your way along the trail to the bridge and enjoy the cascading water, the sound of the rapids, and the breeze that usually blows here above the river.

Options

To stay close to the St. Louis River on this hike, follow the rocky Carlton Trail, which skims the river's shore. Take a right after crossing the footbridge; hike to marker 27 and back for a 2.5-mile trip.

Directions

From St. Paul head north on I-35 East/I-35 for 128 miles. Exit right onto MN-210 for 7 miles. Take a right into the park entrance and visitors center parking lot.

Information and Contact

There is a $5 daily vehicle permit fee. Restrooms and drinking fountains are available at the park office. Dogs are allowed. Maps are available at the park office and on the park website. For more information, contact Jay Cooke State Park, 780 Highway 210, Carlton, MN 55718, 218/384-4610, www.dnr.state.mn.us.

🕄 ROLLING HILLS AND ECHO LAKE TRAIL
Moose Lake State Park, Moose Lake

Level: Moderate

Total Distance: 4.7 miles round-trip

Hiking Time: 2.5 hours

Elevation Gain: 200 feet

Summary: Circle Wildlife Pond and walk through the majestic pine trees near Echo Lake.

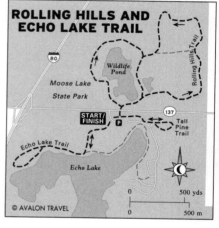

Few symbols evoke the grandeur of the northwoods as succinctly as the moose. And while Moose Lake State Park may not be home to as many moose as in decades past, its trails will still take you through some of the most beautiful northwoods landscape in the region. Head east from the parking lot and follow the blue Hiking Club trail signs to your left at the first trail intersection just a few hundred feet from the parking lot. The grass and gravel trail crosses a park road in another hundred feet and then splits. Take a right, following the Hiking Club trail signs. This 0.1-mile trail section crosses a grassy dam on the south shore of Wildlife Pond. Take a right after crossing the dam to enter the Rolling Hills Trail loop. The path is a wide mowed grass trail lined with thick forest crowded with mature aspen, maple, basswood, and birch trees.

The Rolling Hills Trail is aptly named. In 1.2 miles the path arcs through thick forest and several hills, adding an easy 140 feet of uphill. When you reach the wooden shelter remain left on the wider path that borders the western shore of Wildlife Pond; 0.2 mile from the shelter take a right onto the narrower path that loops around the entire body of water. Take your time here, both to take in the sight of the water and to increase your chances of seeing some animals. Wildlife Pond got its name for a reason, and if you keep your eyes open and your steps light you may see animals varying from muskrat to moose. More common are whitetail deer, beavers, foxes, herons, and raccoons. This 0.7-mile portion of the hike can be wet in the spring and summer thanks for a healthy beaver population.

When you return to the trail intersection near the wooden shelter, take a right onto the grassy path and another right 0.2 mile later to cross the dam. Take a left, leaving the Hiking Club trail and crossing the park road toward the trailhead. Take a left at the intersection after the road onto the Tall Pine Trail. This spur loop leads through tall, majestic red pines. These silent giants whisper in the breeze and have blanketed the trail with their soft brown needles. The 0.3-mile loop takes you up and down both sides of the small hill the pine grove is on and then returns you to the trailhead. Take a left at the parking lot and follow the road to the beach parking lot for 0.2 mile.

The final 1.2 miles follow a section of the northern shore of beautiful Echo Lake. Take a right at the sandy beach (or dip your toes in if you'd like to cool off). You will walk past a shaded picnic

Peaceful pines sway in the breeze along the Tall Pine Trail.

area and then climb a small hill along the Echo Lake Trail loop. More wildlife sightings likely lie ahead on the small wooded hill on the northwest branch of the lake. When you return to the beach walk back north through the parking lot along the park road to the trailhead.

Options

For another 0.5 miles and more time along the lakeshore, keep along the water's edge when you return to the Echo Lake beach. This path winds south to the campground. Turn around at the park road and follow the path back to the beach. Then take a right and head north to the parking lot.

Directions

From St. Paul head north on I-35 East/I-35 for 107 miles. Exit onto MN-73 toward Moose Lake for 0.3 mile. Turn right at County Road 137 for 0.4 mile, crossing over the freeway. Turn right into the park entrance in 0.1 mile. Park in the lot just across from the park office.

Information and Contact

There is a $5 daily vehicle permit fee. Restrooms and drinking fountains are available in the park office. Dogs are allowed. Maps are available at the park office and on the park website. For more information, contact Moose Lake State Park, 4252 County Road 137, Moose Lake, MN 55767, 218/485-5420, www.dnr.state.mn.us.

4 CHRISTMAS TREE TRAIL

Nemadji State Forest, Holyoke

Level: Easy

Hiking Time: 1-1.5 hours

Total Distance: 2 miles round-trip

Elevation Gain: 30 feet

Summary: Walk through thick stands of Norway pine and secluded wetland habitats along the National Christmas Tree Trail deep in the northwoods.

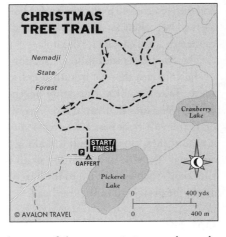

While not a technically challenging hike, the secluded Christmas Tree Trail is worth a visit for anyone who loves the Minnesota outdoors. The trail was created in 1987 to commemorate the location of the National Christmas Tree that was cut in 1977 and used at the White House. Two rings of campsites situated near Pickerel Lake provide access to the many ATV trails that run throughout the forest. While the trails in this area are primarily used for ATV and other off-road-vehicle use, the little-used hiking only Christmas Tree Trail loops through some of the most pristine northwoods forest in this area of the state. With only very small towns and quiet county roads nearby, the silence and solemnity of the Nemadji State Forest is as complete as it comes.

The trailhead begins at the outdoor restroom in the Gaffert Campground and heads straight north. A metal gate blocks access to motor vehicles, opening to a wide and grassy path. Mowed only a few times a year, the first 0.5 mile is a wild tangle of underbrush tallgrass that winds through a dense pine forest. The giant red pines crowd close to the sides of the trail, and their enchanting quietude enhances the already heavy sense of seclusion. When the trail splits, veer to the right. White birch trees huddle along the left side of the trail, a stark contrast against the dark pines. After the turn the trail makes its way east toward Cranberry Lake; 0.75 mile into the hike the wide trail arcs northward and enters a more open area near the creek that flows into Cranberry Lake. This low wetland area is a haven for wildlife. Signs of bears can be found amidst the brush, and whitetail deer, foxes, and raccoons are in high numbers. The numerous pine trees attract the

© JAKE KULJU

Wild blackberries grow along the Christmas Tree Trail.

shy porcupine. Keep your eyes trained to the treetops and look for signs of falling bark to locate these prickly creatures.

Not far from the creek, a spur trail on your right heads north to Net River. The waterway is about 0.2 mile from the trail loop and marks the halfway point of the hike. When you reach the river you'll get a sense of how remote this area is. This completely undeveloped portion of the forest is an example of what much of Minnesota looked like before settlement. When you return to the trail loop, take a right into the thick trees. The red pines are not only numerous here, but large as well. Many of them are too large to wrap your arms around.

The next trail intersection is at the bottom of the loop, 1.6 miles into the hike by the same stand of birch trees that greeted you at the beginning of the hike. Take a right here and follow the trail as it meanders south back to the trailhead.

Options

For more immersion in the thick pines, take a right on the campground road that you drove along to the trailhead and take a right on the narrow gravel road that heads north to Net Lake. This tree-lined road leads to the southeast corner of Net Lake and gives you a wider perspective of the pine forests and wetland areas of the park while adding 1.2 miles to your hike.

Directions

From St. Paul head north on I-35 East/I-35 for 88 miles. Exit right onto MN-23 for 30 miles. Turn right at County Road 8 for 1.1 miles. Veer right to continue on County Road 8 for another 1.7 miles. Turn right at County Road 145 for 0.5 mile. Turn left and stay on County Road 145 for 1.5 miles. The trail parking lot is at the intersection of Harlis Road from the east.

Information and Contact

There is no fee. Dogs are allowed. Maps are available on the park website. For more information, contact the Moose Lake Area Office, 218/485-5410, www .dnr.state.mn.us.

5 QUARRY LOOP TO HIGH BLUFF TRAIL

Banning State Park, Sandstone

BEST ◖

Level: Moderate

Total Distance: 3 miles round-trip

Hiking Time: 1.5 hours

Elevation Gain: 200 feet

Summary: Climb the craggy rock formations along a cascading section of the Kettle River near the area's old rock quarry site.

In the 1890s, more than 500 workers were employed by the Banning Sandstone Quarry works. Before the popular use of structural steel, this strong sandstone was chiseled into blocks and used for the construction of large buildings. Weathered remains of the old stoneworks and the small village around it still exist along the Quarry Loop Trail. The Kettle River tears a rapid-filled ravine through the park, exposing towering sandstone formations and rushing waters below the cliffs.

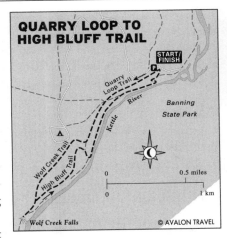

The Quarry Loop Trail leads west from the parking lot. Stone steps take you down close to the cascading Kettle River. Veer right when the trail splits near the trailhead. You will quickly see why this area was chosen as a quarry site. If you aren't completely rapt by the rushing and rocky rapids, you will be stepping around boulders or staring up at sheer stone cliffsides. The packed-dirt trail slips through the exposed bedrock of the park. Stay on the Quarry Loop Trail through three trail intersections. Stands of red and white pine huddle among the rocks, while aspen and birch dominate most of the forested area.

From the trailhead, after 0.8 mile take a right onto Deadman Trail just beyond the old quarry site. The trail here climbs a small hill into thicker deciduous trees. At the top of this 0.1-mile connecting trail take a left onto the Wolf Creek Trail; 0.6 mile of thick forest leads away from the river toward Wolf Creek Falls. You will see some patches of exposed bedrock along Wolf Creek Trail and pools of water in the rocks after rains and during wet seasons. At the bottom of the falls the creek makes a wide, deep pool. This area is the most remote part of the park, where you will have the greatest chance of seeing wildlife. The ubiquitous whitetail deer, shy ruffed grouse, and chattering red squirrels fill the forest around the falls.

Turn around here and walk up from the creek to High Bluff Trail at the top of the hill. Veer right into the gnarled red pine trees that grow amid the boulder field. On top of the cliffs that line the river near Hell's Gate you will be 40 feet above the rushing water. Many times the trail seemingly disappears in the layers of rock and blanket of pine needles. Keep your eyes open for the narrow forest turf trail that winds along the craggy bluff for 0.7 mile back to Deadman Trail. Take a right here back to Quarry Loop. More stone steps take you closer to the river and along the second half of the Quarry Loop. Here you walk through the thickest boulder field, past the old power house and crusher sites from the abandoned quarry works.

Near the end of the loop take a right to Teacher's Overlook. The 0.1-mile spur trail is worth the view over Kettle River. Return to Quarry Loop and take a right. The trailhead is just a few hundred feet from the last intersection.

Options

Upstream from the rock formations, the Skunk Cabbage Trail loop follows a more peaceful stretch of the river and takes you deeper into the woods, adding 2.2 miles to your hike. Take a right after returning to the parking lot onto the Skunk Cabbage Trail. After crossing the park road, the trail makes a wide loop through the forest. Follow signs for the Skunk Cabbage Trail at the two intersections until

Norway pines take root among the rocks near the old quarry site in Banning State Park.

returning to the north side of the parking lot. Cross the park road back to the trailhead to finish the loop.

Directions

From St. Paul head north on I-35 East/I-35 for 88 miles. Exit right onto MN-23 for 0.4 mile. Turn right at Banning Park Road for 0.1 mile into the park entrance. Drive past the park office and veer left for approximately 1 mile, following signs to the picnic area parking lot.

Information and Contact

There is a $5 daily vehicle permit fee. Restrooms and drinking fountains are available in the picnic areas and at the park office. Dogs are allowed. Maps are available at the park office and on the park website. For more information, contact Banning State Park, P.O. Box 643, Sandstone, MN 55072, 320/245-2668, www.dnr.state.mn.us.

6 KETTLE RIVER AND BEAR CREEK TRAIL
St. Croix State Park, Hinckley

Level: Moderate

Hiking Time: 3.5-4 hours

Total Distance: 6.2 miles round-trip

Elevation Gain: 30 feet

Summary: Walk to the confluence of the Kettle and St. Croix Rivers and through the thick forests of this curvy portion of the St. Croix.

Few things are as peaceful as watching the confluence of two Minnesota northwoods rivers. St. Croix State Park is one of the best places to do it. This expansive park has several trail systems, including one that leads to the confluence of the St. Croix and Kettle Rivers. This hike starts out with a beautiful overlook of a sharp bend in the Kettle River. Walk back to the gravel road and take a right. Look for the trail to start on your right-hand side in just a few hundred feet. Head south here along the Kettle River and beside the thick sugar maple and basswood trees that line its bank. On the far southwestern edge of the park, this trail system is one of the more remote and less traveled. The narrow forest turf path and abundance of wildlife are proof of it. Whitetail deer, minks, foxes, and raccoons thrive near the two rivers. You also have a good chance of spotting bald eagles soaring above the waterways. Black bears also roam these woods but are rarely seen.

A trail intersection meets you at 1.3 miles. Across the river is the River's End canoe camp. You may be able to spot it in autumn or winter when the trees are bare but will have a hard time during the lushness of summer. Stay to your right closer to the river at the intersection and continue for another 0.8 mile to the confluence point. The Two Rivers canoe campsite marks the spot of the confluence, though you'd be able to tell that two rivers come together here anyway. The upper arm of the St. Croix is dotted with small islands and sandbars as the Kettle River joins in from the north. Cross the campsite and follow the trail northeast as it now borders the St. Croix River; 1 mile from the campsite the trail passes an intersection. Stay to your right closer to the water and continue heading north. The next

A stand of birch trees grows tall and narrow.

1.1 miles is through the thick of the forest and moves away from the river. The forest turf path is easy to follow and passes through one of the quietest and most serene areas in the entire park. Small forest meadows break up the scenery as you continue north. Look for deer at the edges of the fields, especially at dusk. These secluded meadows are favorite feeding grounds for whitetail.

Only the calls of songbirds and the chatter of squirrels break the silence along this shady, forested path. The trail emerges along the park's gravel road and crosses over to part of the Bear Creek Trail. A mile later at the 5.2-mile mark, Bear Creek Trail breaks to the right. Take a left at this intersection along Kennedy Brook. A mile later you will cross the gravel road back to the parking lot and trailhead.

Options

For 2 more miles along the peaceful Kettle River, take a right along the dirt road before crossing over to the parking lot. Cross the park road in 0.3 mile and follow the hiking trail east toward the Kettle River to another overlook point called Kettle River Highbanks. Turn around and return to the parking lot and trailhead to finish the hike.

Directions

From St. Paul head north on I-35 East for 75.5 miles. Exit right onto MN-48 toward Hinckley for 9.5 miles. Turn right at County Road 21 into the park entrance and follow signs to the Kettle River Overlook for approximately 10 miles. Take a right into the Kettle River Overlook parking lot.

Information and Contact

There is a $5 daily vehicle permit fee. Restrooms and drinking fountains are available in the group center and at the park office. Dogs are allowed. Maps are available at the park office and on the park website. For more information, contact Banning State Park, P.O. Box 643, Sandstone, MN 55072, 320/384-6591, www.dnr.state.mn.us.

7 DEER CREEK LOOP AND RIVER TRAIL

Wild River State Park, North Branch

Level: Moderate

Hiking Time: 4 hours

Total Distance: 7.3 miles round-trip

Elevation Gain: 120 feet

Summary: Walk along a ridgeline forest on an old logging trail and descend to the banks of the St. Croix River.

Wrapped around 18 miles of the scenic St. Croix River, Wild River State Park is a prime Minnesota hiking destination. With more than 35 miles of trails to explore, you can have a different experience almost every time you visit this park. A classic hike that provides plenty of wildlife and river viewing is a combination of the Deer Creek Loop and the River Trail.

From the visitors center parking lot, walk left to the paved Old Logging Trail, then take a right onto the packed-dirt footpath that loops around the visitors center building. Take a right at the information and map kiosk to join the Old Military Road trail. This wide dirt and gravel path is part of the Deer Creek Loop; 0.4 mile from the map kiosk you will cross an old bridge above Deer Creek where it joins the St. Croix River. Just beyond the bridge is the Deer Creek canoe campsite. Continue walking south past the wooden shelter for 1 mile along the gravel trail

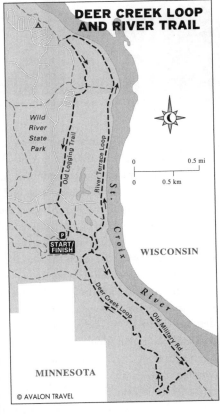

to a trail intersection. Take a right as the trail climbs slightly uphill and begins to head northward through the thick and shady woodland that surrounds Deer Creek. At the top of the loop take a left back to the map kiosk. At 3.6 miles, you're at about the halfway point.

Take a right at the next intersection 0.1 mile away. This trail cuts east toward

© JAKE KULJU

A Chicken of the Woods mushroom grows in a patch of moss in Wild River State Park.

the river and breaks into an open meadow. The transitional zone between the forest and the meadow is always a favorite for wildlife, especially the whitetail deer. Look for the occasional otter and mink, as well, especially near the water. Stay to the right at the next trail intersection and follow the river north to the boat access site. Cross the gravel road at the boat access and continue north. In a few hundred feet you will cross a small creek and submerge once again into the thick forest.

You will pass the Spring Creek canoe campsite 0.2 mile from the road. In another 0.7 mile you will reach the Old Nevers Dam site and trail intersection. An informational kiosk and history display marks the spot of the old dam. The dam was built in 1890 to control the logjams that once plagued the St. Croix during the lumber boom. It was later used to generate hydroelectric power before being demolished in 1955. The site commemorates Minnesota's thriving logging past and the lumbermen that worked in this area.

Continue north from the dam site along the River Terrace Loop. Winding wooden steps climb straight up the 60-foot bluffside here. Stay to the left on the trail that leads away from the steps. The stairs are 5.8 miles into the hike. As the trail leads south it slowly climbs up from the floodplain for 0.5 mile. Go straight at the intersection at the top of the incline on the dirt trail. In 0.2 mile the dirt path intersects the paved Old Logging Trail. This is a straight shot south through the woods and across the boat access park road for 0.7 mile. At the three-way paved intersection take a left to end up at the visitors center and trailhead just 0.3 mile away.

Options

To fit more of a climb into this hike, take a right at the trail intersection at the northern tip of the River Terrace Loop. This trail climbs 164 meandering steps straight up more than 50 feet to the top of the ridge. Turn left at the camper cabins and follow the paved Old Logging Trail back to the visitors center parking lot.

Directions

From St. Paul head north on I-35 East for 40 miles. Exit right onto MN-96 for 11 miles. Turn left at Maple Lane for 0.2 mile. Turn left onto County Road 12/Park Trail for 2 miles past the park entrance. Follow signs to the visitors center parking lot.

Information and Contact

There is a $5 state park vehicle permit fee. Restrooms and a drinking fountain are available at the visitors center and at the boat access site. Dogs are allowed. Maps are available at the park headquarters and on the park website. For more information, contact Wild River State Park, 39797 Park Trail, Center City, MN 55012, 651/583-2925, www.dnr.state.mn.us.

8 RIVER TRAIL TO SANDSTONE BLUFFS

Interstate State Park, Taylors Falls

Level: Moderate/strenuous

Hiking Time: 2.5-3 hours

Total Distance: 3.75 miles round-trip

Elevation Gain: 250 feet

Summary: Pick your way through a field of ancient geologic potholes and climb the steep sandstone bluffs that overlook Folsom Island.

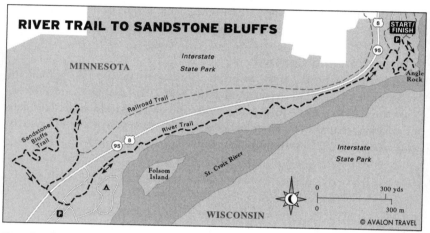

Popular for its awesome geologic abnormalities, Interstate State Park is also a great hiking destination. The first and most impressionable feature of this hike is the glacial potholes the park is famous for. Interstate State Park contains more glacial potholes in a smaller area than any other place on earth. Several theories exist about how they were created, ranging from powerful whirlpools to highly compressed pockets of water and sediment.

Facing the visitors center, take a right toward the pothole field. This 0.25 mile is packed with things to see, including dozens of massive geologic potholes and an outlook over the St. Croix River. You won't gain your stride until starting on the River Trail, so take your time around the potholes. Many of them you can climb in and around.

Veer left toward the Baby Potholes and take another left toward the Lily Pond. Straight south from there a spur trail leads to an overlook at Angle Rock. Return from the overlook and take a left toward the Bottomless Pit and Bake Oven potholes. More than 60 feet deep, Bottomless Pit is the world's largest explored glacial pothole. At the next trail intersection keep to the right toward The Squeeze, then take another left to the Caldron. Return to the main trail and take a right on the trail that runs adjacent to the paved path. Take a left at the interpretive kiosk near the parking lot to join the River Trail.

The River Trail meanders 50 feet above the St. Croix and treats you to three stunning overlooks over the river and Folsom Island. Near the river is also where you are likely to see the most wildlife. In the summer turtles sun themselves near the water, fish jump in the river eddies, and whitetail deer come to the water's edge for a drink. You may also see the tracks of raccoons and foxes near the water.

Just over 1 mile into the hike the trail descends closer to the water to an overlook site. The river bulges around Folsom Island here and provides a beautiful panoramic view of the floodplain forest and wide river. Shortly after the overlook stay to the right at the trail intersection for another 0.2 mile to a park road and parking lot. Turn right here and follow the road past the park information office and underneath Highway 8. On the other side of the highway the path meets the Sandstone Bluffs Trail loop. Take a right to begin the 200-foot climb to the top. This is a rugged climb up a craggy sandstone path—sturdy hiking boots will serve you well.

A stunning overlook hundreds of feet above the river gives you a commanding view of the surrounding area. The overlook is halfway through the loop, 0.5 mile from the base of the bluff and 3.2 miles into the hike. Continue west to another overlook 0.2 mile away before beginning the steep descent to the bottom. Cross under the highway again toward the park office and follow the River Trail back

A butterfly plumbs the depths of a butterfly weed flower in Interstate State Park.

to the parking lot, making sure to stop and enjoy the overlooks along the River Trail a second time. In the spring, especially, you can spot bald eagles soaring over the water searching for prey.

Options

If you want to take another route back to the trailhead, you can finish out the full Sandstone Bluffs loop and then start around again, taking a right onto the Railroad Trail, which leads 1.5 miles back to the trailhead at the visitors center parking lot without adding any miles to your hike.

Directions

From St. Paul head north on I-35 East for 25 miles. Exit onto US-8 East for 22 miles. Turn right at MN-95 into the park entrance for 0.2 mile. Follow signs to the visitors center parking lot.

Information and Contact

There is a $5 state park vehicle permit fee. Restrooms and a drinking fountain are available at the visitors center. Dogs are allowed. Maps are available at the park headquarters and on the park website. For more information, contact Wild River State Park, 39797 Park Trail, Center City, MN 55012, 651/465-5711, www .dnr.state.mn.us.

9 PRAIRIE OVERLOOK AND WOODLAND EDGE LOOP

William O'Brien State Park, Marine-on-St. Croix

Level: Moderate

Hiking Time: 2.5-3 hours

Total Distance: 5.7 miles round-trip

Elevation Gain: 160 feet

Summary: This hike winds through the ponds and rolling prairie hills of William O'Brien State Park on the St. Croix River.

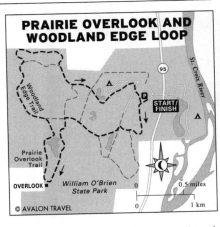

The St. Croix River Valley is famous for its beautiful river scenery and recreational activities, but the surrounding prairie lands in William O'Brien State Park are equally as beautiful. Fields full of wild asters, purple coneflowers, and blooming milkweed turn the prairie hills into natural works of art. From the parking lot walk towards the visitors center and take a left onto the mowed grass trail that enters the open, rolling grassland. You will enjoy the vastness of prairie and wetland landscape for the next mile before climbing to the Prairie Overlook Trail. This gently rolling landscape combined with Minnesota's characteristically wet climate makes the division between grassland and wetland a matter of only a few dozen feet of elevation in places. At 0.2 mile the trail swings west toward the Wetland Trail. Take a left at the next two intersections, 0.1 mile apart, and then a right to stay north of the Beaver Lodge Trail loop. The trail hugs the southern edge of a large wetland area in the middle of the park. A small beaver pond and lodge are to your left as the trail gently climbs upwards. At dawn or dusk you might be lucky enough to spot a reclusive beaver or two.

Take another right 0.2 mile later to keep bordering the wetland. Railroad tracks lie 0.3 mile ahead. Keep going straight to cross the tracks at the next trail intersection and then make a left onto the Prairie Overlook Trail. As you begin to climb the 40-foot incline you will notice how a little elevation makes a big difference in your view. The top of the overlook is 1.8 miles into the hike, marked by a bench and lined with coneflowers, Indian paintbrush, and wild daisies. The hilltop gives you a sweeping view of all the terrain you previously passed through and the hills of the eastern horizon as they rise from the St. Croix River.

The St. Croix River winds through bottomland forest between the hills of William O'Brien State Park.

From the bench walk northwest for 0.7 mile to the Woodland Edge Trail intersection. Take a left onto the forest turf trail, which enters a more heavily wooded area of primarily oak and maple trees. Woodland creatures, like the whitetail deer who feed along the tree line, minks, foxes, and raccoons, dwell in this wooded region. One-third mile after passing a wooden shelter on the Woodland Edge Trail take a left onto the Hardwood Hills Trail, which arcs through a thickly wooded, rolling landscape for 0.8 mile, climbing 40 feet back to the Woodland Edge Trail. Taking a left at the next two trail intersections brings you to a tunnel that passes underneath the train tracks. From here the forest path descends back into the large wetland area and Savanna Campground. Dotted with small ponds, the 0.9 mile from the tunnel leads to the Wetland Trail. Take a left at this intersection back to the visitors center and parking lot.

Options

Head east from the visitors center along the trail that follows the park road down to the river. A trail makes a loop past Lake Alice and Greenberg Island in the St. Croix. This will add 4.2 miles and 100 feet to your hike, making this a challenging all-day outing.

Directions

From St. Paul head north on I-35 East for 16 miles. Turn right onto County Road 14 for 0.6 mile. Continue on Frenchman Road North for 1.4 miles. Turn left at

Forest Boulevard North for 2.8 miles. Turn right at 170th Street North for 8.2 miles. Continue on Ostrium Trail North for 2.8 miles. Turn left at Broadway Street for 0.4 mile. Turn left at Maple Street and make a quick left onto St. Croix Trail North for 2 miles. Turn left at O'Brien Trail North and follow signs to the visitors center.

Information and Contact

There is a $5 state park vehicle permit fee. Restrooms and a drinking fountain are available at the visitors center. Dogs are allowed. Maps are available at the park headquarters and on the park website. For more information, contact William O'Brien State Park, 16821 O'Brien Trail North, Marine-on-St. Croix, MN 55047, 651/433-0500, www.dnr.state.mn.us.

10 GOLDENROD AND FISH LAKE TRAIL LOOP

Tamarack Nature Center, White Bear Township

Level: Easy

Hiking Time: 2 hours

Total Distance: 3.6 miles round-trip

Elevation Gain: 70 feet

Summary: A boardwalk through marshlands, gentle hills covered in majestic oak trees, and open fields of prairie flowers await you.

Just 15 minutes north of St. Paul, this nice little hike is easy to get to after work. Despite its proximity to the freeway, the Tamarack Nature Center trail system is a wonderful respite from the city. From the parking lot walk to the right of the nature center onto the mowed grass trail that leads farther to your right. The trail enters a stand of maple and basswood trees for 0.2 mile, then swings west into open grassland toward Teal Pond. Follow the grassy path as it hugs the tree line north of the pond and dips into stands of young pines.

The sounds of traffic may puncture the silence as you hike farther west. The Goldenrod Trail approaches the I-35 East freeway and briefly runs parallel to it 1 mile into the hike. Tallgrass and prairie flowers like the purple coneflower and Indian paintbrush grow between the young pine trees in the northwest corner of the park. When the trail curves left it makes a short climb into a stand of oak and maple trees, narrowing into a forest turf path. This slightly elevated oak forest is a wildlife-rich zone. Whitetail deer often feed at the forest edge and raccoons meander through the trees. After 0.2 mile through the woods the trail brings you back into grassland at marker 7. Stick to your right here to start on the Fish Lake Trail. This trail soon descends into the wide wetland area that surrounds Fish and Tamarack Lakes; 0.3 mile from marker 7 you ascend 20 feet above the wetland into a thickly forested area. The trail becomes forest turf here and is overgrown in some areas with the roots of nearby trees. If you look to your left as you pass through the woods you can see the waters of Fish Lake and the waving fields of cattails in the surrounding wetlands.

Fish Lake Creek runs in the low place between the elevated forest and the grassland to the north. The trail descends into this miniature valley and crosses the creek, then climbs to the rolling grassland. Stay left at marker 10 and 0.2 mile later go straight ahead at marker 9. In just a few feet you will see marker 8. Take the middle path here on the wide mowed-grass Tamarack Trail. If you start climbing back up the hill you went the wrong way. The path you want wraps around the eastern shore of Tamarack Lake and enters the swath of wetland the park encompasses. At 3.1 miles you will set foot on the Tamarack

The lush forest near the Tamarack Nature Center is a peaceful reprieve from the nearby city.

Lake boardwalk, which floats in the reedy marsh surrounding the lake. When you get to marker 6, take a left to walk out onto the observation dock that floats in the lake. Return to marker 6 and take a left onto the forest turf Oak Trail. And take a right at marker 2 onto the paved Prairie Trail path. Stay on the pavement for 0.2 mile until you return to the nature center.

Options

If you just want to dip into nature for a mile or so, take the 1.5-mile Tamarack Trail around Tamarack Lake. This little loop sends you through the same landscape on the outer edges of the park that the Goldenrod Trail passes through but cuts the distance almost in half.

Directions

From St. Paul take I-35 East north for 9.6 miles. Exit right onto County Road 96 for 1 mile. Turn left at Otter Lake Road for 1.6 miles. The entrance is on your left marked by a sign. The nature center parking lot is a just a few hundred feet from the entrance.

Information and Contact

There is no fee. Restrooms and a drinking fountain are available at the Center. Dogs are not allowed. Maps are available at the Tamarack Nature Center and on the website. For more information, contact Tamarack Nature Center, 5287 Otter Lake Road, White Bear Township, MN 55110, 651/407-5350, www.co.ramsey .mn.us/parks (click on *Nature Center*).

11 EAGLE POINT LAKE TRAIL

Lake Elmo Park Reserve, Lake Elmo

Level: Easy/moderate

Total Distance: 4.5 miles round-trip

Hiking Time: 2.5-3 hours

Elevation Gain: Negligible

Summary: Circumnavigate Eagle Point Lake and its wide-open grasslands.

Lake Elmo Park Reserve has some of the state's most beautiful grasslands. The wide-open expanses surround Eagle Point Lake and make for excellent prairie hiking in the spring and summer. Wild asters, Indian paintbrush, coneflowers, honeysuckle, and several other wildflowers bloom here in the spring and summer months, making this a colorful and refreshing way to spend an afternoon.

Facing Eagle Point Lake from the large paved parking lot, take a right onto the dirt trail heading north. Light tree cover guards the trail as it cuts west on one of the lake's large peninsulas and then breaks into open grassland when it makes a sharp turn to the right. The trail crosses a land bridge between the lake and a smaller pond. At the intersection on the other side, take a left along the tree line that hugs the lake. A narrow swath of mostly maple trees borders the water for 0.5 mile up along the northernmost arm of the lake. As the trail arcs around the northern tip of the water it enters the expansive grasslands that dominate the landscape. Turning to the south the trail briefly enters another stand of trees.

At the upcoming trail intersection, make a sharp right that leads north out of the stand of trees and into the rolling prairie hills. As you leave the trees behind, watch for pheasants in the tallgrass, weasels, foxes, and rabbits. The undulating grassland is a haven for these types of wildlife. At marker 26, keep left as the trail arcs south through the prairie for 0.4 mile. Almost 2 miles from the trailhead you reach marker 27. Choose the middle path here and continue walking south. The grassy trail eventually veers east and rejoins Eagle Point Lake at its wooded southern shore.

The tree cover soon becomes scarce in 0.2 mile and clears to prairie again.

Take a left at the next trail intersection and follow the eastern shore of the lake to marker 19. Take the second right at this junction in just a few hundred feet along the grassy trail that arcs back up to the parking lot.

Options

For a shorter hike that stays closer to the lake, turn left and continue going south at marker 28. Keep closer to the water by taking a left at marker 29 as well. This will shave 0.75 mile off of your hike.

Directions

From St. Paul take I-94 East for 8.8 miles. Exit left onto Keats Avenue for 1.7 miles. Keats Avenue leads right to the park entrance. Follow signs to the Eagle Point Lake parking lot 0.2 mile ahead on your left.

Information and Contact

There is a $5 vehicle permit fee. Restrooms and a drinking fountain are available in the main office near the park entrance. Dogs are not allowed. Maps are available on the park website. For more information, contact Lake Elmo Park Reserve, 1515 Keats Avenue, Lake Elmo, MN 55042, 651/430-8370, www.co.washington .mn.us (click on *Things to Do Here* and then *Parks and Trails*).

© JAKE KULJU

an open meadow under the big sky near Eagle Point Lake

🔢 ST. CROIX RIVER TRAIL

Afton State Park, Afton

Level: Moderate

Hiking Time: 2-2.5 hours

Total Distance: 4 miles round-trip

Elevation Gain: 180 feet

Summary: Shoreline views and blufftop vistas await you along the St. Croix River Trail in Afton State Park.

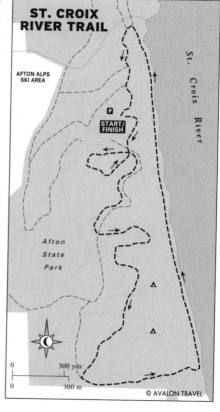

Afton State Park's cache of outdoor beauty is well known by most St. Paul residents. Only 25 minutes away from the city, Afton occupies a choice piece of land in the St. Croix River Valley full of blufftop views and rocky river shore. The trailhead begins at the visitors center and heads south. Take a right onto the paved hiker-biker trail that runs between the center and the parking lot. Stay right at the first intersection behind the visitors center to join the Hiking Club trail. In a few hundred feet an interpretive trail makes a 0.5-mile loop through one of Afton's prairie restoration areas. This grassy path is full of wild daisies, Indian paintbrush, purple coneflowers, milkweed, and tall prairie grasses. You may see groundhogs, gophers, foxes, and bull snakes along this loop.

After completing the prairie loop, cross the paved path and take a right onto the mowed-grass horse/hiking trail. Follow this wide trail through the grasslands on top of the bluff for 0.3 mile to the 1-mile overlook hiking trail that heads east. Take a left onto the narrower path as it gently descends 60 feet to an overlook on the edge of the bluff. The St. Croix runs almost straight north and south here, and the overlook gives you a view of the wide river and the rolling Wisconsin hills on the other side.

Hikers descend wooden steps down to the banks of the St. Croix River.

From the overlook, the path meanders south for 0.8 mile past a group campsite and across two park roads. This trail leads past a wooden shelter 0.2 mile from the next intersection. Take a left when you reach it into the thick oak, maple, and basswood forest that hugs the bluffside near the river. This quick transition into the forest is a favorite lurking place for whitetail deer, who feed at the forest edge.

The gravel hiking path becomes quite steep near the river, dropping 120 feet in 0.1 mile. Use extra caution on wet days or after rainfall, as the path can be slippery. At the bottom of the bluff, the trail swings north on a wide, straight gravel path along the riverbank for 1.7 miles. You will have several opportunities to approach the water from the gravel. The trail is approximately 20 feet above the river, but several sets of overgrown wooden and stone stairways lead through the brush down to the water.

At the end of the 1.7-mile stretch, the paved hiker-biker path cuts sharply to your left. Start taking this up the hill, then veer to the left onto the narrower gravel Hiking Club trail. This climb through the forest gives you another overlook and ends in 0.2 mile when it rejoins the paved path. Follow the paved trail for 0.2 mile back to the visitors center.

Options

To make the steep climb at the southern end of this hike, simply reverse your route, but be prepared for an intense uphill climb. Use caution, especially on wet days.

Directions

From St. Paul take I-94 East for 11 miles. Exit right onto County Road 95 South for 7 miles. Turn left at 70th Street South for 3.5 miles to the park entrance. Follow signs to the visitors center another 1.8 miles ahead.

Information and Contact

There is a $5 state park vehicle permit fee. Restrooms and a drinking fountain are available at the visitors center. Dogs are allowed. Maps are available at the visitors center and on the park website. For more information, contact Afton State Park, 6959 Peller Avenue South, Hastings, MN 55033, 651/436-5391, www.dnr.state.mn.us.

13 KINNI CANYON TRAIL

BEST 🌙

Glen Park, River Falls, Wisconsin

Level: Moderate

Total Distance: 3.7 miles round-trip

Hiking Time: 2.5-3 hours

Elevation Gain: 60 feet

Summary: Explore the lush banks of the playful Kinnickinnic River in western Wisconsin.

Most Minnesotans wouldn't be caught dead hiking in Wisconsin, but when it comes to the Kinnickinnic River trail, most of us make an exception. The trail along this lovely meandering river starts at Glen Park in River Falls, Wisconsin. Wildflowers lean over the water, fish jump in the swirling pools, and tall floodplain trees abound on this little stretch of paradise. Long known as a trout fishing hot spot, the Kinni Creek, as it is called by locals, is also an excellent hiking destination.

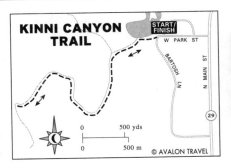

From the parking lot, walk around the tennis courts to the wide tree-lined path that leads to the dam. Take a left and follow the gravel trail along bank of the river. Unless you come here in the dead of winter, you will undoubtedly seen anglers around every river bend. Whether they are casting spinners from shore or fly fishing in waders, anglers come here for the lively trout and beautiful scenery. This entire area of the Kinnickinnic is part of a land trust that preserves and maintains the land along the river.

From Glen Park, the path makes a 0.4-mile arc to the south. The gravel path here is easy walking from the dam, lined with benches and mowed grass. Another wide gravel walking path joins the riverbank trail 0.4 mile in, then quickly narrows into a packed dirt pathway. From here, the narrow path turns into a kind of delta of walkways. Small forest paths and packed dirt trails all head in the same general direction but crisscross each other and branch around difference obstacles as they follow the river. Choose whichever path you'd like. It is almost impossible to get lost, as no path leads far from the water, and the trees aren't thick enough to block your sight of it.

After 0.3 mile of flowing south, the river makes a sharp turn to the north, and the trail follows it. The water splits around several shallow islands and sandbars here for 0.1 mile, then makes another run to the south at the 0.5-mile mark. Just before the top of this northern arc the path narrows to a small dirt footpath that climbs the side of a steep bank. Hold on to tree trunks and roots to gain your balance as you scramble across the bank. This only lasts a few hundred feet before the trail drops back to the water's edge. The river makes a quick southern turn 0.2 mile from the steep bank, creating a deep pool at the point of a horn-shaped piece of land. The sandy banks and dark, quickly moving water swirl here, creating an ominous and beautiful sight. On hot days this makes an excellent swimming hole, deep enough to dive into from shore. Note that this fast-moving river can sweep you away if you aren't careful and can carry fast-moving debris in it as well. Use caution if you plan on going in.

The trail becomes much narrower and hard to follow over the next 0.25 mile. People rarely venture this far, making further hiking more of an exploration than a walk through the woods. Before the next river bend, the brush becomes too thick for recreational hiking. Many anglers don their waders and walk downstream to find the fishing holes that lie ahead, but hiking is a different story. On your way back you may be a little scratched and bruised from the thick brush and the light climbing you need to do to make it through this hike, but the sense of satisfaction and the peacefulness that comes with spending time in a wild bit of nature will be more than enough to send you back to Kinni Canyon for another go.

Trees and heavy brush overhang the quick-moving waters of the Kinnickinnic River.

Options

A trail runs along the other side of the creek as well. At Glen Park you can either choose one path or return and take them both to lengthen your hike.

Directions

From St. Paul take I-94 East for 19 miles into Wisconsin. Exit onto WI-35 South toward River Falls for 7.2 miles. Take the River Falls ramp onto North Main Street for 2.2 miles. Turn right at West Park Street and right again onto Glen Park Road and the Glen Park parking lot.

Information and Contact

There is no fee. Glen Park is a small city park with portable restrooms and seasonal outdoor drinking fountains. Dogs are allowed. Maps are available at the land trust website. For more information, contact the Kinnickinnic River Land Trust, 421 N. Main Street, P.O. Box 87, River Falls, WI 54022, 715/425-5738, www.kinniriver.org (click on *The Kinni*).

14 COTTAGE GROVE RAVINE TRAILS
Cottage Grove Ravine Regional Park, Cottage Grove

Level: Moderate

Hiking Time: 2.5 hours

Total Distance: 2.8 miles round-trip

Elevation Gain: 150 feet

Summary: Walk through the prairie hills, young pine forest, and gnarled stands of oak that line the Cottage Grove Ravine.

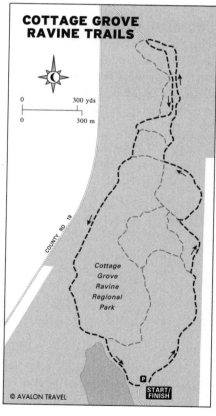

COTTAGE GROVE RAVINE TRAILS

Cottage Grove Ravine Regional Park

COUNTY RD. 19

START/FINISH

© AVALON TRAVEL

Minnesota isn't known for its ravines, but near Cottage Grove the glaciers have spared a 500-acre patch of land that carries the steep sides and deep gouges of a bona fide ravine. Different sun exposures give this area widely varied vegetation that attracts plentiful wildlife. Deep in the ravine shady oaks crowd close, while at the outer edges stands of young pine and open fields roll toward the horizon.

From the parking loop you will see a picnic pavilion and an information kiosk to your right. Walk toward the kiosk and follow the forest turf trail that leads right. This wide, oak-lined path gently climbs through the forest along the eastern edge of the park. Each intersection is marked with a numbered wooden post. You will come to marker 2 at 0.4 mile from the trailhead. Take a right and walk down a small hill to a service road. Powerlines run through the park here, and the trail briefly follows the area where trees have been cleared. The road is quite overgrown and is more of a wide trail than a gravel road. Take another right at marker 5. The trail continues a gradual climb here through oak and maple trees for 0.1 mile and then abruptly enters an open field. The trail is sparsely peppered with young pine trees, but the rolling prairie easily dominates the landscape. The trail bends to the west along this stretch, headed for marker 8.

© JAKE KULJU

A gnarled oak tree frames the trail through the Cottage Grove Ravine.

Take a right here and follow the grassy hilltop trail to a denser pine forest. In a few hundred feet you will come to marker 9. Veer to the right once again and watch the forest transition from straight and sturdy red and white pines to gnarled oak trees. This narrow forest turf path is in the northern section of the park and is a favorite place for grouse and rabbit. Keep your eyes open for weasels and whitetail deer as well. The rare pileated woodpecker can also occasionally be spotted in the ravine.

Marker 12 is the halfway point, 1.4 miles from the trailhead. Take a sharp left onto the paved hiker-biker trail and follow it as it meanders south through the bottom of the ravine. This twisting path explores the lowest points of the ravine and is a shady respite from the hot summer sun. In the spring the grassy shoulders of the trail are lined with wild red asters, wild daisies, and coneflowers.

At marker 16 the trail bends south toward Cottage Grove Ravine Pond and follows its eastern shore. Marker 17 is at the fishing pier that overlooks the pond and the rising hill on the other side of the park. Continue on the paved path to the picnic pavilion and parking loop.

Options

To explore more of the ravine, take a left at trail marker 2 to marker 4, then take a right and walk north, taking a left at trail marker 7. When you get to trail marker 8 you'll be at the 0.75-mile point in the trail description with 0.25-mile more under your belt.

Directions

From St. Paul take Shepard Road East to Warner Road for 2.5 miles. Merge right onto US-10 East/US-61 South for 13 miles. Exit left onto Innovation Road and take a right onto East Point Douglas Road South for 0.5 mile. Turn left into the park entrance. Stay to your right after the fee station and park in the picnic shelter parking loop.

Information and Contact

There is a $5 vehicle permit fee. Restrooms and a drinking fountain are at the picnic shelter. Dogs are allowed. Maps are available at the trailhead and on the park website. For more information, contact Cottage Grove Ravine Regional Park, 9940 Point Douglas Road, Cottage Grove, MN 55016, 763/694-7650, www.co.washington.mn.us (click on *Things to Do Here* and then *Parks and Trails*).

15 VERMILLION FALLS TRAIL

Vermillion Falls Park, Hastings

Level: Easy/moderate

Hiking Time: 2.5 hours

Total Distance: 4.6 miles round-trip

Elevation Gain: Negligible

Summary: Walk from Vermillion Falls, near the Old Mill Ruins, to Bull Frog Pond along one of Hastings's most serene city trails.

When you think of hiking in the St. Croix River Valley, city parks aren't the first things that come to mind. Vermillion Falls Park in Hastings is a different story. Wrapped along the eastern edge of the city near the confluence of the Mississippi, St. Croix, and Vermillion Rivers, this paved trail is a great place to take children for a weekend outing.

This hike starts with a spectacular view of Vermillion Falls. From the parking lot walk straight ahead toward the river. A small pavilion is behind the trees that line the Vermillion River at

the foot of the falls. The waterfall was once a functioning hydroelectric power source for the large brick factory across the river. Follow the river downstream to your right on the paved path. The pavement here is old and cracked, but it's still smooth enough for easy going. The trail heads east and follows the upper bank of the Vermillion River as it heads towards its confluence with the St. Croix and Mississippi Rivers; 0.4 mile from the falls the paved trail turns left and crosses high above the river. Down below you can see small cascades and shallow pools along the rocky riverbed. High stone cliffs make a small gorge here that is full of the sounds of splashing water and chirping birds. In the autumn the changing leaves on the trees that line this miniature canyon are a must-see.

At the bridge the pavement is newer, smoother, and wider. The trail leads north along a tree-lined path into more of a cityscape. Hastings is a beautiful, peaceful town—even though you'll be walking near an avenue, traffic is minimal and a sense of nature prevails. A half mile after the bridge the trail juts left and then north again, running parallel to Tyler Street. At the 8th Street intersection, cross the road

© JAKE KULJU

The Vermillion River gorge in Hastings is rife with rock outcroppings and red pine trees.

to the right and follow the paved path toward Bull Frog Pond. The path crosses over the Vermillion River again and leads to CP Adams Park, about 1 mile ahead on the southern shore of the pond. The park makes a nice clearing in the basswood and maple trees, and it's a good spot to look for wildlife. Some whitetail deer may be around, but the proximity to the city makes sightings of smaller mammals like raccoons, weasels, and cottontail rabbits more common. Follow the looped path around the perimeter of the clearing and head back to the trailhead the way you came. When crossing over the high bridge back to Vermillion Falls Park, you will see the other side of the ravine and the small cascades that winnow through the rocks. When you reach Vermillion Falls, take a left after the pavilion to return to the parking lot.

Options

You can continue on the southern shore of the Vermillion River past the high bridge on a packed dirt trail to add 0.5 mile to this hike and view the Old Mill Ruins. The trail follows the top of the ravine and leaves the park. An old mill building stands 0.25 mile from the bridge with an informational kiosk. Turn around and take a right over the high bridge to continue the hike.

Directions

From St. Paul take Shepard Road East to Warner Road for 2.5 miles. Merge right onto US-10 East/US-61 South for 18 miles. Continue on Vermillion Street after entering Hastings for 1.3 miles. Turn left at 21st Street East for 0.2 mile into the Vermillion Falls parking lot on your left.

Information and Contact

There is a no fee. Dogs are allowed. The park is open from sunrise to sunset. A portable restroom is available near the pavilion at Vermillion Falls Park. Maps are available online. For more information, contact Vermillion Falls Park, 215 21st Street East, Hastings, MN 55033, 651/480-6175, www.ci.hastings.mn.us.

16 LAKE PEPIN OVERLOOK HIKING CLUB TRAIL

BEST ◖

Frontenac State Park, Frontenac

Level: Moderate

Hiking Time: 2 hours

Total Distance: 3.3 miles round-trip

Elevation Gain: 220 feet

Summary: Get some of the best vistas of the Mississippi River's most popular lake and the surrounding bluffs along this clifftop trail.

Without a doubt, Lake Pepin is one of the most picturesque bodies of water in the upper Midwest. People have flocked to this area for more than 100 years to take in the beauty of the lake and the surrounding high bluffs. The Minnesota Hiking Club has designated one of the trails in nearby Frontenac State Park a statewide hiking destination.

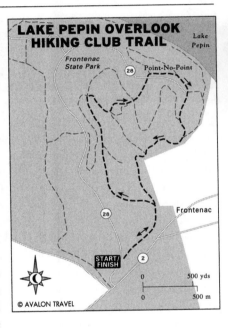

From the parking loop adjacent to the park office head east into the rolling prairie. You will be surrounded by tallgrass, including varieties of pungent sweetgrass, wild asters, daisies, and coneflowers, as well as Indian paintbrush and blooming milkweed. This prairie is rife with wildflowers and is a wonderful way to enjoy the colors and scents of early spring and summer. The grassy path joins the Hiking Club trail 0.3 mile from the trailhead. Take the left branch as it begins to climb uphill into the oak and maple forest. Grouse and pheasants live in this transition zone and you will more than likely hear their crows and wing beats if you come in the early summer. One mile into the trail take a right and follow the Hiking Club signs for another 0.5 mile to the top of the bluff. The trail crosses the paved park road and veers to the right toward a mowed picnic area that overlooks the small town of Frontenac and shimmering Lake Pepin. My favorite times of year to experience this park are early summer and mid-autumn.

In the summer bluebirds and swallows fill the air with song and the lush blufftop

Lake Pepin glistens in the distance from atop the bluffs of Frontenac State Park.

forest provides shade from the sun. The prairie is in full bloom and looks and smells so good you'll want to bottle it up and take it home. Autumn brings more open views through the trees but really wallops you with the blazing oranges, reds, and yellows of the changing trees. The rolling blufftop forests come alive with color and seem to stretch endlessly along the shores of Lake Pepin. Sunset views from the top of the bluff are made of pure gold.

The Hiking Club trail skirts the parking lot near the picnic area and then makes a slight dip down to the edge of the bluff. Follow the trail as it hugs the cliffside and gives you two stunning overlook points. A half mile from the picnic area the trail heads west and zigzags to the south out of the trees and back into the rolling prairie grasses. At the intersection stay left to return to the trailhead and parking lot near the park office.

Options

If you've got strong legs you might want to add 1.3 miles and 250 feet to this hike. After crossing the park road, take a left and head west toward In Yan Teopa Rock. This trail slides down the bluff and cuts back east nearer the lake, then climbs a brutal 250 feet in 0.1 mile up to the Hiking Club trail.

Directions

From St. Paul take Shepard Road East to Warner Road for 2.5 miles. Merge right onto US-10 East/US-61 South for 16 miles. Follow US-10 left into Wisconsin for

3.2 miles. Turn right at Broad Street North in Prescott and continue on WI-35 for 19 miles. Turn right onto US-63 into Minnesota for 3 miles. Turn right at Potter Street in Red Wing and turn right onto Highway 61 for 10 miles. Turn left at County 2 Boulevard for 1 mile. Turn left at County 28 Boulevard for 1 mile to the park entrance. Park at the park office parking lot.

Information and Contact

There is a $5 state park vehicle permit fee. Restrooms and a drinking fountain are available at the park office and at the Point-No-Point picnic area. Dogs are allowed. Maps are available at the park office and on the park website. For more information, contact Frontenac State Park, 29223 County 28 Boulevard, Frontenac, MN 55026, 651/345-3401, www.dnr.state.mn.us.

17 RIVERBEND TRAIL

BEST C

Carley State Park, Altura

Level: Moderate/strenuous

Total Distance: 3.1 miles round-trip

Hiking Time: 2 hours

Elevation Gain: 350 feet

Summary: Winding through pines, climbing up and down the river gorge, and offering a beautiful vista, this hike is a forest gem.

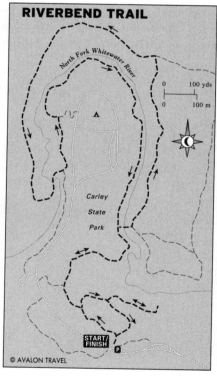

RIVERBEND TRAIL

North Fork Whitewater River

0   100 yds
0   100 m

Carley State Park

START/FINISH   P

© AVALON TRAVEL

Tucked into a quiet river bend of the Whitewater River, this little-used trail is one of the finest in the state. The curvy Whitewater River really outdoes itself at Carley State Park, making an extravagant oxbow that nearly doubles back on itself. The ravine the river has carved is fairly deep for the area and will give you 350 feet of climbing.

As you head north from the parking lot into the woods you will notice tall, thick stands of red and white pine. Hundreds of years ago Minnesota may have been home to trees like these, but it is a rare sight these days. The trees were planted decades ago but thrive in the river gorge and can even evoke a sense of northern pine forests if you can forget that you are in the southern part of the state. Chattering red squirrels and surreptitious whitetail deer linger in this shady sanctuary. Take a left at the first trail intersection just 75 feet ahead and another left in 0.1 mile; 300 feet ahead take a right at the trail intersection onto a forest turf path that leads to a long set of moss-covered stone steps. Be careful after rain or when the steps appear to be wet. They descend 80 feet and can be slippery. After taking the steps you will be down close to the river and in the bottom of the ravine. Follow the trail as it winds north and take a right at the trail crossing that leads to the river. A series of concrete blocks spans the water. You have to jump from block to block to make it across. During high water this can be nearly impossible, and you may want to use a walking stick for balance even when the water is low.

Take a left after crossing the bridge back up the other side of the ravine to the top of the eastern ridge. Pine trees still fill the woods, but maple and oak crowd in here, too, dominating most of the ridgeline forest. Take a left at the trail crossing 0.4 mile from the bridge. Still buried in the forest, this narrow trail arcs along the oxbow of the river and eventually descends the ridge back into the ravine. The trail deposits you at a river crossing with more concrete blocks. As evidenced by the abundance of tracks at this crossing, whitetail deer come here to cross the river and to drink. Look also for raccoon and muskrat along the weedy shores. On the other side take a left at the trail crossing and another left in 0.1 mile. A right would lead you to the campground area. The next stretch of trail leads 0.4 mile along the riverbank in the bottom of the gorge. The thick brush and trees provide plenty of shade, as do the ridges on either side of the river. The temperature can often be 5–10 degrees cooler in the ravine than in surrounding areas.

When you reach the first river crossing point, go south on the trail you took to get there. After you climb the stone steps take a left at the next two trail crossings. You will be back in the thick pine forest again. Take another left to visit an outlook point 600 feet from the last intersection. The overlook is crowded with trees but gives a great perspective of the river gorge and the rolling landscape above it. Return to the main trail from the overlook and take a left to return to the trailhead and parking lot just over 500 feet ahead.

Concrete stepping stones form a crossing point along the Whitewater River in Carley State Park.

Options

To delve deeper into the woods on the east side of the river and add 0.4 mile to your hike take a right after the river's first crossing point and follow a trail that arcs east up and over the ridge, then north, then west back to the main trail.

Directions

From St. Paul take US-52 South for 6.2 miles. Exit to continue on US-52 South for another 56 miles. Turn left onto County Road 12 and continue on MN-247 for 19.5 miles. Turn right at MN-42 for 0.5 mile. Turn left onto County Road 4 for 3.2 miles. Take a right into the park entrance and drive 0.1 mile to the trailhead parking lot just past the park office.

Information and Contact

There is a $5 state park vehicle permit fee. A restroom and a drinking fountain are available at the park office. Dogs are allowed. Maps are available at the park office and on the park website. For more information, contact Carley State Park, c/o Whitewater State Park, Route 1, Box 256, Altura, MN 55910, 507/932-3007, www.dnr.state.mn.us.

18 DAKOTA AND TROUT RUN CREEK TRAILS

BEST

Whitewater State Park, Altura

Level: Strenuous

Hiking Time: 4.5 hours

Total Distance: 6.7 miles round-trip

Elevation Gain: 400 feet

Summary: This hike traverses a dramatically contoured area of the state that was untouched by glaciers during the last ice age.

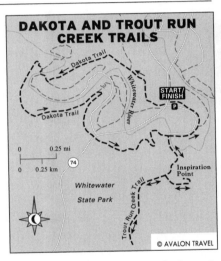

DAKOTA AND TROUT RUN CREEK TRAILS

Minnesota has a lot of great parks and trails, but this one takes the cake. From the climb to Inspiration Point to the bottomlands along Trout Run Creek, this is one of the most entertaining hikes in the state. Start by walking around the Nature Store and following the dirt trail that leads uphill straight away from the parking lot. This is the beginning of the Dakota Trail, which loops around the river to the west. Whitewater State Park is known for its amazing views, deep ravines, and thick maple, oak, and basswood forest. If you could see the park from above, you would see arms of thick trees following the curving river as it winds through the farmland of southern Minnesota.

The trail quickly climbs up to the top of the ridge. Take a left at the next two trail intersections to stay on the Dakota Trail. Oak and maple trees dominate this forested area, providing shade in the summer and blazing colors during autumn. The Goat Point overlook is approximately 0.5 mile from the trailhead at the top of the ridge. The vista over the park as it stretches south is full of the cliffs, bluffs, and thick woods that crowd around the Whitewater River. The trail descends back into the river valley 0.4 mile from Goat Point. Take two right-hand turns to cross the river, followed shortly by a left, all in a 0.2-mile stretch. The Dakota Trail makes one sharp switchback turn on the western bluff and then heads south toward Signal Point. This spur trail is barely 0.1 mile long and gives a beautiful view of the river as it flows east.

Return to the main trail and take a left. The trail climbs another 100 feet in 0.5 mile to Eagle Point overlook. On top of the bluff you may see wild turkeys, foxes, and whitetail deer. At the lookout points, keep your eyes peeled for soaring bald eagles, which live here year-round. Take a right at Eagle Point and follow the Dakota Trail southeast as it gently descends to Highway 74. Cross the road and continue east up another bluff and down a switchback back to the river. Take a right before the bridge onto Trout Run Creek Trail.

This area of the park is one of the most spectacular. Deep in the valley and sandwiched between two 200-foot bluffs, this trail feels like walking in the bottom of a lush and narrow canyon. 0.4 mile from the bridge take a left onto the Inspiration Point spur trail. This path begins climbing the bluff and then leads

Rocky Inspiration Point juts out from the trees high above Trout Run Creek.

to several sets of steep wooden staircases with hundreds of steps leading straight up the bluff. At the top, turn to your left on the narrow rock path. Cedar trees cling to the rocks and sprout from the boulders. The trail leads to a narrow outcropping of rock that juts into the air. If you are afraid of heights, you may not be able to stomach the view. Out on the rock, the view is beyond words. The entire park and its lush forests, rolling blufftops, and winding river lie more than 200 feet straight below.

Make your way back to Trout Run Creek Trail and take a left for 0.6 mile to the turnaround loop at the trail's end. This creek trail gets wild in some places, as it isn't often traveled. Several wooden bridges cross different branches of the creek. The narrow dirt path can be lost sometimes in the overhanging brush, so keep your eyes open. After returning to the bridge at the head of Trout Run Creek Trail, take a right and cross the river on the trail that follows the gravel road back to the parking lot at the Nature Store.

Options

You don't have to go all the way down Trout Creek to get a look at Inspiration Point. After returning from the point, take a right to finish the hike and shave a mile off your hike.

Directions

From St. Paul take US-52 South for 6.2 miles. Exit to continue on US-52 South for another 56 miles. Turn left onto County Road 12 and continue on MN-247 for 19.5 miles. Turn right at MN-42 for 0.5 mile. Turn left onto County Road 4 for 3.5 miles. Continue on County Road 10 for another 3.5 miles. Turn left at County Road 2 for 3 miles. Continue on County Road 39 for 2.5 miles. Turn right at MN-74 for 0.3 mile to the Nature Store parking lot.

Information and Contact

There is a $5 state park vehicle permit fee. A restroom and a drinking fountain are available at the park office. Dogs are allowed. Maps are available at the park office and on the park website. For more information, contact Whitewater State Park, Route 1, Box 256, Altura, MN 55910, 507/932-3007, www.dnr.state.mn.us.

19 RIVERVIEW TRAIL TO BLUFFTOP TRAIL

Perrot State Park, Trempealeau, Wisconsin

BEST (

🏛 🚶 🐕

Level: Strenuous

Total Distance: 4.5 miles round-trip

Hiking Time: 3 hours

Elevation Gain: 420 feet

Summary: Stunning vistas of the towering bluffs along this portion of the Mississippi are easy to come by in Perrot State Park.

The next best thing to hiking the bluff trails in Minnesota near the Mississippi River is seeing the Minnesota bluffs from the other side. The trails in Perrot State Park from the riverbank to the rising bluffs give hikers views of the rolling bluff landscape in Minnesota and the wild Wisconsin forests that dominate the park. Black walnut, hickory, and oak trees make up most of the forest here, with some stands of birch, maple, and basswood.

RIVERVIEW TRAIL TO BLUFFTOP TRAIL

© AVALON TRAVEL

Start hiking south from the nature center parking lot by walking behind the building and taking a left near the water. The dirt path follows the eastern edge of Trempealeau Bay, where the river forms a confluence with the Mississippi River. The trail passes directly by an ancient Indian burial mound. Signs give some history of the site. Keep walking south to the picnic area and bay overlook point. Looking west you will see Trempealeau Mountain rising like a volcanic island at the confluence point of the two rivers. Covered in trees, the landform looks enchanted, like a bluff standing on its own in the water.

The trail crosses the boat landing road and parking lot 0.3 mile from the lookout point. Cross the road and follow the trail south toward the Mississippi River. The Riverview Trail runs between the park road and the railroad tracks that skirt the riverbank. Through the trees you can see the towering bluffs on the Minnesota side of the river. At 1.5 miles from the trailhead choose the middle trail option, which crosses the parking loop and park road, heading northeast. This begins the blufftop trail that leads farther into the forest away from the water and climbs the park's highest bluffs. The trail starts climbing to Reed's Peak about 0.6 mile

© JAKE KULJU

A dragonfly basks in the sun.

from the park road crossing. At the top of the bluff the trail arcs west to the Perrot Ridge overlook point. This high point looks over the river and gives views of Brady's Bluff and the Minnesota bluff line.

The trail quickly descends a steep slope to the base of the bluff and crosses a ski trail. Keep going south for 0.4 mile toward the park road and stay to the right at the trail intersection near the road. The forest turf trail winds through the oak woods for 0.6 mile before climbing Brady's Bluff. This bottomland forest is full of whitetail deer, foxes, and raccoons. Wild turkeys may also congregate in the open patches amidst the trees. At the top of Brady's Bluff a ski shelter is near the overlook point. Take a left back down the bluff toward the boat landing. Cross the road and walk through the parking lot toward the water and picnic area. Here you rejoin the Riverview Trail. Take a right to head back to the nature center parking lot.

Options

You can take in the grandeur of the bluffs without climbing all of them. The Riverview Trail provides sweeping views of the river valley and the bluffs on both sides of the river and will turn this into a 2.7-mile hike. Just turn around at the parking loop and follow the trail along the river back to the nature center.

Directions

From St. Paul take US-52 South for 6.2 miles. Exit to continue on US-52 South for another 76.5 miles. Turn left to merge onto I-90 East toward Lacrosse for 34 miles. Exit left onto MN-43 toward Winona for 7 miles. Follow MN-43 for 2 miles through Winona to the MN-43/WI-54 bridge that crosses the Mississippi into Wisconsin. Turn right onto WI-54 for 6 miles. Turn right at West Prairie Road for 3.8 miles. Turn right at Lehmann Road for 0.5 mile.

Information and Contact

There is a $5 resident vehicle permit fee and a $10 nonresident fee. Restrooms and a drinking fountain are available in the nature center by the parking lot. Dogs are allowed. Maps are available at the park office and nature center. For more information, contact Perrot State Park, P.O. Box 407, Trempealeau, WI 54661, 608/534-6409, www.dnr.state.wi.us (click on *Find a State Park or Forest*).

20 KING'S AND QUEEN'S BLUFF TRAIL

BEST ☾

Great River Bluffs State Park, Winona

🏕 🦌 🐕 👨‍👩‍👧

Level: Moderate

Total Distance: 4.5 miles round-trip

Hiking Time: 2.5-3 hours

Elevation Gain: 220 feet

Summary: Get views of the expansive river system and the dynamically shaped landscape that make this an awe-inspiring hike.

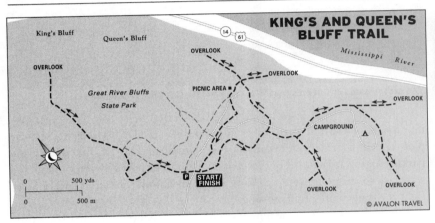

Everyone knows that southeastern Minnesota is bluff country, but no one knows it more than those who have been to Great River Bluffs State Park. Home of King's and Queen's Bluffs, the park offers views of the river valley and undulating landscape that are fit for royalty. Facing north with the parking lot at your back, take a right, crossing the road and starting east on the mowed-grass trail.

Stay to your right at the first trail intersection less than 0.1 mile ahead. This trail section slides along the open bluffside. Interspersed trees, tall grasses, and prairie flowers live here and are a nice transition before delving into the thicker forested portions of the hike. Wild daisies, asters, coneflowers, and prairie smoke give color and character to the grassland. Bull snakes and turtles love this area and can often be seen sunning themselves in the summer.

Take another right at the next two trail crossings. The path continues through the grassy landscape interspersed with prairie shrubs and trees, and then it leads to the group camp parking lot. Follow the trail behind the parking area to the Pioneer Group Camp site. Two overlook points branch off from the campsite and give views to the lush valley below. Return to the maintenance building area and

The grassy sides of Queen's Bluff rise from the Mississippi River Valley.

take a right on the trail on the other side of the park road. This leads you into the pine forest and farther east toward the campground parking lot. Take a left at the parking lot toward another overlook point, then return the way you came all the way back to the group camp parking area. Stay to your right and take another right at the upcoming trail crossing.

This trail snakes along the tops of the Mississippi River's most majestic bluffs, which tower hundreds of feet about the river valley. You will climb approximately 50 feet to the picnic area. Take a left at the picnic area on the trail that leads to an overlook point on the eastern edge of Queen's Bluff. No trail leads to Queen's Bluff, but you can see it jutting out over the valley from the overlook point. Across the river are the rolling hills and bluffs on the Wisconsin side of the water. Return to the picnic area and walk across the parking lot to the trail that follows the road back to the place you parked. Take a right here to join the interpretive trail. This is the most scenic part of the hike and will take you to the end of King's Bluff. The mowed-grass path skirts the northern edge of a grassland and enters a thick stand of pine trees. Follow the packed-dirt and forest turf trail when it enters the trees all the way to the open grassland on the end of King's Bluff. From here you can see Queen's Bluff and the panoramic vistas of the Mississippi River Valley for miles on either side.

After you've seen all you can see, head back to the parking lot along the interpretive trail. At dusk the woods on King's Bluff are usually active with whitetail deer, wild turkeys, and ruffed grouse. You can also see bald eagles soaring over the valley during all times of the year. Between the prairie flowers, the majestic pine trees, the abundant bluff wildlife, and breathtaking views, this park trail system is one you will never forget.

Options

If you want a great view without stopping at every overlook in the park, take the 1.5-mile interpretive trail out to King's Bluff and back. This is the most popular trail, and it leads to the most sweeping view of both the river valley and of Queen's Bluff.

Directions

From St. Paul take US-52 South for 6.2 miles. Exit to continue on US-52 South for another 76.5 miles. Turn left to merge onto I-90 East toward Lacrosse for 48 miles. Turn left onto County Road 12 and take a quick right in 0.2 mile onto County Road 3 for 1 mile. Turn right at Lynch Road for 2 miles past the park entrance to the interpretive trail parking lot.

Information and Contact

There is a $5 state park vehicle permit fee. A restroom and a drinking fountain are available at the park office. Dogs are allowed. Maps are available at the park office and on the park website. For more information, contact Great River Bluffs State Park, 43605 Kipp Drive, Winona, MN 55987, 507/643-6849, www.dnr .state.mn.us.

MINNESOTA RIVER VALLEY AND SOUTHERN MINNESOTA

© JAKE KULJU

BEST HIKES

❰ Historical Hikes
Pike Island Loop, **page 219.**
Sugar Camp Hollow and
    Big Spring Trail, **page 267.**

❰ River Hikes
Pike Island Loop, **page 219.**

❰ Viewing Wildlife
Big Woods Loop to Timber Doodle Trail, **page 252.**

❰ Waterfalls
Hidden Falls to Hope Trail Loop, **page 255.**

❰ Wildflowers
Seppman Windmill Trail, **page 249.**
Hidden Falls to Hope Trail Loop, **page 255.**

Known as the land of 10,000 lakes, Minnesota

is home to countless lakes, watersheds, rivers, bogs, and wetlands, which are a deeply important part of the Minnesota wilderness identity. Chief among them is the Minnesota River Valley region. The state was named after the river; *minnesota* is a Lakota word describing the appearance of its waters.

In places, the valley cuts a 5-mile-wide swath through the gentle hills that flow west from the Twin Cities. Unlike most rivers, the Minnesota River becomes more protected and has more wilderness and wildlife habitats the closer it gets to the urban center it flows to. These dense wilderness areas are a national anomaly because of their proximity to urban areas. Just a few miles from St. Paul, the Minnesota Valley National Wildlife Refuge covers more than 14,000 acres of land, and it is the largest of only four urban national wildlife refuges in the nation.

While many of the areas surrounding the Twin Cities are well protected, the Minnesota River Valley enjoys the close watch of the National Refuge Service, ensuring that its pristine critical habitats are protected and accessible for anyone who wishes to enjoy them. Visits in the spring and autumn are particularly spectacular, when tens of thousands of birds are migrating.

From Mankato to its confluence with the Mississippi River at Pike Island, the Minnesota River forms an invaluable migratory corridor for more than 50,000 waterfowl during the spring and fall migration seasons. One hundred different species of birds nest in the valley, which is designated an Important Bird Area. Great blue herons, bald eagles, and tundra swans are commonly seen. Rarer finds include the black-crowned night heron, the prothonotary warbler, and the green heron.

Next to waterfowl, beavers are especially prominent, and their signs can be found throughout the valley. The Louisville Swamp is a particularly choice beaver territory. Their dams routinely flood the swamp, sometimes necessitating creative ways of navigating the blocked trails.

Part of educating the public about how important these critical habitats are is through allowing access to them. The Minnesota River Valley provides miles of wetland trails, forest turf paths, and riverside walkways. Even the most remote places have some access trails, which allow people to observe rare and beautiful wildlife. A notable example is the trek along the marshes of Black Dog Lake, a favorite gathering place for waterfowl well into the winter months due to its warm waters. This important Scientific Natural Area and the trail that runs through it are perfect examples of how Minnesota prioritizes its wetland wilderness.

Whether you have all day to hike the hills and explore the abandoned town of historic Forestville in Forestville State Park, or have only a few hours to take a stroll around nearby Pike Island or the Bass Ponds in the Minnesota Valley National Wildlife Refuge, the Minnesota River Valley and southern Minnesota trails will treat you to the best of Minnesota's wetlands, Big Woods forests, and wetland wildlife.

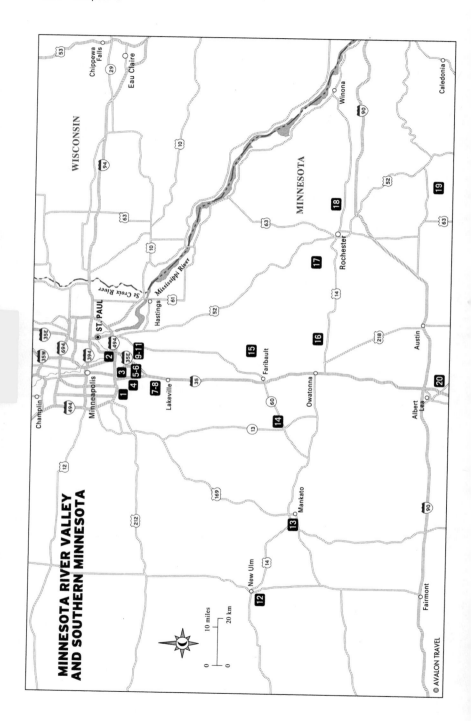

MINNESOTA RIVER VALLEY
AND SOUTHERN MINNESOTA

© AVALON TRAVEL

TRAIL NAME	LEVEL	DISTANCE	TIME	ELEVATION	FEATURES	PAGE
1 Hyland and Bush Lakes Loop	Easy/moderate	4.5 mi rt	2.5-3 hr	Negligible		216
2 Pike Island Loop	Easy	3.5 mi rt	1.5-2 hr	Negligible		219
3 Bass Ponds and Old Cedar Bridge Trail	Easy	3 mi rt	1 hr	Negligible		222
4 Wilkie Rookery Trail	Moderate	6.1 mi rt	3.5 hr	Negligible		225
5 Louisville Swamp Loop	Moderate	5.7 mi rt	3 hr	100 ft		227
6 Black Dog Lake Trail	Easy	4 mi rt	2 hr	Negligible		230
7 Hanrehan Lake Trail	Easy/moderate	5.1 mi rt	2.5 hr	10 ft		232
8 Murphy Lake to Minnregs Lake Trail	Moderate	6.3 mi rt	3-3.5 hr	100 ft		234
9 Western Lebanon Hills Hiking Trail	Easy	2.5 mi rt	1.5 hr	60 ft		237
10 Jensen Lake Trail	Easy	3.3 mi rt	2 hr	60 ft		240
11 Holland and O'Brien Lakes Trail	Moderate	4.6 mi rt	3 hr	70 ft		243
12 Cottonwood River and Hiking Club Trail	Moderate/strenuous	5.6 mi rt	3 hr	210 ft		246
13 Seppman Windmill Trail	Easy	4 mi rt	2 hr	50 ft		249
14 Big Woods Loop to Timber Doodle Trail	Moderate/strenuous	6.1 mi rt	3-3.5 hr	270 ft		252
15 Hidden Falls to Hope Trail Loop	Easy/moderate	4.7 mi rt	2.5 hr	90 ft		255
16 Rice Lake Trail	Easy	3.5 mi rt	1.75 hr	Negligible		258
17 Zumbro River and High Meadow Trail	Moderate	5.1 mi rt	2.75 hr	120 ft		261
18 North Trail, Prairie Ridge Trail, and the Dam Overlook	Moderate	5.6 mi rt	3 hr	100 ft		264
19 Sugar Camp Hollow and Big Spring Trail	Strenuous	11.8 mi rt	7-8 hr	520 ft		267
20 Big Island to Great Marsh Trail	Easy/moderate	6 mi rt	3 hr	Negligible		270

1 HYLAND AND BUSH LAKES LOOP

Hyland Lake Park Reserve, Bloomington

Level: Easy/moderate

Hiking Time: 2.5-3 hours

Total Distance: 4.5 miles round-trip

Elevation Gain: Negligible

Summary: Enjoy this lakeside hike through mature hardwood forests and an open prairie in a more than 1,000-acre park reserve.

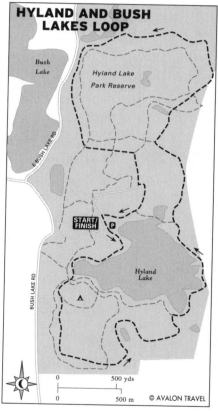

As Minneapolis's most popular first-ring suburb, Bloomington is better known for its malls and hotels than its wildflowers and butterflies. To the surprise of many Twin Cities residents, Hyland Lake Park Reserve, in the heart of Bloomington, has some of the most breathtaking prairie trails in the southern half of the state.

Start by walking behind the visitors center toward Hyland Lake. Take a right as you near the water and head south toward the fishing pier. The turf trail follows the oak-lined lakeshore around the western arm of Hyland Lake and then delves into the thicker forest that covers the southern and eastern shores. Take a right at the first trail intersection and cross over the paved hiker-biker path. A drinking fountain marks this intersection, 0.4 mile from the trailhead. This is the quietest part of the park and the area where you may see the most wildlife. The ever-present whitetail deer and the occasional fox peruse these woods.

Keep to the right at the next trail intersection and follow the turf trail as it arcs through the park's southern forest and around one of the park's small ponds. One mile from the drinking fountain take a right at the turf trail intersection and head north along Hyland Lake's eastern shore. The trail runs parallel to a set of train tracks and comes quite close to them on the eastern end of the lake. Take another

a view of the prairie hillside in Hyland Lake Park Reserve

right at the northern end of the lake and you will soon break out of the forest into the broad prairie meadows that Hyland Lake Park Reserve is known for.

After another right-hand turn you come to a four-way intersection. Take the middle path, which leads north and crosses the paved hiker-biker path; 0.2 mile from the paved intersection the trail meets a gravel road that leads to the maintenance facility. Turn left and follow the turf trail west here for 0.6 mile to another intersection with the paved hiker-biker trail. This 0.6-mile stretch passes through an open prairie corridor between two stands of trees. At the paved intersection, take a left on the turf trail into the heart of the prairie. Just east of Bush Lake, the grassy meadow trail here is lined with wild purple asters, creeping bellflowers, purple coneflowers, and blooming milkweed. Look for wild daisies, one-eyed susans, and Indian paintbrush. Bluebirds and the occasional meadowlark flit between the shrubs and grasses, and their songs can be heard across the prairie.

In 0.6 mile take a left on the gravel road that leads east. Follow it as it curves to the south through the middle of the prairie grassland past a parking lot on your right. At the intersection with the paved hiker-biker path, take a left and follow the pavement south toward the lake and past the visitors center. Leave the trail at the visitors center and find the parking lot on the other side of the building.

Options

Another turf trail near the Bush Lake trail intersection leads north to the Richardson Nature Center trail system. Turn right at Bush Lake to enter the interpretive trails that surround the ponds, forests, and prairie of the park's northern section.

Directions

From Minneapolis take I-35 West south for 7.2 miles. Merge onto I-494 West for 2.7 miles. Exit left onto East Bush Lake Road for 0.5 mile. Turn right to continue on East Bush Lake Road for another 2.4 miles. Turn left at Highland Lake Park Road for 0.2 mile to the visitors center parking lot.

Information and Contact

There is no fee. Restrooms and drinking fountains are available at the visitors center. Dogs are allowed. Maps are available at the park office and on the park website. For more information, contact Hyland Lake Park Reserve, 10145 Bush Lake Road, Bloomington, MN 55438, 763/694-7687, www.threeriverspark district.org/parks.

2 PIKE ISLAND LOOP

BEST ☾

Fort Snelling State Park, St. Paul

Level: Easy

Total Distance: 3.5 miles round-trip

Hiking Time: 1.5-2 hours

Elevation Gain: Negligible

Summary: Make an easy loop around the peaceful confluence of the Minnesota and Mississippi Rivers.

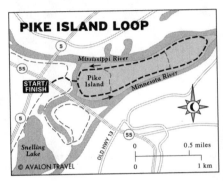

Fort Snelling is infamous for its whiskey-drinking soldiers, its influence on the founding of St. Paul, and its dark past during the Native American conflicts of the 19th century. The fort is on the bluff high above the confluence of the Mississippi and Minnesota Rivers. The best trail in the park, however, is down below on the island at the confluence of the rivers. The packed-dirt path loops through the majestic bottomland forest along the two legendary rivers that Minnesota takes so much of its identity from.

From the parking lot, walk north to the visitors center to get some historical background on the area. The Mdewakantonwan Dakota that once peopled this area considered Pike Island the site of the source of creation. The sacred land was a meeting ground for members of tribes from all over the region. The visitors center also has detailed maps of the area.

From the visitors center, follow the paved walking path east. Signs indicate the direction of Pike Island. Cross the footbridge to the island and take a right onto the smooth packed dirt and turf trail. A brass plaque gives historical information about the island and commemorates Zebulon Pike, the white explorer whom the island is named after. From the moment you set foot on Pike Island, you'll see why it was considered a holy place by the Dakota. The plush bottomland forest fills every inch of the island and creates a canopy over the wide walkway. A feeling of enchantment pervades the place as water from two rivers eddies and swirls on either side.

Maple and basswood trees provide plenty of shade, but the real beauties are the massive cottonwood trees. Several of these giants still live on the island, and their mammoth trunks stand out boldly from the rest of the forest. Whitetail deer,

© JAKE KULJU

Elm, maple, oak, and cottonwood trees line the packed dirt path that loops around Pike Island.

foxes, and badgers all find homes in this shady paradise. You will almost certainly see a deer or two. The non-venomous fox snake is sometimes seen coiled in the underbrush, but for the most part the island is quiet and peaceful. High summer is the best time to visit, when light filters through the thick tree canopy and provides a cool, shady respite from the sun.

You will come to two trail intersections on the south side of the island. Keep straight ahead at each one to complete a full loop around the island. At the eastern tip of the island where the two rivers become one a bench overlooks the channel and downtown St. Paul. Continue counterclockwise around the island from the confluence point, heading west back toward the footbridge. At the southern end of the island you walk along the shore of the Minnesota River; on the northern end you walk along the Mississippi River. Across the river you can see Crosby Farm Park, St. Paul's largest city park. Several large cottonwood trees line the bank across the river. Stay straight ahead at the two trail intersections until you reach the footbridge. From here, trace your steps back to the visitors center and parking lot.

Options

You can island hop onto Picnic Island for a little more distance and another view of the Minnesota River. Take a left after crossing the Pike Island bridge after finishing the loop and follow the paved path south along the river-bend to the Picnic Island bridge. Take another left and follow the turf trail loop around the island to get another 2.2 miles in. Watch for the Kentucky coffee trees that grow here. The tree has the broadest leaves of any in the state, and the state's largest coffee tree is on the southern end of the island.

Directions

From St. Paul take MN-5 west for 7 miles. Take the Post Road exit and turn left for 420 feet. Continue on Snelling Lake Road past the park exit for 2.1 miles to the visitors center.

Information and Contact

There is a $5 daily vehicle permit fee. Restrooms and drinking fountains are available in the park office. Dogs are allowed. Maps are available at the park office and on the park website. For more information, contact Fort Snelling State Park, 101 Snelling Lake Road, St. Paul, MN 55111, 612/725-2724, www.dnr.state.mn.us.

3 BASS PONDS AND OLD CEDAR BRIDGE TRAIL

Minnesota Valley National Wildlife Refuge, Bloomington

Level: Easy

Hiking Time: 1 hour

Total Distance: 3 miles round-trip

Elevation Gain: Negligible

Summary: You'll find trails teeming with wildlife and sky-blue waters along this river bottomland trail loop.

Little and Big Bass Ponds were dug by hand during the 1930s when the Works Progress Administration (WPA) created a bass-farming site here. Today, a small spring-fed creek and shallow wetlands make this a favorite place for migrating waterfowl. In the spring, ducks, especially, come to feed at the bottom of the shallow ponds formed by the rains. Puddle ducks, egrets, great blue herons, redwing blackbirds, and swamp sparrows actively use this area, and the entire Minnesota River Valley, as a major source of food and nesting grounds.

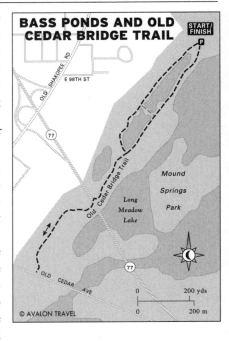

The trail starts just 2 miles from the Minnesota Valley National Wildlife Refuge Visitor Center. There is a parking area where the road dips down into the lowlands near the ponds. The gate from the parking area to the trailhead is always locked, but you can walk around either side of it or obtain a key from the visitors center.

Start on the 0.5-mile, figure-eight interpretive trail as it heads to your left on the other side of the gate. An information kiosk there has a map and brochures that detail the history and use of the Bass Ponds area. The interpretive trail passes by the foundation of an old WPA building, Minnow Pond, and Wood Duck Pond, where you will see installations of wood duck nests. During nesting times, the wetland is full of birds, with their colorful plumage and feeding activities on display. You'll see many signs of wildlife on this 0.5-mile stretch, and it is very common to encounter beavers, deer, foxes, and raccoons while hiking. Drooping willow trees line the entire length of this section of the hike.

After you loop back to your starting point in the figure eight, continue to the right of the parking lot and follow the path about 0.25 mile from the parking lot, where it joins the Old Cedar Bridge Trail. On the Old Cedar Bridge Trail, you will walk under MN-77 (Cedar Avenue) after about 0.75 mile of graveled pathway through a dense marshy area. Cattails, swamp reeds, and lily pads encroach on both sides of the hiking path, eventually giving way to a sprawling marsh and several small ponds. From this relatively open area, the trail continues for another 0.25 mile to the Old Cedar Bridge. The bridge

A delicate Virginia Waterleaf blooms near the Bass Ponds.

is a remnant of the former route of Cedar Avenue and now serves as little more than a trail landmark and fishing pier for local anglers.

Turn around once you reach the bridge parking lot. Retrace your steps through the dense greenery along the edge of the lake, which is a haven for songbirds and wildlife. When you reach the interpretive trail, keep walking straight ahead to the middle of the figure eight and then take a left to finish the loops around the two ponds.

Options

Continue hiking once you get to the Old Cedar Bridge Trail parking lot to add an extra 2 miles to your hike. This additional stretch follows the roadway that was formerly used as Cedar Avenue. Much of the trail is built up in the lake, giving you wide, open views of the surrounding shoreline.

Directions

From Minneapolis take I-35 West south for 7.4 miles. Exit onto I-494 East for 2.3 miles. Exit onto Highway 77 South for 0.4 mile, then keep right and merge onto Killebrew Drive for 1 mile. Turn right at East Old Shakopee Road for 0.3 mile. Turn left at East 86th Street for 0.3 mile to the Bass Ponds parking lot.

Information and Contact

There is no fee. Dogs are allowed. Maps are available at the trailhead kiosk. For more information, contact the Minnesota Valley National Wildlife Refuge, 3815 American Boulevard East, Bloomington, MN 55425, 952/854-5915, www.fws .gov/refuges.

4 WILKIE ROOKERY TRAIL
Minnesota Valley National Wildlife Refuge, Jordan

Level: Moderate

Hiking Time: 3.5 hours

Total Distance: 6.1 miles round-trip

Elevation Gain: Negligible

Summary: Follow trails and abandoned farm roads through the marshes and lakes that surround the state's largest great blue heron rookery.

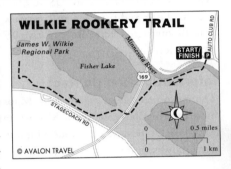

Before you pack your binoculars and bird book, take note that the rookery section of the Wilkie Unit at the Minnesota Valley National Wildlife Refuge is closed March–August each year to accommodate the shy pairs of herons (600 each year) that nest during the spring and summer. But don't worry—you'll still see plenty of birds no matter when you go. Trails with viewing areas outside of the rookery remain open all year.

From the Bloomington Ferry parking lot walk to the pedestrian footbridge just a few hundred feet southwest. The bridge crosses the Minnesota River toward Rice and Fisher Lakes, leading through some hardwoods that line the river. The trail is essentially an abandoned road. Wide and overgrown in places, it is a strange reminder of nature's staying power.

This area is home to three adjacent lakes and the Minnesota River. The large amounts of water can make trail conditions wet, especially after rains and in wet seasons. Call the park ahead of time to find out about trail closings. One mile from the pedestrian bridge you come to the boat ramp that provides access to Rice Lake. Continue on the trail as it passes under the US-169 freeway bridge. The trail widens to a gravel road here and leads for another 0.9 mile to the Wilkie parking lot.

As you head west, you will begin hiking on the Minnesota River Trail. At 0.3 mile from the Wilkie parking lot, take a right at the trail intersection to head north toward the river. The trail makes a 1-mile loop, borders the southern shore of the river and then heads back south. This area is a soggy river marsh, full of reeds, swamp grasses, and open water. The large cottonwood trees that grow in this floodplain are homes to the herons that nest in the Wilkie Unit.

Options

Instead of crossing the river from the Bloomington Ferry parking lot, shorten this hike by parking at the Wilkie entrance on the other side of the river. Cross the river on US-169 and exit right to the Wilkie entrance and parking lot. Take a left on the trail that heads northwest toward the river.

Directions

From Minneapolis head south on I-35 West for 7.2 miles. Take the I-494 West exit for 4.5 miles. Exit onto US-169 South for 3.5 miles. Take the Old Shakopee Road exit and turn left at Riverview Road. Drive 0.7 mile and take a right onto Bloomington Ferry Road. Drive 0.7 mile to Bloomington Ferry Circle and parking lot.

Information and Contact

There is no fee. Dogs are allowed. Maps are available on the park website. For more information, contact the Minnesota Valley National Wildlife Refuge, 3815 American Boulevard East, Bloomington, MN 55425, 952/854-5900, www.fws.gov/midwest/minnesotavalley (click on *Wilkie*).

5 LOUISVILLE SWAMP LOOP
Minnesota Valley National Wildlife Refuge, Jordan

Level: Moderate

Hiking Time: 3 hours

Total Distance: 5.7 miles round-trip

Elevation Gain: 100 feet

Summary: Delve into the lush floodplain of the Louisville Swamp, viewing one of the richest wildlife areas in the Minnesota River Valley.

Minnesota is known as the perfectly seasoned state. The wilderness areas, trails, and hiking spots are beautiful all year-round. That being said, you'll definitely want to come to the Louisville Swamp Unit of the Minnesota Valley National Wildlife Refuge in the late summer, when flooded trails and high water are less common than in the spring and fall. Walk south from the parking lot on the gravel entryway to the grassy trail that starts this hike.

The trailhead on the southern end of the parking lot is easy to find. There's a large map, and an information kiosk gives a brief history of the area, explaining that elk and buffalo once grazed the vast oak savannas that are now a scarcity across the entire continent. A patch of remnant savanna remains intact in this unit of the refuge. Take a right at the trail intersection 0.4 mile from the trailhead. The next mile of trail leads west through the savanna. Two short spur trails lead left to the edge of the bluff that overlooks the Louisville Swamp and the creek that runs through it. The sweeping view is a beautiful way to observe the wetland habitat that lies below. Turn around and you will see an entirely different habitat where you stand, a hundred feet or so above the swamp. The prairie grasses and gnarled oak trees are home to foxes, whitetail deer, raccoons, and bull snakes, whereas the swamp houses cranes, egrets, geese, and bullfrogs.

At the western end of the trail, take a left at the intersection and begin a fairly steep descent through the oak and maple forest to the bottomlands. The trees transition to basswood and cottonwood the closer you get to the wetland. Follow the turf trail across the creek that runs west through the swamp. This can be quite

© JAKE KULJU

Flooded tree stumps and swamp grass fill the Minnesota River Valley at the Louisville Swamp.

difficult during wet seasons and after rains. You will more than likely get your feet wet trying to cross this portion of the trail no matter what time of year it is. The Louisville Swamp Unit of the refuge floods three out of every five years, and the trails in the bottomlands can often be submerged under several feet of water. Make your way south to Jabs Farm, where three original buildings still stand on the 1880 farmstead. Then follow the trail that veers left toward the glacial boulder. The glacial boulder, 1.6 miles from the historical farm site, is a remnant of the last ice age, deposited here when the massive sheets of ice receded north.

Turn left at the boulder intersection to head north for a mile across the swamp and up the ridge to the oak savanna and prairie. As you leave the wetland below and break from the trees into the grassland, look for the wild asters, lupines, and Indian paintbrush flowers that mingle with the grass. The diversity of habitat here can be overlooked if you don't pay attention, but with the right eye you can pick out dozens of different wildflowers among the grass. Take a right at the intersection on top of the ridge to return 0.4 mile to the parking lot and trailhead.

Options

After climbing out of the wetland back up to the savanna, take a left instead of heading back to the trailhead and finish out the Little Prairie Loop trail that winnows through the tallgrass and wildflower prairie on top of the hill. The loop is nearly 2 miles long and will return you to the trailhead on the western end of the parking lot.

Directions

From Minneapolis drive south on I-35 West for 7.2 miles. Exit onto I-494 West for 4.5 miles. Take the US-169 South exit and drive south for 16 miles to 145th Street West. Turn right and look for the Louisville Swamp Unit parking lot on your left in 0.5 mile. A park sign is posted at the entrance.

Information and Contact

There is no fee. Dogs are allowed. During the spring and early summer, flooding can block sections of the trail, especially in the low-lying areas. Call the park ahead of time for information about trail closings. Maps are available at the trailhead kiosk and the refuge website. For more information, contact the Minnesota Valley National Wildlife Refuge, 3815 American Boulevard East, Bloomington, MN 55425, 952/854-5915, www.fws.gov/midwest/minnesotavalley (click on *Louisville Swamp*).

6 BLACK DOG LAKE TRAIL

Minnesota Valley National Wildlife Refuge, Bloomington

Level: Easy

Hiking Time: 2 hours

Total Distance: 4 miles round-trip

Elevation Gain: Negligible

Summary: Black Dog Lake is home to the rare calcareous fen habitat – one of the most protected wetland areas in the refuge.

Black Dog Lake is the centerpiece of the Black Dog Preserve Unit of the Minnesota Valley National Wildlife Refuge. The area is notable for its preservation of prairie landscape and calcareous fen. Calcareous fen is considered the rarest wetland community in the Midwest and one of the rarest in North America. Fens of this type have their own internal water flow, which is rich in calcium and other minerals and which creates a rather harsh habitat that only rare and limited plant species can survive in. Because of their rarity, the plants that grow in them are almost all endangered. It is very important to stay on the established trail to maintain the integrity of the fen and its plant community. Some of the plants you may see here include shrubby cinquefoil, sterile sedge, and wild timothy. You may need a plant book on hand to help you identify them, since you probably haven't seen them anywhere else.

From the parking lot, follow the dirt path to the northern edge of the soccer fields through the tree line and across the railroad tracks. The tall wavy grasses here are examples of what much of this part of the state used to look like. Prairie land and its tallgrass once covered more then one-third of Minnesota. Black Dog Lake is a particularly good place to observe big bluestem, sideoats grama, and smooth brome. The trail makes a 0.5-mile arc to the northeast, then evens out into a straight line for 1.25 miles as it approaches the wetland fen near the lake. The trail is intermittently lined with trees, mostly cottonwood. But the prairie and wetland clearly dominate this habitat. Croaking bullfrogs, dazzlingly colored dragonflies, and leaping grasshoppers fill the reeds and tallgrass that surround the tree-lined path.

Three-quarters of a mile from the trailhead the path threads between an outcropping of Black Dog Lake to the north and a marshy wetland pond to the south. Depending on the time of year and the amount of rainfall, the pond can look like a small lake or a dry swamp. There is always abundant wetland wildlife in this area, however. Great blue herons, egrets, and marsh hawks seek food in this marshy landscape. You will likely see turtles sunning themselves on grass hummocks and perhaps a shy beaver or two groping in the mud. During the migratory seasons you can see birds of all feathers moving through this area. Flocks of pelicans, mergansers, wood ducks, and even green herons can be seen. Call the park office to get information about the peak migration times, and make sure to bring your binoculars.

After passing by the pond, the trail veers right to a parking lot on River Hills Drive. Turn around here and retrace your steps for 2 miles through the marsh and back through the prairie grasses near the trailhead.

Options

If you have two vehicles in your hiking party you can turn this into a shuttle hike instead of a "there and back" hike. Park one car at the River Hills Drive parking lot by taking a left on Cliff Road and another left onto West River Hills Drive for 1.2 miles. The road ends at the gravel parking lot. This cuts the hike in half, turning it into a 2-mile trek from prairie grasses through calcareous fen marshes and wetland ponds.

Directions

From Minneapolis head south on I-35 West for 12.7 miles. Take exit 4A for Cliff Road and merge onto Cliff Road in 0.3 mile. Continue on River Ridge Boulevard/Cliff Road West for 0.8 mile. The Cliff Nicollet Park parking lot will be on your left next to the soccer fields.

Information and Contact

There is no fee. Dogs are allowed. Maps are available on the park website. For more information, contact the Minnesota Valley National Wildlife Refuge, 3815 American Boulevard East, Bloomington, MN 55425, 952/854-5900, www.fws .gov/midwest/minnesotavalley (click on *Black Dog*).

7 HANREHAN LAKE TRAIL

Murphy-Hanrehan Park Reserve, Lakeville

Level: Easy/moderate

Hiking Time: 2.5 hours

Total Distance: 5.1 miles round-trip

Elevation Gain: 10 feet

Summary: Weave your way through the woods and ponds in the gentle hills that surround Hanrehan Lake.

HANREHAN LAKE TRAIL

HANREHAN LAKE BLVD

Hanrehan Lake

START/FINISH

MURPHY LAKE BLVD

Murphy-Hanrehan Park Reserve

© AVALON TRAVEL

0   500 yds
0   500 m

The land south of Burnsville is what anyone from the Twin Cities would call "out in the country." The landscape varies from large tracts of farmland to untouched swaths of woods. The rest is filled in with grasslands, lakes, ponds, and rivers. Murphy-Hanrehan Park Reserve is one of the pockets of woods and water that gives southern Minnesota its country feel.

Start hiking south from the parking lot. The trail almost immediately splits, at which point you should veer right. The turf trail crosses a grassy meadow and then enters the maple and oak woods that arc along the north shore of an approaching pond. The trail continues southeast through the woods, occasionally passing through patches of meadow. Look for deer and foxes loitering along the tree lines of these areas. Bluebirds and meadowlarks may have homes in these secluded meadows as well. The splashes of color and sunlight that these forest meadows provide make the Hanrehan Lake Trail an especially beautiful one in mid-spring when flowers like wild lilies, wild purple asters, and lupines are boldly blooming. This trail is also popular in the early autumn when the dynamic maple leaves begin to turn color before the rest of the forest. Their blazing red leaves give a spectacular dimension to the forest.

A cross-country ski trail breaks to the right 0.75 mile from the trailhead. Stay to the left to intersection 10 and take a right to continue through the forest. Stay to the right at the next intersection in 0.3 mile. Over the next 0.5 mile, two more cross-country ski trails lead south. Stay eastward at the first, and take a left at the second to head almost straight north for another 0.75 mile. The trail makes a hard turn to the left and in 0.5 mile arcs south along the upper arm of Hanrehan Lake. When the turf trail doubles back northeast you will cross through a larger section of meadow. Surrounded on all sides by trees, this swatch of grass and prairie flowers is one of the quietest, most secluded open spaces in the park.

Another cross-country ski trail branches from the trail 0.75 miles from the lake. Keep walking south to intersection 9 and take a right. Take another right in 0.2 mile to intersection 3. Take another right here onto the north-leading wetland trail. This 0.75-mile arc passes through the marsh that hugs the eastern shore of Hanrehan Lake. A boardwalk leads through the reeds before the trail enters the higher wooded grounds farther to the south. At intersection 1 stay to the right, walking straight west back to the trailhead and parking lot.

Options

You can take a shorter hike that gives you a view of the lake and takes you over the boardwalk by taking a left at intersection 10 and heading north toward Hanrehan Lake. After crossing over the boardwalk and walking along the lake's southern shore, take a right at intersection 1 to return to the trailhead. This 2-mile hike weaves through several of the park's ponds and gives you plenty of time in the woods and patches of meadow.

Directions

From Minneapolis head south on I-35 West for 15.2 miles. Take the County Road 42 exit and turn right. Drive for 2 miles and take a left at West Burnsville Parkway; 1.1 miles later merge onto Hanrehan Lake Boulevard for 1.2 miles. Turn left at Murphy Lake Boulevard. The park entrance is a few hundred feet on your left. The parking lot is to the left.

Information and Contact

There is no fee. Dogs are allowed. A drinking fountain and restroom are in the trailhead shelter. Maps are available at the park website. For more information, contact Murphy-Hanrehan Park Reserve, 15501 Murphy Lake Road, Savage, MN 55378, 763/559-9000, www.threeriversparkdistrict.org.

8 MURPHY LAKE TO MINNREGS LAKE TRAIL

Murphy-Hanrehan Park Reserve, Lakeville

Level: Moderate

Hiking Time: 3-3.5 hours

Total Distance: 6.3 miles round-trip

Elevation Gain: 100 feet

Summary: Trek through wide meadows and thick forests nested with dozens of ponds and two of the park's primary lakes.

South of Hanrehan Lake, Murphy Lake has its own trail system through the ponds and forests of the park. From the parking lot, cross the road and follow the turf trail east into the thick woods. You have entered a large counterclockwise loop that tours the wooded ponds of the park's central section. Maple, oak, basswood, and aspen fill this forest with filtered sunlight during the summer. In early autumn when the maple trees begin to turn colors before the rest of the forest, the stark contrasts make their blazing red pop out from the rest of the forest.

On the northern end of the loop, two cross-country ski trails lead north at intersections 16 and 15. Stay to the left at all trail intersections until you reach the parking lot at the completion of the 2.2-mile loop.

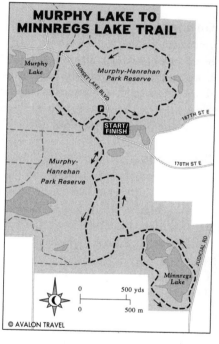

After returning to the parking lot, walk west on the unpaved hiking trail that skirts the northern shore of a small park pond. The landscape here is scattered with trees and meadows, but as the trail turns south it enters thicker hardwood forest. Maple and oak provide a nice shade canopy for 0.5 mile before the trees give way to prairie. The trail hugs the edge of the grassland at the tree line for another 0.6 mile, then crosses the shallow creek that flows from the park's pond system to the west. At intersection 40 take a left. After the creek the trail reenters the forest and meanders northeast toward Minnregs Lake. While you walk through the prairie notice the wild asters, daisies, coneflowers,

© JAKE KULJU

Fallen leaves line the path in early autumn in Murphy-Hanrehan Park Reserve.

and Indian paintbrush that give color to the grass. In the forest of the northern loop you may have seen whitetail deer, foxes, skunks, and raccoons, whereas here in the grasslands the flowers and prairie shrubs give shelter to gophers, small snakes, and badgers. Up above fly hawks and eagles. Wild turkeys also like the diverse landscape of this park and can be seen scurrying along the tree line in huddled clusters.

The trail splits in 0.25 mile. Take a right to enter the loop that circles the lake. The trail soon splits again at the top of the loop. Take a left if you want to take in the sights of the prairie that dominate the eastern side of the water. As the trail leads north again, you will enter a woodland all the way to the top of the loop. If you'd rather finish the loop in the waist-high grass, take a right.

After returning to intersection 38, take a right and then another right at intersection 37 in 0.5 mile. The final stretch leads north to the parking lot through patches of meadow and forest between the scattered ponds that characterize Murphy-Hanrehan Park Reserve.

Options

Getting to Minnregs Lake can take about half the time if you cut out the first loop of the hike. Just head south from the parking lot, take a left at intersection 40, and loop counterclockwise around the lake. At intersection 38, take a right. Take another at intersection 37 and head north back to the trailhead. This shorter hike is 4.1 miles long.

Directions

From Minneapolis head south on I-35 West for 17 miles. Continue south on I-35 after the merger of I-35 East for another 2 miles. Take the County Road 5 exit and merge onto Kenwood Trail for about 0.5 mile. Turn left at Klamath Trail and drive 0.7 mile to 168th Street West. Take a left for 0.5 mile and continue straight on Judicial Road. Turn right at 170th Street East and continue on Sunset

Lake Road for another 0.4 mile. The parking area and trailhead are on the left just before the Equestrian Group Camp.

Information and Contact

There is no fee. Dogs are allowed. A drinking fountain and restroom are in the trailhead shelter at the group campsite. Maps are available at the park website. For more information, contact Murphy-Hanrehan Park Reserve, 15501 Murphy Lake Road, Savage, MN 55378, 763/559-9000, www.threeriversparkdistrict.org.

9 WESTERN LEBANON HILLS HIKING TRAIL

Lebanon Hills Regional Park, Eagan

Level: Easy

Hiking Time: 1.5 hours

Total Distance: 2.5 miles round-trip

Elevation Gain: 60 feet

Summary: Enjoy a woodsy hike through the pine trees and hardwoods of Lebanon Hills Regional Park's western territory.

The less visited western portion of Lebanon Hills Regional Park is mostly known for its mountain-biking trails, which wind through the rugged terrain of gently rolling hills filled with hardwood forests and small open meadows, but there is some excellent hiking to be done here as well. From the parking lot head west along the packed dirt trail that leads through the thick pine trees. This stand of evergreens is about 0.2-mile wide and is a gorgeous setting for starting this hike any time of year. In the summer the sun shimmies through the breezy pine branches, in the autumn the dark green needles stand out against the changing colors of the surrounding hardwood forest, and in the winter the stark contrast between the white snow and green trees is a beautiful sight.

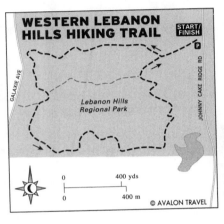

The pines give way to the maple and oak woods that dominate most of the park. Several mountain-biking paths cross the hiking trail, but don't be tempted to go down them. Most of the them are single-lane one-way bike paths, and bikers can come crashing along with little notice. Stick to the turf trail that heads west through the trees. When you reach the spur trail that leads out of the forest to Galaxie Avenue, take a left to mosey your way south. You will encounter two more hiking trail intersections. Stay right at the first and left at the second to remain on the larger trail loop this hike follows.

These woods are thick and don't see a lot of visitors, so animals have naturally sought it as a refuge. You will more than likely see whitetail deer, woodpeckers, red squirrels in the pine stands, and raccoons. Although the woods are thick, there are some small meadow openings. Look for wild turkeys huddled near the tree lines.

Transition zones between forest and meadow create a unique habitat for local wildlife.

When the trail begins to head eastward, it weaves through several very small ponds. In the spring the sound of the frogs in these water holes is nearly deafening. All summer long the chirping rhythm of frogs and crickets hardly ceases, creating a kind of natural music that is a joy to hike in step to. The trail swings north near the large pond close to Johnny Cake Ridge Road and passes through the largest of the forest meadows along this hike. Make sure to check the sky as well as the land for wildlife here. Some hawks may use this area as a hunting ground. The last 0.5 mile of this hike crosses another mountain-biking trail and a hiking trail intersection. Take a right and follow the turf trail 0.25 mile back to the trailhead and parking lot.

Options

Across Johnny Cake Ridge Road, you can follow Sherwood Way above Gerhardt Lake and take a right onto the hiking trail that runs through the forests between Johnny Cake Ridge and Pilot Knob Road. Sherwood Way is just 200 feet south of the parking lot. Walk along the road and follow Sherwood Way to the trailhead on your right. At Pilot Knob, turn around and head back to the parking lot. This will add about 2 miles to your hike.

Directions

From St. Paul drive 13 miles south on I-35 East. Take the Cliff Road exit, keeping left at the fork to continue toward Cliff Road. Turn left, then take a right at

Johnny Cake Ridge Road in 0.7 mile. The parking lot is 0.5 mile ahead on your right just to the south of a baseball diamond.

Information and Contact

There is no fee. Dogs are not allowed. A portable restroom is available at the trailhead parking lot. Maps are available at the park website. For more information, contact Lebanon Hills Regional Park, 860 Cliff Road, Eagan, MN 55123, 651/554-6530, www.co.dakota.mn.us (click on *Leisure & Recreation* and then *Park Locations*).

10 JENSEN LAKE TRAIL

Lebanon Hills Regional Park, Eagan

Level: Easy

Hiking Time: 2 hours

Total Distance: 3.3 miles round-trip

Elevation Gain: 60 feet

Summary: Get a taste of the grassy hills and forested lakeshores along Bridge Pond and the forests that surround Jensen Lake.

Jensen Lake is one of the primary lakes in Lebanon Hills Regional Park. Surrounded by hardwood forests of maple and oak, this beautiful lake is in the central region of the park, a quiet, peaceful area where hiking is more of an exercise in relaxation than exertion.

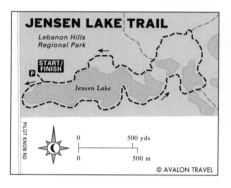

From the picnic shelter, head southeast on the packed-dirt trail that leads through the meadow to the lake. Take a right at the trail intersection to start a counterclockwise loop around the water. The trail almost immediately delves into the woods. The lakeshore does have some contour to it, but the hills aren't serious challenges. Small animals love this forested lakeshore. Squirrels, toads, salamanders, and turtles poke their way through the brush, while elusive foxes and raccoons do much of their food gathering near the water. Summer is always a good time to hike in Minnesota, but late autumn is a real treat along this trail. The dark blue water of Jensen Lake against the reds, oranges, and yellows of the changing leaves is nature at its finest.

As the path turns to the east, it follows the lakeshore closely, not leaving it until the far eastern edge of the water. A midsized peninsula juts into the lake near the small island in its eastern arm. You can catch views of it through the trees, especially in autumn when the leaves are gone. At intersection 10, between the lake and a park pond, take a right to move toward Bridge Pond. When you get to the water you'll cross the pond's namesake bridge. The trail passes through an open meadow briefly before reaching the footbridge. On the other side, it's back into the woods.

The trail splits north and south after the bridge. Take a left to head north along the eastern edge of the pond. A grassland borders the water here. Trees still

Prairie and oak savanna blanket the gentle hills.

clump together near the water, but meadow struggles to maintain its dominance in this transitional habitat zone. There is enough open space for prairie flowers like wild asters and blooming milkweed to take root. Look also for grasshoppers and butterflies that linger in the grass. Several will probably hitch a ride on your shoulder if you let them.

As you head north, the trail crosses a wider horse trail. Keep north for another 0.25 mile to intersection 15. Take a left here and recross the horse trail in another 0.15 mile. The next 0.2 mile is through a larger meadow, with scattered trees. Occasionally pheasants or prairie chickens may be seen here, though they are a rare sight. In the early summer you might hear the calls of rooster pheasants from the grass. Take a left at intersection 9 and a right at the next trail intersection 0.1 mile later. This is the final 0.75 mile of the hike along Jensen Lake's north shore. Thick woods dominate the terrain once again. When you reach the meadow opening along the shoreline, take a right to return to the trailhead and parking lot near the picnic shelter.

Options

Shorten this hike by forgoing the Bridge Pond section of the hike. Just take left turns at intersections 10 and 8 to make one 2.2-mile loop around Jensen Lake. The forest trail will give you plenty of views of the water and the wildlife in the park.

Directions

From St. Paul drive 9.6 miles south on I-35 East. Take the Pilot Knob Road exit and turn right. Drive for 3.5 miles to Carriage Hills Drive. Take a left and an immediate right onto Coach Road. Coach Road is a large parking loop. The picnic shelter and trailhead are east of the parking lot.

Information and Contact

There is no fee. Dogs are not allowed. Restrooms and a drinking fountain are available at the picnic shelter near the trailhead. Maps are available at the park website. For more information, contact Lebanon Hills Regional Park, 860 Cliff Road, Eagan, MN 55123, 651/554-6530, www.co.dakota.mn.us (click on *Leisure & Recreation* and then *Park Locations*).

11 HOLLAND AND O'BRIEN LAKES TRAIL

Lebanon Hills Regional Park, Eagan

Level: Moderate

Hiking Time: 3 hours

Total Distance: 4.6 miles round-trip

Elevation Gain: 70 feet

Summary: Explore the hardwood forests and occasional open meadows and prairie hills surrounding some of the many lakes of Lebanon Hills Regional Park.

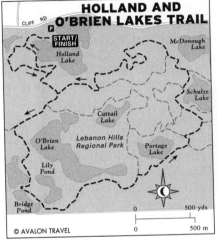

This hike is for the map-loving hikers who don't mind exercising their orienteering skills as much as their legs. The several intersections and trail crossings of this hike can be challenging to navigate, but the beautiful landscape and rolling hills of Lebanon Hills Regional Park are worth the effort. That being said, make sure you have a map before you go on this hike. Use the one provided in this book or print one from the park's website.

Start from the Holland Lake trailhead and walk south toward the water. The turf trail cuts west and then arcs to the south between the lake and a smaller pond. Take a right at intersection 19 for 0.2 mile to intersection 16. Take a left here for 0.25 mile to intersection 25, then turn right. At intersection 29, take another right and cross the wider horse trail that passes through the center of the park. The terrain here switches from thick woods to scattered trees and meadows. This is a transitional habitat zone, so look for bluebirds in the fields as well as wild turkey and pheasant. Whitetail deer come to the tree line to feed, and if you're patient enough you may see a fox slinking through the grass near the trees.

Continue south for 0.1 mile to intersection 24 and take a right. Intersection 15 lies 0.25 mile ahead through the thick hardwood forest. Take a left here and walk south to Bridge Pond for 0.5 mile. You will cross another horse trail at intersection 18 and a hiking trail near the bridge. Stay to your left on the eastern side of the pond and follow the trail south to intersections 22 and 23 between Bridge and Lily Ponds. Stay to the right on the forest turf trail. The wider horse

Indian paintbrush and butterfly weed flowers bloom amidst the prairie grass.

trail isn't the way you want to go. Horse riders abound at Lebanon Hills Regional Park and would rather not deal with lost hikers in their paths.

For the next 0.7 mile the trail leads northeast near the south shore of O'Brien Lake. More thick woods line the path. It's a rare day that you won't see white-tail deer bounding through the hills and fallen trees of this section of the park. Woodpeckers pound away at the tree trunks. In the colder months, chickadees flit through the trees, often landing startlingly close to you, especially if you stand still for a moment. At intersection 35 take a right to continue heading northeast near the south shore of the much smaller Portage Lake. Take a left at intersection 49 after crossing a horse trail, and a right just 0.1 mile later at intersection 45. There is a bit of a hill here as you head north toward Schulze Lake. 0.2 mile up the trail at intersection 53 take a left. You will really need to pay attention during the next 0.5 mile. Take a left at intersection 46 and walk along the western tip of Schulze Lake to intersection 43. Take a right and head north to intersection 47. Stay to the right here as well continuing north on the western shore of the lake to intersection 50. Take a left here and walk 0.2 mile to intersection 40. The trail finally breaks into the grasslands between McDonough and Schulze Lakes. Take another right and follow the winding forest and meadow trail for 0.8 mile to intersection 32. Take a right here through more meadow and forest mixed landscape to intersection 29. Take a right and another right at intersection 25 along the western shore of Holland Lake. At intersection 19 take a right to head 0.25 mile back to the trailhead and parking lot. Dizzy yet?

Options

Instead of arcing east all the way to Schulze Lake, you can make a shorter loop around O'Brien and Cattail Lakes. Take left turns at intersections 35 and 33, and a right at intersection 24 to head back north along the trail that leads from the parking lot. The trail portion between the north shores of Cattail and O'Brien Lakes is part of the canoe route portage. Make sure to give right of way to passing portagers.

Directions

From St. Paul drive south on I-35 East for 9.6 miles. Take the Pilot Knob Road exit and turn right onto Pilot Knob for 2.8 miles. Turn left at Cliff Road for 1 mile and take a right onto Lexington Avenue South. Park in the parking loop at the end of the road.

Information and Contact

There is no fee. Dogs are not allowed. Restrooms and a drinking fountain are available at the picnic shelter near the trailhead. Maps are available at the park website. For more information, contact Lebanon Hills Regional Park, 860 Cliff Road, Eagan, MN 55123, 651/554-6530, www.co.dakota.mn.us (click on *Leisure & Recreation* and then *Park Locations*).

12 COTTONWOOD RIVER AND HIKING CLUB TRAIL

Flandrau State Park, New Ulm

Level: Moderate/strenuous

Hiking Time: 3 hours

Total Distance: 5.6 miles round-trip

Elevation Gain: 210 feet

Summary: Visit the sand-bottom swimming pond, oxbow marshes, and oak grove bluffs along the Cottonwood River in Flandrau State Park.

Tucked inside the river valley between the Cottonwood River and the bluff ridge, Flandrau State Park is one of the coziest in the state. The trail system here ranges from bottomland forest loops to blufftop overlooks, and the park is just a hop, skip, and a jump away from New Ulm. The Minnesota Hiking Club liked it so much they designated one of the hikes as their own. The historical August Schell Brewery is just down the river, near the old dam site on the Cottonwood. The brewery is America's second-oldest family-owned brewery and still distributes its beer within the region. It is open to the public for scheduled tours.

From the parking lot walk west away from the park road to the beach house shelter. Just south of here is the sand-bottom pond swimming area. Take a right at the beach house to begin on the Hiking Club trail. Once upon a time tallgrass prairie covered this entire region. The land was valuable to settlers as farmland, and much of the oak savanna and prairie grass was plowed under for crops. Today, large cottonwood trees fill the low-lying river areas, and oak forests line the bluffs. Some remnant goat prairie still clings to the south-facing bluffsides, blooming blazing star and butterfly weed throughout the growing season.

You will come to a short spur trail 0.3 mile from the parking lot that leads to the first overlook point. Take a left onto the trail and take a moment to look over the Cottonwood River. The sandy waterway snakes through the valley, often rearranging its channel with the sediment it carries in its current. Return to the trail and take a left. Keep left at the trail intersection 0.2 mile up the trail, staying on the Hiking Club path. As the trail leads north it slowly climbs up the valley away from the river; 0.5 mile from the overlook point the trail passes by a walk-in campsite and crosses a gravel park road and parking lot into an open grassland. A few stands of trees huddle in the grass, but prairie takes over this section of the park. Grasshoppers and butterflies flit between the Indian paintbrush and blazing star. Look also for the small white lady's slipper orchid near the tree lines in the shady areas at the edge of the grass. Continue north, following the Hiking Club trail signs; 0.3 mile from the park road the trail arcs east along the ridgeline that forms the boundary of the park. The trail follows the ridge for 0.9 mile to the Indian Point spur trail. Take a left here and climb 110 feet up the ridge. Take a

Driftwood and fallen logs are left behind from a recent flood.

left on the Ridge Trail to the overlook point. This sweeping view covers the entire park and river as it winds its way southeast.

Return to the Hiking Club trail and take a left past the trailer sanitation station for 0.3 mile. The forest encroaches once again on this trail section; 0.3 mile from the Indian Point trail the Hiking Club trail crosses two park road intersections. Follow the trail southeast, keeping on the Hiking Club trail, which is marked with signs. In 0.3 mile take a left up the steps to climb a ridge up to another overlook point. Continue south from the overlook on the River Trail on the Old Island Loop. Here in the floodplain of the river cottonwood trees and meadows tangle together near the water. Take a right 0.6 mile from the last intersection to yet another overlook point. Take another right onto the River Loop, which passes by the dam site that once blocked the Cottonwood River. The dam held water back, forming an island upstream. Now that the dam no longer functions, the river has reformed into one channel, hence the Old Island Loop trail. From the dam, finish the loop back to the overlook point and retrace your steps for 0.1 mile. Take a right at the intersection on the north end of the Old Island Loop and follow the ridgeline back to the Hiking Club trail. Take a left down the steps and another left to head west on the Hiking Club trail back to the beach house and parking lot.

Options

If climbing isn't your strong suit, you can forgo the 100-foot climb to Indian Point overlook. Just keep to the right when you come to the spur trail that leads up the hill. This will shave 0.4 mile off of your hike and keep you in the bottomlands formed by the Cottonwood River.

Directions

From Minneapolis drive south on I-35 West for 7 miles. Take the I-494 West exit. In 4.5 miles exit onto US-169 South. Drive 65 miles and merge onto US-14 West for another 24 miles. Turn left at 20th Street South into New Ulm and take a right onto MN-15 in 1.1 miles. In 1 mile turn left at 10th Street South, then left at Summit Avenue. Take a right into the park entrance. The office is 0.3 mile ahead. Follow signs to the parking lot 0.2 mile ahead. Park in the southern lot near the beach.

Information and Contact

There is a $5 daily vehicle permit fee. Restrooms and drinking fountains are available in the park office. Dogs are allowed. Maps are available at the park office and on the park website. For more information, contact Flandrau State Park, 1300 Summit Avenue, New Ulm, MN 56073, 507/233-9800, www.dnr.state.mn.us.

13 SEPPMAN WINDMILL TRAIL   BEST ◖

Minneopa State Park, Mankato

Level: Easy

Hiking Time: 2 hours

Total Distance: 4 miles round-trip

Elevation Gain: 50 feet

Summary: See the stone grist mill, Seppman Windmill, and the grasslands that surround the Minnesota River in Minneopa State Park.

Oak savanna and native prairie grasslands are a rarity in North America, but you wouldn't know it at Minneopa State park. The Minnesota River Valley is a haven for these native landscapes, and the gnarled branches of old oak trees and the bright prairie flowers of the native grasslands fill this portion of the Minnesota River Valley.

Start by walking south from the parking loop toward the picnic area on the Hiking Club trail. Follow the trail as it swings northwest past the park office and crosses the park road. From start to finish, this hike is primarily through the beautiful native prairie and oak savanna just south of the Minnesota River. Songbirds such as the eastern bluebird, the western meadowlark, and the yellow-shafted flicker are common here, though you will be hard-pressed to see them in other parts of the state. Tree sparrows, king birds, redwing blackbirds, red-tailed hawks, and sometimes bald eagles are common, depending on the season.

Continue west on the Hiking Club trail; 1.3 miles from the trailhead take a left at the prairie spur trail that leads to the Seppman Windmill. You will already have seen it standing tall above the grass, but it is worth it to get an close-up look. Made from native stone and lumber, the historic Seppman Windmill was built in the German style with a wind-driven grist mill inside. Brought to ruins by lightning and a tornado, the mill didn't operate for long after it was built in 1864. It is a rare and beautiful example of what wind-powered grain milling once looked like.

From the windmill, return to the main trail and take a left to continue touring the park's grassland and oak savanna. The trail crosses the park road just after the windmill intersection. Stay on the Hiking Club trail as it swings southeast toward the campground. The oaks gain some ground on the grassland along this portion

© JAKE KULJU

A dragonfly rests on the undergrowth in Minneopa State Park.

of the trail. Watch for pheasants in walking in the grass near the trees. In the early summer you can hear the roosters calling loudly from the grass.

After crossing the park road once more, take a left off of the Hiking Club trail on the spur trail that leads northeast along Minneopa Creek to its confluence point with the Minnesota River. The trail crosses some railroad tracks through the forest near the river and passes an overlook point. Return to the Hiking Club trail and take a left to return to the parking loop, just a few hundred feet to the south.

Options

This park was originally created to preserve the waterfall on the Minneopa Creek in the southern portion of the park. You can drive south from the parking lot across Highways 68 and 69 to the parking lot at the head of the falls. A small trail loops around the area. Limestone steps lead down to the cascade, and the turf trail climbs the wooded hills across the creek to give a view of the bottomlands from above. This adds 0.4 mile to your hike and gives you a beautiful waterfall view.

Directions

From Minneapolis head south on I-35 West for 7.2 miles. Take the I-494 West exit. Exit onto US-169 South in 4.5 miles; 70 miles later turn right at MN-68 past Mankato. Drive 1.6 miles and turn right at Minneopa State Park Road. After the information office, take a right into the parking lot and trailhead.

Information and Contact

There is a $5 state park vehicle permit fee. Restrooms and a drinking fountain are available at the information office and picnic area. Dogs are allowed. Maps are available at the information office and on the park website. For more information, contact Minneopa State Park, 54497 Gadwall Road, Mankato, MN 56001, 507/389-5464, www.dnr.state.mn.us.

14 BIG WOODS LOOP TO TIMBER DOODLE TRAIL

Sakatah Lake State Park, Waterville

BEST ☾

Level: Moderate/strenuous

Total Distance: 6.1 miles round-trip

Hiking Time: 3-3.5 hours

Elevation Gain: 270 feet

Summary: Climb the hills that roll south from the southern shores of Upper Sakatah Lake.

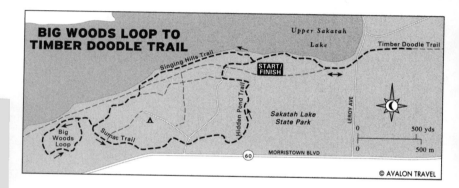

Most southern Minnesotans know of the Sakatah Lake Singing Hills Trail. The beautiful paved trail makes a clean pass through the beautiful rolling hills in the southern portion of the state. But if you'd like to get off the pavement, Sakatah Lake State Park has wonderful turf trails that line the lake and delve into the wooded hills that surround it.

From the parking lot head north for a few hundred feet on the turf trail that leads downhill to the lake. Take a left and follow the lakeshore west for 0.6 mile to the paved Singing Hills Trail. Walk up the hillside and cross the trail, taking a right at the turf trail intersection. The maple, oak, and basswood are thick here, creating a tight forest canopy that is a cool, shady paradise in the summer. The mosquitoes can be bothersome in the late spring but are usually endurable by midsummer. Make sure to bring bug spray along on this hike.

The trail enters the Big Woods Loop 0.4 mile from the paved trail crossing, climbing the undulating hills that characterize this portion of the state. You walk up 100 feet of hillside through this thick basswood, oak, and maple jungle and walk right back down it on this 0.6-mile loop. Big Woods forests were once much more pervasive, but many of them have been cleared for farmland. Sakatah

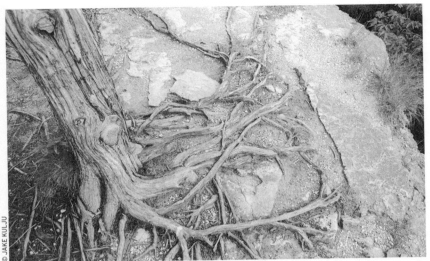

© JAKE KULJU

The roots of a cedar tree search for footholds along a rock surface in the thick Big Woods of Sakatah Lake State Park.

Lake State Park is a remnant of Big Woods among the sprawling fields of corn and soybeans that now grow here. This island of thick forest is home to whitetail deer, foxes, skunks, and raccoons. If you don't see any deer, you will certainly see their tracks. Their hoofprints are easily seen on the turf trails that run through the woods.

After leaving the loop, take a right to continue a gradual uphill climb along the Sumac Trail. Stay to the right at the next two trail intersections, crossing the park road near the park office onto the Hidden Pond Trail. The trail crosses it again 1 mile from the park road, this time heading west. Take a right at the road and follow it north for just a few hundred feet to the picnic area parking lot. Retrace your steps downhill to the lake and take a right this time, past the fishing pier toward the boat access ramp. Continue east past the group campsite on the Timber Doodle Trail. There is little landscape variation, as you plow through more hills and thick Big Woods forest. Take a right on the loop at the end of the trail and retrace your steps heading west to the parking lot and trailhead.

Options

Remain in the hills and shorten this hike by 2.1 miles by not taking the Timber Doodle branch of the trail. After making the Big Woods Loop and returning to the parking lot, find the trailhead and call it a day after 4 miles of hiking through rolling hills and thick maple and oak forest.

Directions

From Minneapolis drive south on I-35 West for 16.6 miles. Continue south for another 31 miles after the I-35 East merger in Burnsville. Take the MN-60 exit and merge onto 30th Avenue Northwest in Fairbault. Drive 12.8 miles to the Sakatah Lake State Park entrance on your right. Follow signs to the picnic area and fishing pier parking lot.

Information and Contact

There is a $5 state park vehicle permit fee. Restrooms and a drinking fountain are available at the picnic area. Dogs are allowed. Maps are available at the park office and on the park website. For more information, contact Sakatah Lake State Park, 50499 Sakatah Lake State Park Road, Waterville, MN 56096, 507/362-4438, www.dnr.state.mn.us.

15 HIDDEN FALLS TO HOPE TRAIL LOOP

BEST 🅲

Nerstrand-Big Woods State Park, Nerstrand

Level: Easy/moderate

Total Distance: 4.7 miles round-trip

Hiking Time: 2.5 hours

Elevation Gain: 90 feet

Summary: View the hidden falls of Prairie Creek in this island of thick oak, maple, and basswood trees in the middle of the prairie.

The most famous of the remaining stands of Big Woods forests in the state is in Nerstrand-Big Woods State Park. The park's trails are beautiful places to enjoy nature any time of year. Home to rare wildflowers in the spring, such as the dwarf trout lily and bloodroot; full of thick tree canopy and creekside grasses in the summer; and ablaze with bursts of color in the fall, this park easily makes the best of list of most Minnesota hikers.

HIDDEN FALLS TO HOPE TRAIL LOOP

From the southeastern corner of the parking lot follow the trail east for 0.1 mile, then take a left toward the picnic area. The trail arcs northeast for 0.5 mile through the woods to Hidden Falls. Take a left at the falls across Prairie Creek, and then turn right about 100 feet after the bridge, continuing north on the Fawn Trail. Follow this 1-mile arc into the northernmost region of the park. The thick woods here abound with wildlife. Whitetail deer, raccoons, skunks, and foxes all seek the Big Woods habitat for their homes. The park also has a notable warbler population. Keep your eyes peeled for the rare flowers that bloom under the canopy in the spring. Park officials claim that the rare and endangered dwarf trout lily blooms only in Nerstrand-Big Woods State Park.

Take a right on the Hope Trail, near a large open meadow in the middle of the woods. Walk northwest for 0.2 mile and take a right on the Hope Trail Loop. This 1.2-mile loop leads through more thick woods and skirts the edge of another open meadow before swinging south and east. Retrace your steps

a view up the creek above Hidden Falls

on the Hope Trail for 0.2 mile, then take a right to finish the Fawn Trail. Take a right onto the Beaver Trail, which leads to the creek. You cut west here and meander through more woods and hills to a trail intersection 0.6 mile ahead. Take a right and cross the oak footbridge that crosses Prairie Creek. Continue for 0.2 mile and take a left, then another left 0.1 mile later. This path leads around the walk-in campsites into a thick stand of white oaks. Take a left at the trail intersection. The parking lot and trailhead are 0.3 mile ahead.

Options

If you'd like to enjoy the view of hidden falls without the full 4.7-mile hike, you can take a shorter 1.5-mile jaunt to the creek and back to the trailhead. After reaching the falls, either turn around and follow your steps back to the parking lot or take a left at the first intersection south of the falls. This path arcs south around the trail maintenance station and emerges back on the park road that leads to the campground. Cross the road and take a right. The trail back to the parking lot leads to your left just a few hundred feet to the east.

Directions

From Minneapolis drive south on I-35 West for 16.6 miles. Continue south for another 28.8 miles after the I-35 East merger in Burnsville. Take exit 59 toward Faibault and merge onto MN-21 for 1 mile. Turn left at 20th Street Northwest and drive for 1 mile. Turn right at 2nd Avenue Northwest and left at 14th Street

Northwest. In 1.4 miles turn left at 14th Street Northeast for 0.5 mile. Continue on Cagger Trail for 1.4 miles. Turn left at Cannon City Boulevard and drive for 0.8 mile. Turn right onto Cannon City Path and continue on Nerstrand Boulevard for 3.3 miles. Turn left at Hall Avenue for 1 mile and turn right at 170th Street East for 1.5 miles. The park entrance is on the left. Take a left after the visitors center into the parking lot.

Information and Contact

There is a $5 state park vehicle permit fee. Restrooms and a drinking fountain are available at the picnic area. Dogs are allowed. Maps are available at the park office and on the park website. For more information, contact Nerstrand-Big Woods State Park, 9700 170 Street East, Nerstrand, MN 55053, 507/333-4840, www.dnr.state.mn.us.

🔟 RICE LAKE TRAIL
Rice Lake State Park, Owatonna

Level: Easy

Total Distance: 3.5 miles round-trip

Hiking Time: 1.75 hours

Elevation Gain: Negligible

Summary: Explore the transition zones between hardwood forest, marshy wetland, lakes, and prairie.

Rice Lake was named for its abundant stands of wild rice, which once fed countless Native Americans. The rice harvest was a central part of the Native American culture and a major source of nutrition. Wild rice no longer grows here in the abundance it once did, but migratory waterfowl and wetland wildlife still abound in the lake's waters and along its shores. The Rice Lake area is notable for its diversity of habitat. Marshes, lakes, meadows, and woods are all found here and attract a significant amount of wildlife. The rare pileated woodpecker is often seen here, for example, as well as whistling swans, blue geese, and black terns.

From the north end of the parking lot follow the turf trail to the right toward the wooden trail shelter. Continue following the trail north as it breaks out of the trees and makes a 0.6-mile arc to the west, parallel to Highway 19. Patches of shrubs and trees linger in this area, but the landscape is primarily treeless here. Look for animals on the tree line, such as fox and whitetail deer. Just before the trail crosses the park road, it enters the maple, oak, and aspen forest that characterizes most of the park. Cross the road and walk south for 0.5 mile to the boat access road. The trail leaves the trees once more and passes through the wide prairie meadow. Wild asters and coneflowers bloom here, as well as wild daisies and some lilies.

Take a right on the gravel road to the boat access ramp and another right on the turf trail that leads north where it crosses the road. The trail makes a 0.9-mile loop through the woods and along the marshy shore of the lake. This little island of trees lies between the water and prairie and is a good spot to find whitetail deer

The reedy shores of Rice Lake are a haven for wildlife and waterfowl.

and other forest creatures, especially several of the seven species of woodpeckers that live in the park. Look for waterfowl here as well, especially near the water during the spring and fall migratory seasons.

After finishing the loop, return to the boat access ramp and follow the trail as it crosses the park road. The next mile of trail closely follows the lakeshore. The thick marsh grasses, lily pads, and sedge swamp that borders the water is rife with waterfowl and makes for great bird watching. As the trail bends away from the lake, its returns to the wooden shelter. Take a left here and return to the parking lot, just 0.2 mile to the west.

Options

If you'd rather not walk along the park road, you can take a right at the first trail intersection and follow in the inner curve of Rice Lake to the loop at the end of the trail, then turn around and follow your steps back to the trailhead and parking lot. This will add 0.1 mile to your trip and keep you closer to the marshy shores of the lake throughout the hike.

Directions

From St. Paul drive south on I-35 East for 19.2 miles. Continue on I-35 South after the merger of I-35 West in Burnsville for another 45.4 miles. Take exit 42A for Owatonna. Merge onto Hoffman Drive and drive for 1.2 miles. Turn left at Highway 19 and drive for 6.4 miles. Veer right to stay on Highway 19 for 2.2

miles to the park entrance. Turn right into the park. Turn left after the park office for 0.3 mile, and make another left after 0.3 mile following signs to the walk-in campsite parking lot.

Information and Contact

There is a $5 state park vehicle permit fee. Restrooms and a drinking fountain are available at the picnic area. Dogs are allowed. Maps are available at the park office and on the park website. For more information, contact Rice Lake State Park, 8485 Rose Street, Owatonna, MN 55060, 507/455-5871, www.dnr.state.mn.us.

17 ZUMBRO RIVER AND HIGH MEADOW TRAIL

Oxbow Park, Rochester

Level: Moderate

Hiking Time: 2.75 hours

Total Distance: 5.1 miles round-trip

Elevation Gain: 120 feet

Summary: Take a walk along the winding oxbows of the Zumbro River and the prairie meadows that rise above.

Until 1967, this park was patches of unused farmland and degraded forests that saw no use. Tucked into the ridge that borders the large bend of the Zumbro River, Oxbow Park is now a beautifully preserved area full of hardwood forests and riverside trails.

From the parking lot and picnic area, cross the first bridge and take a right onto the Zumbro Trail. The trailhead is located in the middle of the oxbow that the park derives its name from. The river nearly doubles back on itself, almost forming a circle as it winds northward along the ridgeline. Follow the Zumbro Trail for 1.5 miles as it follows the curve of the river. The trail leads primarily through the maple,

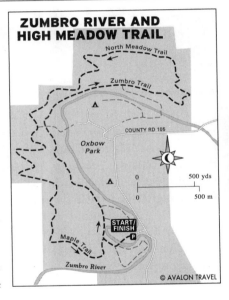

aspen, and basswood trees on the floodplain, though several meadows have wedged their way between the trees. After the trail arcs eastward, the trees completely take over, and the thick forest dominates the landscape. Whitetail deer and raccoons love this forest and are often seen among the trees. When the Zumbro Trail splits on the north bank of the river take a left and follow the North Meadow Trail as it climbs the ridge up to the patch of prairie on top of the bluff.

A trail cuts through the diameter of the North Meadow Loop. Stay to the right at both of its intersection points to stay on the tree line trail that borders the meadow. Prairie grasses and some wildflowers bloom here, including milkweed, asters, and coneflowers. Since this area is not a native prairie, many of the wildflowers that thrive in other meadowlands in the state are not as common here. The trail

A large moth spreads its wings on a cedar branch in Oxbow Park.

swings south and follows the eastern shore of the Zumbro River, though this time from up above. The trail dips into a small valley but soon climbs back up along the Maple Trail; you guessed it—maple trees dominate this forested portion of the park. Squirrels and nuthatches, chickadees, and some wrens live in this maple forest and give an energy to the peaceful forest that only small creatures can.

The Maple Trail leads for 1.5 miles south, twisting through the forest and eventually descending to the bottomlands near the first bridge. Take a right at the Zumbro Trail intersection and a left to cross the bridge back to the picnic area and parking lot at the trailhead.

Options

You can add 0.5 mile to this hike and see some different terrain by taking a left after crossing the bridge from the oxbow parking lot. This loop is called the River Loop and leads you through the sumac and meadow grasses that line the bottomlands near the river. Sumac is a transitional plant between prairie and forest and shows how the nature is constantly reshaping itself. As you finish the loop and continue north on the Zumbro Trail, watch how the plants and trees thicken into a forest.

Directions

From St. Paul drive east on I-94 for 1.3 miles. Take the US-52 South exit. Drive 59 miles to Pine Island. Take a right on Main Street and head south for 1.4 miles. Turn right at 8th Street Southwest and left at Highway 3. In 0.6 mile turn right at Highway 5. Drive for 9.8 miles to Valleyhigh Road Northwest. Turn left at Highway 105 for 0.5 mile. Turn left at Oxbow Park Drive into the picnic area parking lot.

Information and Contact

There is no fee. Dog are not allowed. Restrooms and drinking water are available in the Oxbow parking lot, as well as in the picnic area near the campground. Maps are available on the park website. For more information, contact Oxbow Park, 5731 County Road 105 Northwest, Byron, MN 55920, 507/775-2451, www.co.olmsted.mn.us/parks.

18 NORTH TRAIL, PRAIRIE RIDGE TRAIL, AND THE DAM OVERLOOK

Chester Woods Park, Rochester

Level: Moderate

Hiking Time: 3 hours

Total Distance: 5.6 miles round-trip

Elevation Gain: 100 feet

Summary: This loop climbs through thick woods and open meadows on the rugged bluffs north of Bear Creek and its headwaters.

Chester Woods Park is a collection of fields, oak woods, and bluff prairie lands that surround Chester Lake. Formed by the dam on the lake's southern end, Chester Lake has three large branching arms bordered by thick woods.

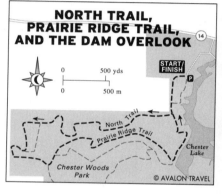

From the parking lot follow the North Trail as it leads west and then juts sharply south along the park border. This broad prairie is full of the beautiful tallgrass and prairie flowers that once covered much of the state. Beautiful wild asters, Indian paintbrush, blazing stars, and prairie smoke flowers bloom here in the spring and summer, along with some lupines near the gravel roads. At the Prairie Ridge Trail intersection take a right to continue on the North Trail. Keep to the right at all trail intersection for the next 2 miles. The wide dirt trail borders a thick stand of trees for about 0.2 mile, then breaks into open prairie again. Look for deer feeding on the tree line, as well as eastern bluebirds and meadowlarks in the fields.

At the third trail intersection stay to the right and follow the path as it curves to the south through the oak forest. Take another right and then a left to join the Prairie Ridge Trail. It's helpful to have a map along, as the trail intersections can get tricky over the next mile. The Prairie Ridge Trail leads straight east for 0.25 mile before turning south toward Bear Creek. Take a left at the creek and continue on the Prairie Ridge Trail as it angles northeast on the ridge above the waterway. Stay to the left at the next trail intersection and to the right at the following two. The wide dirt path is shared by riders on horseback. Make sure to give right of way to horses and their riders. This portion of the trail is through a mixture of oak forest and prairie. The

a view over the tree canopy above Bear Creek in Chester Woods Park

savanna-like landscape is beautiful and frequented by squirrels, raccoons, and bluebirds.

At the Dam Overlook Trail intersection take a right and walk 0.2 mile to the dam overlook area. Look for wood ducks and mergansers feeding along the lakeshore; grasshopper sparrows and bobolinks can also be seen in this prairie corridor. Painted turtles, bull snakes, and broad-winged hawks are also attracted to this habitat. Continue north on the Dam Overlook Trail loop and take a right at the next intersection. This path leads through the oak woods and another patch of meadowland to one of the park's gravel roads. Take a left for 0.1 mile to the horse trail parking area and trailhead.

Options

You can cross Bear Creek on the western end of the park by taking a right at the bridge that leads south from the Prairie Ridge Trail. Cross the bridge and take a left, following the South Sand Prairie Trail east to another creek crossing. Take a right after crossing back to the north of the creek to the dam overlook. From here, follow the Dam Overlook Trail north back to the horse trailer parking lot.

Directions

From St. Paul drive east on I-94 for 1.3 miles. Take the US-52 South exit. Drive for 76.8 miles and take the US-14 East exit. Merge onto US-14 and drive for 8.7

miles to the park entrance on your right. Take your first right and then a left, following signs to the horse trailer parking lot.

Information and Contact

There is a $5 daily vehicle permit fee. Dogs are not allowed. Restrooms are available at the park information office. Maps are available on the park website. For more information, contact Chester Woods Park, 8378 Highway 14 East, Eyota, MN 55934, 507/285-7050, www.co.olmsted.mn.us/parks.

19 SUGAR CAMP HOLLOW AND BIG SPRING TRAIL

BEST ☾

Forestville/Mystery Cave State Park, Preston

Level: Strenuous

Total Distance: 11.8 miles round-trip

Hiking Time: 7-8 hours

Elevation Gain: 520 feet

Summary: You'll discover a natural spring, a hilltop cemetery, and an abandoned 19th-century town on this explorative hike.

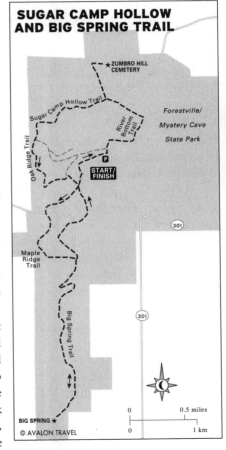

SUGAR CAMP HOLLOW AND BIG SPRING TRAIL

Forestville/Mystery Cave State Park is truly a gem of southern Minnesota. The park surrounds the old town site of Forestville, an abandoned trade town founded in 1853. Area farmers came to the town to sell and trade goods, and the town once had a grist mill, general stores, and even hotels. The only remnants now are reconstructed buildings and a faded grid of streets that once made up the framework of the town. During the summer months, pioneer-era actors recreate village life of the 1850s.

From the parking lot take a right onto the turf trail that follows the creek. The trail borders the northern edge of historic Forestville before crossing the park road. You will quickly see why the town was named Forestville. It is literally a clearing in a thick forest of maple, oak, basswood, aspen, and pine trees. Take a left onto the trail across the road and follow it north to the River Bottom Trail. The landscape opens into a large meadow here. Look for red and gray foxes on the tree line, and opossums and minks near the wooded riverbanks. Half a mile from the park road the trail cuts northwest toward the old 1880 high school and brickyard sites. Another 0.5 mile from the trail

© JAKE KULJU

a whitetail deer track sunk deep in the mud

curve and just past the brickyard is a hitching rail at the bottom of the Zumbro Hill Cemetery Trail. Tighten your boot laces and make the 180-foot climb to the top of the hill. There isn't much of an overlook, but there is a lot of wildlife to see. Wild turkeys and ruffed grouse thrive in these thick woods, as do squirrels and barred owls. Also keep on the lookout for the timber rattlesnake, which lives here. There are only a handful of them in the park, and they remain harmless unless agitated, but it doesn't hurt to practice caution while in the woods.

Crash back down the hill to the hitching post and take a right on the Sugar Camp Hollow Trail. This trail leads through more thick forest and the undulating hills that roll through the area. Choose the middle path at the trail intersection 0.8 mile from the hitching post and continue south on the Oak Ridge Trail. Oak forest dominates this portion of the park. The trail goes quickly downhill toward Forestville Creek, then splits. Take the right fork and cross the creek, then take another right on the trail that parallels the park road; 0.5 mile from the creek the trail crosses the park road and leads south past the park office on the Maple Ridge Trail for 0.75 mile to the Angler's Parking Lot. Cross the road and follow the trail south back the group camp down the hill as the trail arcs east. Take a right at the next trail intersection and cross the South Branch Root River, then take another right on the Big Spring Trail. The path continues through the thick woods, with occasional openings of meadow. Always be alert for wildlife in the transitional zones between forest and field.

The Big Spring Trail follows Canfield Creek to its source at Big Spring. The creek valley is lined by thick forest and is open to public hunting. When visiting the trail during hunting seasons, make sure to wear blaze orange clothing. This 2.8-mile trek through the creek valley forest is worth it to see the gushing waters at Big Spring. Turn around and follow the trail back north, cross the river, and take a right. This trail leads north along the park road and crosses at the parking lot for anglers. Take a right at the parking lot past the amphitheater and up the hill past the trailer sanitation station. The path crosses the road again and arcs northward along the river and crosses the park road once more. Take a right on the other side of the road and walk 0.2 mile back to the parking lot and trailhead.

Options
You don't have to bust your butt through almost 12 miles of trails to get the essence of Forestville/Mystery Cave State Park. From the parking lot you can head north and follow the River Bottom Trail to the Zumbro Hill Cemetery spur trail, then link onto the Sugar Camp Hollow Trail heading west. This shortens the hike by more than 7 miles, still giving you a 4-mile uphill workout through the woods.

Directions
From St. Paul head east on I-94 for 1.3 miles. Take the US-52 South exit. Drive for 108.8 miles to MN-16. Take a left and drive for 3.1 miles. Turn left at Highway 11. Drive for 1.2 miles and turn right at Highway 118, which leads into the park. In 3.8 miles turn right at Highway 12 and park in the Root River parking lot.

Information and Contact
There is a $5 state park vehicle permit fee. A restroom and a drinking fountain are available at the park office. Dogs are allowed. Maps are available at the park office and on the park website. For more information, contact Forestville/Mystery Cave State Park, 21071 County 118, Preston, MN 55965, 507/937-3251, www .dnr.state.mn.us.

20 BIG ISLAND TO GREAT MARSH TRAIL

Myre-Big Island State Park, Albert Lea

Level: Easy/moderate

Hiking Time: 3 hours

Total Distance: 6 miles round-trip

Elevation Gain: Negligible

Summary: Loop around Big Island and the wetland plains of the Great Marsh on the north shore of Albert Lea Lake.

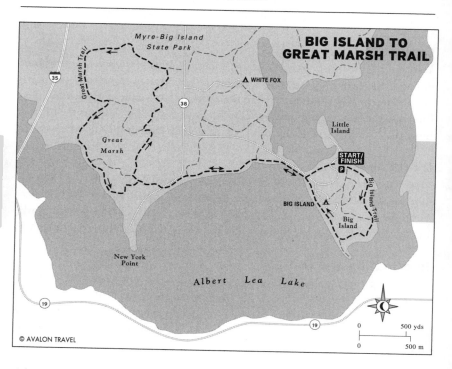

A large tree-covered island in the middle of a marsh-bordered lake filled with exotic migratory waterfowl sounds like the setting of a fantasy novel, and it might well be, but it is also the setting of Myre-Big Island State Park in southern Minnesota. The wetland marshes, oak savanna, and maple and basswood forests along this trail system are one of Minnesota's finest natural outlets.

From the parking lot take a right on the Big Island Trail, which circles the island. The thick maple and basswood forest on the island is home to some whitetail deer and gray foxes. You will also see some squirrels among the trees. Before you finish the 1.1-mile loop around the island, take a left before crossing the park road. This path leads to the mainland and the wide prairie that leads to the Great Marsh. Take a left at the next trail intersection 0.3 mile from Big Island and follow the north shore of Albert Lea Lake. A stand of trees hugs the water here before opening to more prairie and wetland. As the trees give way to the open wetland, look for the muskrats, snapping turtles, and frogs that live near the marsh. If you do a little rock turning you may also see salamanders and red-bellied snakes. Half a mile from the intersection the trail crosses the park road into the Great Marsh; 0.25 mile from the road the trail passes by a parking lot. Take a right at the parking lot and head north on the Great Marsh Trail.

This massive wetland is full of sedge grass, marsh plants, and water. Leopard frogs call from the pools of water, and birds of prey like the red-tailed hawk, kestrel, and marsh hawk glide above looking for food. You may also see the rose-breasted grosbeaks, indigo buntings, and an occasional oriole. Waterfowl such as wood ducks, mallards, and blue-winged teals thrive along the lakeshore, as do egrets, great blue herons, and American bitterns.

Take a right 0.3 mile north of the parking lot through the wetland and prairie, then turn left on the Blazing Star State Trail. Follow this wide path west for 0.5 mile, then take a left at the Great Marsh Trail intersection. Walk south through the marsh for 0.3 mile before taking another right onto the interpretive portion of the Great Marsh Trail. Signs and kiosks with photos and information about the marsh habitat and the creatures that dwell here show up intermittently along the trail, as well as information kiosks that give insight into the Native American history of the area. When you return to the marsh parking lot cross the road and retrace your steps to Big Island. Take note of how the marsh transitions to prairie and the prairie transitions to forest on your way back to the wooded isle. Keep your eyes peeled for wildlife in these transitional zones. Back on the island, take a left and walk for 0.2 mile back to the picnic area and trailhead parking lot.

Options

For a much shorter hike that stays in the trees, just make the 1.5-mile loop around Big Island. Or, if you are more interested in the Great Marsh than the wooded island, park in the Great Marsh Trail parking lot on the way to the group center and make the Great Marsh loop. This will make a 4.5-mile hike through the wetland plain and keep you on the mainland.

Directions

From St. Paul drive south on I-35 East for 19.2 miles. Continue on I-35 South for 76.1 miles after the merger of I-35 West in Burnsville. Take the County Highway 46 East exit and turn left at MN-116. Turn right at 780th Avenue in Albert Lea.

Drive for 2 miles to the park entrance and take your second left. On Big Island, take a left, following signs to the picnic area parking lot.

Information and Contact

There is a $5 resident vehicle permit fee and a $10 nonresident fee. Restrooms and a drinking fountain are available in the nature center by the parking lot. Maps are available at the park office and nature center. Dogs are allowed. For more information, contact Myre-Big Island State Park, 19499 780th Avenue, Albert Lea, MN 56007, 507/379-3403, www.dnr.state.mn.us.

RESOURCES

PARK INFORMATION SOURCES
Minnesota State Parks
For more information on these state parks, visit www.dnr.state.mn.us.

Afton State Park
6959 Peller Avenue South
Hastings, MN 55033
651/436-5391

Banning State Park
P.O. Box 643
Sandstone, MN 55072
320/245-2668

Carley State Park
c/o Whitewater State Park,
Route 1, Box 256
Altura, MN 55910
507/932-3007

Charles A. Lindbergh State Park
1615 Lindbergh Drive South
Little Falls, MN 56345
320/616-2525

Crow Wing State Park
3124 State Park Road
Brainerd, MN 56401
218/825-3075

Father Hennepin State Park
41294 Father Hennepin Park Road
Isle, MN 56342
320/676-8763

Flandrau State Park
1300 Summit Avenue
New Ulm, MN 56073
507/233-9800

Forestville/Mystery Cave State Park
21071 County 118
Preston, MN 55965
507/352-5111

Fort Snelling State Park
101 Snelling Lake Road
St. Paul, MN 55111
612/725-2389

Frontenac State Park
29223 County 28 Boulevard
Frontenac, MN 55026
651/345-3401

Great River Bluffs State Park
43605 Kipp Drive
Winona, MN 55987
507/643-6849

Interstate State Park
P.O. Box 254
Taylors Falls, MN 55084
651/465-5711

Jay Cooke State Park
780 Highway 210
Carlton, MN 55718
218/384-4610

Lake Maria State Park
11411 Clementa Avenue Northwest
Monticello, MN 55362
763/878-2325

Mille Lacs Kathio State Park
15066 Kathio State Park Road
Onamia, MN 56359
320/532-3523

Minneopa State Park
54497 Gadwall Road
Mankato, MN 56001
507/389-5464

Minnesota Valley State Park
19825 Park Boulevard
Jordan, MN 55352
952/492-6400

Moose Lake State Park
4252 County Road 137
Moose Lake, MN 55767
218/485-5420

Myre-Big Island State Park
19499 780th Avenue
Albert Lea, MN 56007
507/379-3403

Nerstrand Big Woods State Park
9700 170 Street East
Nerstrand, MN 55053
507/333-4840

Rice Lake State Park
8485 Rose Street
Owatonna, MN 55060
507/455-5871

Sakatah Lake State Park
50499 Sakatah Lake State Park Road
Waterville, MN 56096
507/362-4438

Sibley State Park
800 Sibley Park Road Northeast
New London, MN 56273
320/354-2055

St. Croix State Park
30065 St. Croix Park Road
Hinckley, MN 55037
320/384-6591

Whitewater State Park
Route 1, Box 256
Altura, MN 55910
507/932-3007

Wild River State Park
39797 Park Trail
Center City, MN 55012
651/583-2125

William O'Brien State Park
16821 O'Brien Trail North
Marine-on-St. Croix, MN 55047
651/433-0500

National Wildlife Refuges
For more information on these refuges,
visit www.fws.gov/refuges/.

**Minnesota Valley
National Wildlife Refuge**
3815 American Boulevard East
Bloomington, MN 55425
952/854-5900

**Rice Lake National
Wildlife Refuge**
36298 State Highway 65
McGregor, MN 55760
218/768-2402

Wisconsin State Parks
101 South Webster Street
P.O. Box 7921
Madison, WI 53707
608/266-2621
www.dnr.state.wi.us/

County Parks

State parks don't have all the best trails! These county parks provide beautiful natural settings full of wildlife, wildflowers, and wilderness.

Anoka County Parks

550 Bunker Lane Boulevard NW
Andover, MN 55304
763/767-2820
www.anokacountyparks.com

Carver County Parks

11360 Highway 212 West, Suite 2
Cologne, MN 55322
952/466-5250
www.co.carver.mn.us

Dakota County Parks

14955 Galaxie Avenue
Apple Valley MN 55124
952/891-7000
www.co.dakota.mn.us

Ramsey County Parks

5287 Otter Lake Road
White Bear Township, MN 55110
651/748-2500
www.co.ramsey.mn.us/parks

Three Rivers Park District

3000 Xenium Lane North
Plymouth, MN 55441
763/559-9000
www.threeriversparkdistrict.org/parks/

Washington County Parks

11660 Myeron Road North
Stillwater, MN 55082
651/430-4300
www.co.washington.mn.us

Wright County Parks

1901 Highway 25 North
Buffalo, MN 55313
763/682-7693
www.co.wright.mn.us

City Parks

City of Roseville Parks & Recreation

2660 Civic Center Drive
Roseville, MN, 55113
651/792-7006
www.ci.roseville.mn.us

Minneapolis Park & Recreation Board

2117 West River Road
Minneapolis, MN 55411
612/230-6400
www.minneapolisparks.org

St. Paul Parks & Recreation

50 West Kellogg Boulevard, Suite 840
St. Paul, MN 55102
651/266-6400
www.stpaul.gov/index.asp?nid=243

MINNESOTA HIKING CLUBS

Meet new people and enjoy the outdoors with your friends.

Minnesota Hiking and Backpacking Clubs

www.hikingandbackpacking.com/minnesotaclubs.html

Minnesota Rovers Outdoors Club

www.mnrovers.org

Minnesota State Park Hiking Club

www.dnr.state.mn.us/state_parks/
  clubs.html

Outdoors Club

www.outdoorsclub.org

Sierra Club, Minnesota North Star Chapter

http://northstar.sierraclub.org/

OTHER SOURCES FOR MINNESOTA OUTDOOR INFORMATION

Bird-Watching Clubs

www.geocities.com/RainForest/5835/
www.zumbrovalleyaudubon.org/

Hiking Gear and Trail Reviews

www.cascadegear.com
www.rei.com
www.backcountry.com

Minnesota Speleological Survey

www.mss-caving.org/

Minnesota Wildflower Information

www.dnr.state.mn.us/wildflowers/
  index.html

Index

Acknowledgments

Rambling over the hills, through the forests, and along the lakes and rivers of Minnesota with a notebook in hand and a camera slung over my shoulder made for one of the happiest summer months of my life. Being able to stop to smell the wildflowers, wait for turtles to rustle out of the prairie grasses to lay their eggs, and watch speckled fawns amble through the trees was not possible on my own.

With all of the sincerity I can muster, I thank my beautiful wife Kerstin for enduring the many days I spent out on the trail and for her support of this project.

My sensational parents also deserve a direct thank you, especially for supplying me with a mode of transportation.

Without Kadie's lavish hospitality, Jacob's eager ear, Andy's steady support, Trevor's companionship, and the enthusiasm of so many of my friends and family, this book would lack the passion and poetry I so happily translated from forest, lakes, and prairies to paper.

Thank you, as well, to Avalon Travel for recognizing Minnesota as the beautiful wilderness that it is. A special thanks to Annie Blakley, my editor, for her patience and helpful encouragement.

Special thanks to the Minnesota State Park system for granting me access to their parks and trails.

And to the people of Minnesota: thank you for preserving, protecting, and cherishing your wild and wonderful state. May you do so for countless generations to come.

Notes

Notes

Notes

Notes

www.moon.com

DESTINATIONS | ACTIVITIES | BLOGS | MAPS | BOOKS

MOON.COM is all new, and ready to help plan your next trip! Filled with fresh trip ideas and strategies, author interviews, informative blogs, a detailed map library, and descriptions of all the Moon guidebooks, Moon.com is all you need to get out and explore the world—or even places in your own backyard. As always, when you travel with Moon, expect an experience that is uncommon and truly unique.

OUTDOORS

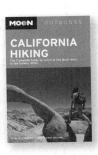

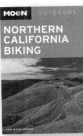

"Well written, thoroughly researched, and packed full of useful information and advice, these guides really do get you into the outdoors."

—GORP.COM

ALSO AVAILABLE AS FOGHORN OUTDOORS ACTIVITY GUIDES:

250 Great Hikes in
   California's National Parks
California Golf
California Waterfalls
California Wildlife
Camper's Companion
Easy Biking in Northern
   California
Easy Hiking in Northern
   California

Easy Hiking in Southern
   California
Georgia & Alabama Camping
Maine Hiking
Massachusetts Hiking
New England Biking
New England Cabins
   & Cottages
New England Camping
New England Hiking

New Hampshire Hiking
Southern California
   Cabins & Cottages
Tom Stienstra's Bay Area
   Recreation
Utah Camping
Vermont Hiking
Washington Boating
   & Water Sports

934654 917.M604Ku $17.95
*MN Sticker
Coffee Stains
notes/1-27-90
7/09

MOON TAKE A HIKE
MINNEAPOLIS & ST. PAUL

Avalon Travel
a member of the Perseus Books Group
1700 Fourth Street
Berkeley, CA 94710, USA
www.moon.com

Editor: Annie M. Blakley
Series Manager: Sabrina Young
Copy Editor: Deana Shields
Graphics Coordinator: Kathryn Osgood
Production Coordinator: Darren Alessi
Cover Designer: Kathryn Osgood
Interior Designer: Darren Alessi
Map Editor: Brice Ticen
Cartographers: Lohnes and Wright, Kat Bennett

ISBN: 978-1-59880-202-3
ISSN: 1947-413X

Printing History
1st Edition – May 2009
5 4 3 2 1

Some photos and illustrations are used by permission and are the property of the original copyright owners.

Front cover photo: Minnehaha Falls in Minneapolis © John Noltner
Title page photo: St. Louis River © Jake Kulju
Table of contents photos: © Jake Kulju
Back cover photo: © Peter Cade / Getty Images

Printed in the United States by RR Donnelley

Although every effort was made to ensure that the information was correct at the time of going to press, the author and publisher do not assume and hereby disclaim any liability to any party for any loss or damage caused by errors, omissions, or any potential travel disruption due to labor or financial difficulty, whether such errors or omissions result from negligence, accident, or any other cause.

KEEPING CURRENT

We are committed to making this book the most accurate and enjoyable hiking guide to the Minneapolis and St. Paul region. You can rest assured that every trail in this book has been carefully reviewed in an effort to keep this book as up-to-date as possible. However, by the time you read this book, some of the fees listed herein may have changed and trails may have closed unexpectedly.

If you have a favorite gem you'd like to see included in the next edition, or see anything that needs updating, clarification, or correction, please drop us a line. Send your comments via email to feedback@moon.com, or use the address above.